Women in Ireland

Voices of Change

Jenny Beale

Gill and Macmillan

Published in Ireland by Gill and Macmillan Ltd
Goldenbridge Dublin 8
with associated companies in
Auckland, Dallas, Delhi, Hong Kong,
Johannesburg, Lagos, London, Manzini,
Melbourne, Nairobi, New York, Singapore,
Tokyo, Washington
© Jenny Beale 1986
5 4 3 2 1
0 7171 1484 8

Photoset in Times by
CAS Typesetters, Southampton

Printed in Great Britain

Published in Great Britain by Macmillan Education Ltd
as part of a feminist list entitled 'Women in Society'
edited by Jo Campling

For Pat, in sisterhood

Contents

Preface

This book is about the extensive changes in the lives of women in the Republic of Ireland during the past twenty to thirty years. During that time, Ireland has developed from a predominantly rural country into an industrialising member-state of the European Economic Community. Rural life has all but disappeared, to be replaced by an urban, materialist culture and a class structure more akin to that in other Western European countries. Many aspects of these social and economic changes are reflected in women's lives. Women now living a relatively sophisticated city-based existence, whose daughters watch the latest videos and go to discos, can recall childhood memories of rural poverty and overcrowding. Many women no older than forty had to leave their jobs on marriage and had no access to contraception, whereas their daughters expect equal opportunities at work and take the local family planning clinic for granted.

Women in both the countryside and towns have been affected by the rapid pace of this transition from rural to urban life. Yet the transition has been neither easy nor complete. The old and the new frequently rub shoulders, and there is tension between them. Issues relating to the changing status of women have acted as focal points for controversy over the wider changes in values and attitudes in Irish society. This is still apparent in the 1980s as debates about divorce, contraception and the family continue unabated.

Because relatively little has been written about women in Ireland (though there has recently been a welcome expansion in women's writing and publishing), there is a danger that women's experiences of this period could be lost. This book is intended to be a contribution towards averting that danger. I set out to describe the background to the transition in women's lives, and to reflect the changing experience of women. The interview material in the book is taken from taped conversations with twenty-seven women of different ages and from a variety of backgrounds. Some of the women live in Dublin, others are from smaller towns and country areas, particularly in the west. A social profile of the interviewees appears in the Appendix. The interviews do not make up a formal survey, but are intended to illustrate a range of different experiences in a way that statistics and information are unable to do.

Every book is coloured by the author's own background and attitudes, in this case by my situation as an Englishwoman living and working in Ireland. I write in a spirit of sisterhood with Irish women, and hope that the book will be of interest to all those who care about the position of women in Irish society.

The term 'Ireland' is used to refer to the twenty-six counties of the Republic of Ireland unless otherwise indicated. Although I am aware of the problems associated with limiting the scope of the text to the Republic, trying to include the very different traditions of women in the North in a book of this size would present even greater difficulties. I have, however, included some comparative material on the position of women in Northern Ireland.

JENNY BEALE

Acknowledgements

I am very grateful to all the women who agreed to be interviewed and who talked so freely about themselves. I also owe a great deal to the women in my classes over the past few years. I have learned an enormous amount through my work with them in adult education and training. I would also like to thank Beth Brownfield, Anne Coughlan, Bernie Divilly, Betty Gosling, Kathleen Lough, Rosemary Cullen Owens and Tony Varley for their comments on the first draft. Pat Farrell helped me to develop my ideas, and both she and Colin Brown provided great support throughout. A big thank you to them both. Finally, my thanks to Jo Crampling for her encouragement and for her belief that women have something important to say.

J. B.

Editor's Introduction

In 1983 I contacted Jenny Beale to write a book on women and trade unions for Women and Society, only to discover that she was then living and working in the Republic of Ireland. We met, and it became clear that she really wanted to write a book about women in Ireland today. At that time, she was teaching courses for married women who wanted to return to work, and some classes in Women's Studies. This work gave her a strong sense of the rapid changes that had occurred in women's lives in Ireland and personal contact with many women who had lived through them. Some women had spent their childhood in rural poverty and others had emigrated to Britain to find work and had returned to Ireland in the 1970s, as so many did. Then there were the younger women who had experienced none of this, but who had modern, urban lifestyles.

Many of the changes are very recent: as late as the 1950s many people in the west of Ireland were living peasant lives; the industrialisation of much of the Republic only took place in the 1960s; and the marriage bar in certain occupations was not removed until 1973. Add to this the fact that many of the most controversial issues in Irish society such as contraception, divorce and the rights of the family are essentially about the role and rights of women, and it becomes clear that something very important has been happening to women which deserves to be recorded. This book does just that. It is intentionally wide-ranging in scope as it is the first book to give an overview of women's experiences in the period since about 1960.

The central themes of the book revolve around the family and sexuality, both of which are connected with the Roman Catholic Church and its enormously important influence, not only on the structures of Irish society, but also on people's deepest emotions and ways of looking at the world. The book does not, however, fall into the trap of being anti-Church, but includes the experiences of Christian women. A particularly interesting and original section of the book explores the changing lives of nuns and the exciting new ways in which some of them are interpreting their roles.

Through the interview material in the book Irish women speak
for themselves, and give the text a direct and authentic tone that is a
pleasure to read. It is a book in the emerging feminist tradition in
that the author uses women's descriptions of their experiences to
illustrate themes and to fire off thoughts and reflections in the
reader. As well as providing analysis and background information,
the book captures the feelings behind the transition in ordinary
women's lives. As a result it is lively and enjoyable as well as
informative.

Because little has been written about women in the Republic of
Ireland, people both inside and outside the country lack information about recent issues and developments. This book will help to
communicate something of the reality of Irish women's situation to
a wider audience, and will contribute to the understanding between
women of different cultures that is so important to the women's
movement internationally.

JO CAMPLING

1 Introduction: Women and the Family

Talking to women about the differences between their own lives and those of their mothers or daughters, two main themes emerge. The first is the enormous change in living standards over just one generation, and how women's day-to-day work has been transformed by hot water, electricity and modern housing. The second theme concerns a change in women's perceptions of themselves; a noticeable shift towards a stronger sense of identity, towards women actively choosing their way of life rather than simply accepting a predestined role. As one woman put it, her teenage daughter is 'what I wish women would be and what I should have been at her age – an independent individual'. Another woman, Tracy, reflects on her mother's life, saying that her mother would never have considered the idea of looking at herself and asking if she had what she wanted in life:

> Sometimes I feel like saying to her, 'Are you happy? Are you really doing what you want?' She would probably say 'yes', but I don't think the idea of questioning it would have been a part of how she approached things. It's possibly religion – her life has been guided very strongly by it so the need to ask questions was never there.

Maura is in her early thirties, and the comparison between her mother and herself reflects both themes:

> My mother came from a very primitive cottage in the west of Ireland. She went to National school in her bare feet. She showed

1

us a picture of her class – all shaved heads and bare feet. She came
up to Dublin when she was 18. It must have been amazing for her
to live in a nice house with taps and hot water. She had no
qualifications whatsoever as she had left school very young, but
she got into the Civil Service. Then she married and lost her job
because of the marriage bar. She had five children and never took
a job again.

And me, how different my life is! I was born in Dublin. I've
been to university and I was in a women's group there. I am a
teacher, and I am still working although I have a child. There isn't
a little pattern I can slot into – I have to make decisions and
choices for myself that my mother didn't have to make.

For Anne, a mother of seven, the biggest change in her
generation is in her surroundings. She has a comfortable bungalow
with central heating, an up-to-date kitchen and a washing machine,
whereas her mother had to manage with a turf range and a cold tap
in the backyard. In other respects their lives are similar. Like her
mother, Anne's main focus is the house and children, and she has
not worked outside the home since she married. It is between
herself and her daughters that she sees a big difference in attitudes:

That's where the change is. They are more adventurous, they
have more courage to do things than I had. They had a better time
in school and made more use of it. I'd say they look at marriage
differently. Orla says to me, 'I'm not going to get married for
years and years, I'm not going to get tied down. You've had a
hard life and Granny had a hard life and I'm not going to'.

Audrey is of a similar age and is aware of great differences
between her two daughters and herself as a girl. Although she
comes from a middle-class family, her dominant childhood memories are of a cold, damp house in the countryside and of 'poverty,
absolute poverty around'. She now lives in Dublin and her
daughters live a comfortable urban life:

I would say my daughters are very assertive and full of self-
confidence. Very different to how I was at that age. They are also
in better health, which is very important. They are certainly more
indulged, there is no doubt about that. They are the kids I saw in

American pictures way back, they are living the life I fantasised about! Even at 11 or 12 they are having their discos. It is pretty innocent stuff really, just good fun. They dress up with nail varnish and skirts up to here and glitter in their hair. The equivalent of what I would be wearing at 12 would have been a vest, a serge dress and ribbed stockings.

Their relationship with their father is totally different. I mean they refer to him by his first name, and in the morning if I'm away and he's seeing them to school its 'Tom, where are my knickers?'. That would have been unthinkable with my father.

These personal accounts reflect the social and economic changes of recent years, during which significant changes in the status of women have taken place. It has been a period in which Irish society as a whole has undergone a rapid transformation. As Basil Chubb writes, 'the country has altered more in the last fifteen years than it did during the whole of the previous half-century'.[1] In a relatively short space of time Ireland has shed its identity as a predominantly rural country dominated by traditional values and attitudes. It has begun to adopt a more urban, industrial culture which reflects standards and practices common to much of Western Europe. The women's movement is a product of this process in that it first developed in urban areas as women came together to discuss their situation in the light of the approach taken by feminists in other countries, particularly the USA. But the campaigns and debates initiated by the women's movement have themselves fuelled the pace of change, notably through the feminist challenge to traditional attitudes in the areas of sexual morality and the role of women in the family.

When women formed the first women's liberation group in Dublin in 1971, there was, from a feminist point of view, a great deal that needed to be changed. Women in Ireland had fewer rights than in most European countries, and many aspects of women's situation in the Republic compared unfavourably with that of their counterparts in Northern Ireland. Contraception was illegal, divorce was banned in the Constitution and abortion was a criminal act. Single mothers and separated women were ineligible for welfare payments, and women were openly discriminated against in education, employment and the tax and welfare systems. A marriage bar was in operation in the Civil Service and other occupations, forcing women to give up their jobs on marriage. Women had few rights under family law, and were in a highly vulnerable position if their marriages broke down. The illegitimacy law stigmatised children born out of wedlock, and their mothers with them.

In 1971, few of these issues were even discussed. Some, like contraception and abortion, were taboo. Others were dismissed as irrelevant or went unrecognised, as many people prefered to hold to a vision of Ireland as a good Catholic society in which people were committed to family life, rather than face the more uncomfortable reality.

Some of the ideas of women's liberation took longer to take root in Ireland because of the subordinate position of women in Irish society. But to the women who *did* become involved, the extent of women's oppression made the struggle for change all the more urgent. The particular form taken by the women's movement in Ireland had some advantages. Several members of the founder-group in Dublin had media jobs. Through their positions in the *Irish Times*, the *Irish Press* and *Radio Telefeis Eirean* they were able to bring women's issues to public attention in a direct way. Although Ireland was in some ways more conservative and un-feminist than many other European countries, feminists achieved a high media profile for women's issues.

One example of this was the night in March 1971 when women's liberation was the main topic on RTE's popular Saturday evening programme, 'The Late Late Show'. The status of women was debated between panel and audience with anger and passion. In the wake of the publicity which followed, the women's group called a meeting in the Mansion House in Dublin and over a thousand people turned up. As June Levine, a member of the founder group recalls:

We had done what comes naturally to a radical group so full of media people. We'd broken the news. We'd told Ireland about the women's movement. We'd turned women on. We'd revealed the underground anger in women's lives, we'd blown the cover.[2]

Meanwhile, in response to mounting pressure, the Government had established a Commission on the status of women. When it reported at the end of 1972, the Commission made forty-nine recommendations and seventeen suggestions 'designed to eliminate

all forms of discrimination against women in the fields of employment, social welfare, education, the taxation code, property rights
and in all areas of central and local administration'.[3] The number of
recommendations alone indicated the size of the problem. The
report provided the first systematic investigation into discrimination against women in the Republic, though some sensitive areas
such as abortion and discrimination against lesbians were not
included.

In the early 1970s, women in Ireland were concerned with many
of the same issues as women in other European countries.
Campaigns for equal pay, better child-care facilities and anti-
discrimination legislation were taking place right across Europe. In
other ways, the situation of women in the Republic differed
significantly from that in other countries. In Britain and Northern
Ireland, for instance, divorce and contraception were available, and
a more comprehensive welfare state gave women access to a wider
range of social security and health facilities. Married women
formed a substantial proportion of the labour force in both
Northern Ireland and Britain, whereas in the Republic only one in
fifteen married women worked outside the home and women's
traditional roles as family-based wives and mothers were more
firmly established. As a result, the pressure for social change in the
Republic tended to be limited to certain areas. Even now, issues
such as divorce and abortion are unresolved and have proved to be
far more contentious than in many other countries.

The family, the Church and the State

The differences in the situation of women north and south could be
traced back to the struggle for independence. 'Fix your minds on the
ideal of Ireland free, with her women enjoying the full rights of
citizenship in their own nation', had been Countess Markievicz's
advice to nationalists in 1909.[4] Women won the vote in independent
Ireland, but in other ways they paid part of the price of partition.
The ideology adopted by the new State as a symbol of national unity
was both Catholic and nationalist. It was an ideology that glorified
rural Irish life and romanticised the Catholic family. The problem
for women was that this family was rigidly defined and patriarchal.
The only roles for women were as wives and mothers; women were

denied economic independence, were discouraged from taking employment and had very limited rights.

In 1926, nearly two-thirds of the population of the twenty-six counties lived outside towns and even villages, and over half the workforce was in agriculture.[5] Farms were generally small, providing little more than a subsistence living for the majority of country people. Two groups of men – the farmers and tradesmen – dominated the political and social thinking of the new State. Both were essentially conservative, and were backed by an equally conservative Catholic Church. In Terence Brown's words, 'their economic prudence, their necessarily puritanical, repressive sexual mores and nationalistic conservatism, encouraged by a priesthood and Hierarchy drawn considerably from their number, largely determined the kind of country which emerged in the first decades of independence'.[6] At this time 93 per cent of the population was Catholic, and both class and sexual divisions in society were obscured by the dominant ideology.

The industrial base of the country was very small, and the isolationist policies of successive governments prevented any significant industrial development until the 1960s. Economic policy was based on the idea of national self-sufficiency, relying on farming and indigenous industry. The small farm was the key economic unit, and to support it, the family was the key social unit. To politicians the family was the basic unit of the rural economy; to the Church it was the basis of Catholic society. The family had such an important function that its role was enshrined in the 1937 Constitution:

Article 41.1.1 The State recognises the Family as the natural primary and fundamental unit group of Society, and as a moral institution possessing inalienable and imprescriptible rights, antecedent and superior to all positive law.
2. The State, therefore, guarantees to protect the Family in its constitution and authority, as the necessary basis of social order and as indispensable to the welfare of the Nation and the State.[7]

This article clearly reflected Catholic teaching. The virtues of family life were frequently lauded from the pulpit, but as three bishops made clear in 1947, the only true Christian family was that based on marriage: 'The sanctity and permanence of the marriage bond are not a matter of indifference to Catholics. They are fundamental truths of their religion. They are sacred principles of Christian morality necessary for the moral health of the family and the nation'.[8] To both politicians and Churchmen, 'the family and the nation' were inextricably linked, and any threat to the Catholic family was seen as a threat to the stability of society as a whole. This teaching was also reflected in the ban on divorce, contained in Article 41.3 of the Constitution.

The family, as envisaged by both Church and State, was strongly patriarchal. The father was expected to be the head of the household and the breadwinner. His was a strictly disciplinarian, often authoritarian, role. 'By natural and divine law', claimed the Bishop of Clonfert in 1944, 'the father of the family is bound to maintain his home for himself, his wife and his family.'[9] In rural families, the father owned the farm and passed it on to a son when he chose to do so. The continuity of the family and survival of the farm were closely related and were controlled by a strict system of marriage. Women rarely owned land, and had little formal control over farm and financial affairs. The woman of the family was expected to be wife, mother and home-maker. In practice, of course, many women did not accept a secondary position in the family but were strong and assertive individuals who took pride in themselves and their achievements. But the role of women in the ideal family was defined by both Church and political leaders as a strictly home-based existence – so much so that it too was written into the Constitution. Interestingly, the terms 'woman' and 'mother' are used interchangeably in this Article:

Article 41.2.1. In particular, the State recognises that by her life within the home, woman gives to the State a support without which the common good cannot be achieved.

2. The State shall, therefore, endeavour to ensure that mothers shall not be obliged by economic necessity to engage in labour to the neglect of their duties in the home.[10]

In practice, the State ensured that women did not work outside the home not by removing 'economic necessity' but by active prevention. Marriage bars were introduced into many occupations. The State categorised all married women as economically dependent on their husbands so that they could not pay tax separately or claim welfare benefits in their own right, and, as contraception was illegal, women who might have wanted to stay in employment after marriage had difficulty in limiting their families and ended up as full-time mothers instead.

The ideology of the family was further reinforced by Catholic moral teaching. Until very recently, the Irish Church's concern with morality has been largely directed towards sexual matters. The Church denounced sex outside marriage, and saw the procreation of children as the only proper function of sex within marriage. In the 1920s and 1930s, the Irish bishops were concerned about a decline in sexual morality for which they blamed undesirable new influences from abroad:

> The evil one is ever setting his snares for unwary feet. At the moment, his traps for the innocent are chiefly the dance hall, the bad book, the indecent paper, the motion picture, the immodest fashion in female dress – all of which tend to destroy the virtues characteristic of our race.[11]

Anything which challenged the bishops' puritanical and repressive view of sexual morality was denounced as a sin and as a threat to family life. And with such a high percentage of Catholics in the population, together with a tradition of uncritical obedience to Church authority, the bishops' views were generally supported by the majority of the people.

Church and State worked hand in hand to protect Catholic morality and institutionalise the Catholic family. One of the most notorious measures taken by the government was the Censorship of Publications Act of 1929, which led to the banning of books by large numbers of twentieth-century authors, including many Irish ones. The same Act made it illegal to advocate the use of contraceptives. In 1935, the Criminal Law Amendment Act tightened State control over family planning by prohibiting the sale and importation of contraceptives. In the same year, an Act to control public dance halls was introduced. Although it proved to be an ineffective piece of legislation, it was, as J. H. Whyte comments, 'one more attempt to enforce Catholic moral standards by legislation'.[12] Another piece of restrictive legislation for women was the Conditions of Employment Act 1935, which allowed the government to prohibit women from working in certain industries and fix the proportion of female workers in certain circumstances.

The 1937 Constitution was the culmination of this process of institutionalising Catholic doctrine. It afforded a special position to the Catholic Church and reflected Catholic teaching in its articles on the family, education and private property. The new Constitution owed much to de Valera, a man with conservative views on religious and social matters. But his approach was supported by the Catholic majority, and few were prepared to oppose the main thrust of the Constitution. Women's organisations campaigned for the deletion of the articles on the family, education and social policy, but failed to get any member of the Republic's legislature, the Dáil, to champion their cause.[13] This failure reflected both the weakness of women's organisations in the decades following independence and the lack of women in politics. As a result, the Catholic family (and the subordinate status of women within it) was laid as a foundation stone of the new State.

Until the late 1950s, the position of women in Irish society remained relatively static. Ireland was still a predominantly rural country, industrialisation was slow and there was little public challenge to the ideology that had formed the basis of the 1937 Constitution. Women lacked economic and political power, and the problems of the 1940s and 1950s – economic stagnation, a disintegrating rural system and high emigration levels – made it difficult for any group to achieve real social progress. It was not until the 1960s and 1970s that economic development and political change opened up new possibilities for women. 'The Ireland of the 1970s', proclaimed the *Irish Times*, 'contrasts strongly with the internationally popular image of a sleepy backwater on the fringe of Europe. No longer is this the rural island of the emigrants, but a fast-growing industrializing frontier on the edge of industrial Europe'.[14] The new economic policies of Lemass's government encouraged multinational companies to set up plants in Ireland and promoted economic growth based on export-oriented industry. Ireland's entry into the European Economic Community in 1972 marked the end of economic isolation and an over-dependence on Britain, and the integration of the Irish economy with that of capitalist Europe.

Throughout much of the 1960s and 1970s economic growth was sustained, living standards rose and Ireland underwent a rapid modernisation. Factories and roads appeared where none had been before. Emigration slowed down and towns expanded as new housing estates were built to cater for the growing population.

Rural families replaced their cottages with modern bungalows, and rising incomes enabled many people in both town and countryside to furnish their homes with consumer goods. The introduction of television in the 1960s aided the process and brought American and British values into Irish sitting-rooms. Service industries expanded, as did Government programmes for education, health and welfare. The class structure of Irish society reflected these developments as farmers dwindled in number and there was a substantial shift towards skilled manual work and white-collar occupations.[15]

All these changes affected women's lives in ways which will be explored throughout this book. Economic growth made some changes for women inevitable. Women were required to work in many of the new industries, and the development of suburbia brought with it the new and often problematic role of the stay-at-home urban housewife. But positive changes in women's position in society did not come easily. Women had to fight for them. Although the economic situation was now very different, the ideology of the family and the dominant view of a woman's rightful place had changed little. On almost every issue, whether it was equality at work or reproductive rights, women found themselves in opposition to the whole weight of traditional values.

Whatever the difficulties, women achieved a great deal in just a decade. Some well-known landmarks were the removal of the marriage bar in 1973, followed by legislation on equal pay in 1974 and on employment equality in 1977, both of which were facilitated by directives on equality from the European Economic Community. Two years later contraceptives were legalised, although in a very limited fashion, and maternity leave was introduced in 1981. In addition, some important changes were made in family law which gave women increased property rights and greater protection.

Women were having fewer children, and more married women were looking for work. An attitude shift was taking place. Women's expectations were rising, and they were becoming aware of inequalities that previous generations might have taken for granted. 'They have gone on television to talk about being single mothers, admitted publicly to being battered, deserted and sexually frustrated; they have even talked to Gay Byrne about it on the radio.'[16] Women highlighted problems and raised issues for public discussion for the first time.

Feminists played an important role in these developments. The women's movement has never been a monolithic organisation, but a loose network of groups and organisations, some radical and others reformist, some consciousness-raising and others actively campaigning. Groups such as the AIM group for family law reform, the Dublin Rape Crisis Centre and Cherish, an organisation for single parents, were all started by women who wanted to tackle a particular set of problems. Others set up the Contraceptive Action Programme or campaigned to get a Working Women's Charter accepted by trade unions and related organisations. Groups of women also worked on issues like lesbian rights, the treatment of women in the media and violence against women.

A question of values

It was mainly women's issues, such as contraception and marriage reform, that provided the focus for the wider controversy about the liberalisation of Irish society that accompanied the economic and social changes of the 1960s and 1970s. As J. H. Whyte writes:

> as the psychological climate changed rapidly in Ireland, it was natural that laws inherited from past periods should come under increasing scrutiny. Did such laws still accurately enshrine Irish values? If not, how should they be changed? The problem was nowhere more acute than in the area of sexual and marital morality.[17]

He notes the three main areas of controversy: abortion, divorce and contraception. All are issues of particular interest to women, which were brought to public attention largely as a result of the development of the women's movement. It was over the contraception issue in particular that 'the State in Ireland first confronted the law and morals dispute in its modern form'.[18]

This dispute concerned both the nature of morality and the proper role of the State in legislating on moral issues. The traditional Catholic view of morality, and the one which had influenced the 1937 Constitution, was based on the notion of 'natural law'. This assumes that there are basic moral principles which are unconditional and absolute, and which can be applied to specific moral issues to determine what is right and wrong. Natural law is frequently invoked in support of Catholic teaching on the family and on sexual morality. An example of this approach was given in a statement by Archbishop McQuaid of Dublin in 1971:

> Any . . . contraceptive act is always wrong in itself. To speak, then, in this context, of a right to contraception, on the part of an individual, be he Christian or non-Christian or atheist, or on the part of a minority or of a majority, is to speak of a right that cannot even exist.[19]

The recourse to natural law tends to lead to a somewhat rigid notion of morality as a set of rules governing right and wrong. As a working party set up by the Catholic bishops in the 1970s reported, 'a majority of Catholics see morality as keeping rules/laws rather than as a commitment to values'.[20]

In the 1970s, an alternative viewpoint developed which challenged the traditional morality based on natural law. Critics noted that natural law is a problematic doctrine in that it never clearly explains the origins of its principles. As one philosopher pointed out: 'to claim that they are self-evident is merely to dodge the problem of giving reasons for them; and to say that any rational person would accept them is to discreetly imply that one is more rational than one's dissenting neighbours'.[21] The other problem with natural law was its use in justifying legislation which enforced Catholic teaching on issues such as contraception and censorship. This effectively imposed Catholic morality on the Protestant and other minorities in the State, and also encouraged State interference in areas of life which people increasingly believed should be of personal concern only. The use of natural law as the basis of social legislation was clearly at odds with the more progressive view of Ireland as a secular and pluralist society in which everyone had freedom of religious belief.

This latter view gained much ground during the 1970s, and reflected a morality based not on absolutes but on an understanding that moral values vary according to religious background and personal experience. Pressure mounted for legislative and constitutional reform that would aid the transition from the 'confessional state' to a modern, pluralist society. The women's movement was an important part of this trend. It also encompassed a section of the new middle class who wanted social reform to enable Ireland to take its place alongside its EEC partners, and those committed to Irish unity who sought to rid the 1937 Constitution of articles unacceptable to Northern Protestants.

It was perhaps the women's movement which articulated most forcefully the arguments for individual freedom and personal choice within a pluralist society. After all, it was women who felt the full impact of the traditional moral code in their personal lives. Women who wanted to plan their families were prevented from doing so and women who wanted to stay at work after marriage were often blocked by a marriage bar. All too often, women were prevented from making their own decisions. Their husbands were expected to make financial decisions for them, and the priest dealt with moral questions. Feminists fought against every form of restriction and prohibition, arguing that every woman should have the right to control her own destiny and should be free to make choices about every area of her life, whether sexual, economic or social. 'The personal is political' has been for many years a key phrase in the women's movement. Through sharing information about the events and circumstances which shaped their lives, women exposed the link between personal experience and the rules and laws laid down by Church leaders and politicians. As a result, most feminists became strongly opposed to the imposition of the dominant morality, especially in the areas of sexuality and relationships.

During the 1970s a slow but definite separation of Church and State took place, which paved the way for a number of legislative reforms. In 1972, a proposal to remove the special position of the Catholic Church from the Constitution was approved in a referendum with the acquiescence of the Hierarchy. A year later the bishops acknowledged publicly that the State was not obliged to defend the moral teaching of the Catholic Church through legislation. The statement was made with reference to contraception, and although the Church campaigned vigorously against the evils of the 'contraceptive mentality', it held back from exerting its full force directly on the government. In the same year, Mrs Mary McGee brought a case against the State for confiscating a contraceptive cream she had ordered from abroad. The Supreme Court held that the 1935 Act which prohibited the importation of contraceptives violated a married couple's right to privacy. The judgement was significant not only because it was the first step towards reform of the contraception laws, but also because it effectively limited the State's power to interfere with a moral decision taken by an individual in private.

Irish society was becoming more secular, whether the Church liked it or not. Until the 1970s, Ireland had been well-known for its exceptionally devout population, as measured by the numbers attending Mass regularly. A survey in 1971 found that 95.5 per cent of Catholics claimed to have attended Mass the previous Sunday.[22] Just a decade later, the picture had altered dramatically. An Irish survey for the European Values Study Group in 1980 showed that the overall rate of regular Mass-going had fallen to 82 per cent, while among young people it was as low as 72 per cent.[23] The drop-out rate was particularly high among younger people and city-dwellers. According to a more recent study of young Dubliners, only 64 per cent of 17-year-olds go to Mass weekly and only 12 per cent of this age group make a monthly confession to a priest.[24] The author of the survey concluded that 'the socio-religious ethos of the past is no longer as strong as it was formerly in Ireland', and warned that 'the decreasing participation by young people may become a permanent feature of Irish Catholicism'.[25] The past strength of the Church had become its weakness. The Irish Church had been run on a strictly disciplined basis, stressing obedience to its rules and submission to the authority of the priest. As a working party set up by the bishops in the late 1970s commented: 'for many, the practice of religion is more a matter of law/routine/social pressure, rather than a result of intellectual and personal conviction'.[26] Once the faithful started to break their routines and question Church authority, many found that they had little to fall back on. And as religious practice declined, adherence to the Church's moral rules tended to decrease also. The bishops' working party, for example, found that three out of four young people in cities did not regard extra-marital sex as always wrong, and almost one in two young women and men disagreed with the Church's teaching on contraception.[27]

As a result of these changes, the institutional Church and groups who supported traditional Catholic values were becoming concerned by what they perceived to be a decline in moral standards and a threat to family life. Many of their fears were voiced by Pope John Paul II on his visit to Ireland in 1979. But the Pope's interest in restoring traditional values in the areas of sexual morality and family life led him to the view that Ireland had a special role to play in this process, as it was one of the few Catholic countries that had not legalised either divorce or abortion. He called on Ireland to 'continue to give witness before the modern world to her traditional commitment, corresponding to the true dignity of man, to the sanctity and indissolubility of the marriage bond'.[28] The Pope's visit was a call to arms for those who believed that even in Ireland traditional values were being eroded, and that the tide of liberalisation should be stemmed.

One way of preventing legislative reform on a particular issue is to prohibit it in the Constitution. At the time of the Pope's visit divorce was banned in the Constitution, but abortion was not. It was a criminal act under the 1861 Offences Against the Person Act, but this was open to reform at any time by the normal parliamentary procedures. The proposal by 'Pro-Life' groups in 1982 to amend the Constitution to prohibit abortion was a conscious attempt to prevent any such reform. It seemed a safe issue as the majority of the population was against abortion, but it turned into a bitter and divisive campaign. The amendment became the focus for a major confrontation between progressive and traditional opinion. A referendum was eventually held in 1983 over the proposal to insert a clause into the Constitution giving the foetus a right to life equal to that of the mother. Although it was passed, the poll was low and the strength of the opposition to the amendment was evidence of the extent to which people were now prepared to challenge the Church's authority on certain matters. In the campaign against the amendment, women's groups were joined by the Protestant Churches, some politicians, the Irish Congress of Trade Unions and sections of almost every profession, from journalists and doctors to lawyers and academics. This is not to say that all these groups were sympathetic to a feminist view on abortion. Many took great trouble to advertise their anti-abortion stance. The factor uniting such disparate groups was their opposition to writing the Catholic Church's teaching on abortion into the Constitution.

The amendment campaign showed up the enormous gap between the moral standpoints of traditional and non-traditional groups. To traditionalists, the issue was straightforward: abortion is murder and should be outlawed. To opposers of the amendment, the debate was far more complex as it raised many questions about the role of the Constitution, about medical and legal ethics and about the power of the Catholic Church.

The same arguments about the relationship between morality, the law and individual people's lives are made on a day-to-day basis on many other women's issues such as rape and the treatment of unmarried mothers. They came to the fore once again in the debate over the 1985 Act to amend the family planning legislation. The Act removed the need for a prescription for non-medical contraceptives such as condoms, and allowed them to be sold freely to persons over the age of 18. Although the effect of the Act was to legalise practices which were already established in certain areas, it was only narrowly passed by the Dáil after strong opposition from both the Fianna Fáil party and the Catholic Church. Statements by the Archbishop of Dublin, Dr McNamara, and the Bishop of Limerick, Dr Newman, were particularly notable as they seemed to contradict the Hierarchy's previous acceptance of a degree of separation between Church and State. 'Let me remind all politicians who profess to be Catholics', said Dr Newman, 'that they have a duty to follow the guidance of their Church in areas where the interests of Church and State overlap.'[29] Dr McNamara, too, asserted that Catholic politicians cannot separate their religious beliefs from their legislative duties. How, he asked, could they 'justify passing a measure which, in the eyes of young people, will give the appearance of legal sanction to what is against God's law, and will progressively result in our teenage population being presented with increased opportunities and inducements to do what is morally wrong?'[30]

Stressing the seriousness of the proposed legislation, Dr McNamara echoed the sentiments of Pope John Paul II when he said 'our society as a whole stands at a decisive moral crossroads. At this turning-point in history Ireland must choose'.[31] Dr McNamara's appointment to the powerful position of Archbishop of Dublin suggests that any further attempt to loosen the bonds between Church and State is likely to meet with significant opposition.

As a campaign for divorce begins in earnest, the stage is set for another round in the fight between traditional and progressive forces on yet another issue of direct concern to women. Once again, the traditional view is clear-cut and is based on the ideology of the family. 'We are totally and utterly opposed to divorce because it is the ultimate and most deadly attack on the family', said the chairman of a newly-formed group, Family Solidarity. According to their motto, 'the family is the true measure of the greatness of the nation'. The group's leaders believe in legislation to support their moral views, as shown by the chairman's comments on the proposal to make contraception available to unmarried people: 'Family planning for people who are not forming a family is merely a licence to fornicate and we think this is a threat to the family . . . If you have unmarried people of 18 who are not prepared to make the commitment of marriage then we take the view that they have no right to sexual indulgence'.[32]

On the other hand, feminists argue that every adult should have the right to both divorce and contraception, and that it is up to individuals whether or not they choose to avail themselves of them. With this view goes a rejection of the idea that there is one 'correct' form of the family. Rather, the women's movement has supported the idea that people should be able to decide for themselves how they conduct their relationships, and that single parents, lesbians or unmarried people should not be discriminated against for not being 'proper' families.

In Ireland today, there are many who hold a traditional view of the family and of women's place within it. But this view no longer automatically holds sway over politicians and public opinion as it did in the past. The homogeneity of attitudes in Irish society is gone. Today, moral issues that relate to the family or to sexual matters are highly controversial, and opinions are guaranteed to be sharply divided.

A noticeable increase in self-awareness and assertiveness among very many women has meant that more women are prepared to say what they think, and act on their beliefs. But women are still underrepresented in all decision making levels in society, including the Dáil, and often lack the political power necessary to make their voices heard on major social questions. Organisations such as the Employment Equality Agency, Rape Crisis Centres and local women's groups can speak out on particular issues, but do not command the institutional power of established bodies such as the Church. There is now a Department of Women's Affairs, with its own Minister, which is supposed to promote women's interests, though this has been criticised by women's organisations for being a token gesture with too small a budget and too little influence on government.

In many practical aspects, the situation of women in the Republic still compares unfavourably with that of women in Northern Ireland. In a submission to the New Ireland Forum in 1983, Clara Clark and Eileen Evison compared women's lot north and south of the border. They found that out of twenty-one points of difference only four favoured the south. In many areas including divorce, family planning, health care and family welfare, women were better off in the north.[33] The women most disadvantaged by the lack of rights in these areas are those who rely most on the State for financial support and other services: families on low incomes or welfare allowances, women with large families and those whose marriages have broken down. Amongst those living in poverty in the Republic, women and children form the largest group. Women who are financially secure can avoid many disadvantages. They can afford to pay a good doctor or travel to a family planning clinic and they are not entangled in the welfare net. On top of this class divide in the Republic there are notable differences between urban and rural women in terms of opportunities and facilities. Women in rural areas tend to have more limited employment prospects than their urban sisters, and have poorer access to facilities such as family planning clinics and legal advice centres.

There is still a long way to go before women reach a position of real equality in Irish society. As the debates about the family and the role of women continue, the second half of the 1980s will no doubt see further changes and controversies. Yet many women are aware that the situation today is vastly different from what it was when the Republic was still a strongly rural country and women were closely tied to narrow roles within their families. In comparison with the generation reared in the period before the 1960s, younger women have higher expectations of life, and take for granted a certain degree of equality between the sexes. They are generally less religious than their mothers, and are more critical of their surroundings. Although large class differences remain, their material circumstances are generally better and their schooling lasts longer. Unlike their mothers, younger women can control their fertility, and are freer to make choices about many aspects of their lives.

Women have been through a period of rapid transition from the old to the new, from the rural to the urban. Values and norms which the majority of people accepted without question thirty years ago are now queried and debated; the economy and the class structure have been transformed by industrialisation and urbanisation. In order to understand the nature of this transition, and the degree to which it has affected women's lives, we must first turn to rural life in the pre-1960s period and look in more detail at the roles women played in the post-independence countryside.

2 Maidens and Myths: Women in Rural Life

> That Ireland that we dreamed of would be . . . a land whose countryside would be bright with cosy homesteads, whose fields and villages would be joyous with the sounds of industry, with the romping of sturdy children, the contests of athletic youths, the laughter of comely maidens, whose firesides would be the forums for the wisdom of serene old age. Eamonn de Valera, 18 March 1943.[1]

> It was a hard, hard life, looking back on it. Molly, Co. Galway, aged 87.

In his famous speech of 1943, de Valera described the romantic view of Irish rural life. It was an ideal which had inspired 'poets and patriots', but which bore little resemblance to the harsh reality of most country people's lives. For the majority, living on the land was a matter of survival at a low standard of living. Half the farms in the country were less than 30 acres, and in many counties much of the land was poor – boggy, rocky or mountainous. It was hard work producing enough food for the family to eat, and diets were simple. The standard rural home was a three-roomed cottage, except in areas where farms were larger and families could afford better housing. In western counties such as Mayo, Donegal and Kerry, at least one in three families lived in grossly overcrowded conditions, with more than two persons per room. For those in Dublin too, conditions were notoriously bad, especially in the tenements of North Dublin city. Over 62 000 families in Dublin were overcrowded in one and two-roomed dwellings.[2]

20

Molly was brought up on Co. Galway in the early years of this century. She was the eldest of fourteen children and remembers the family home:

> We lived in a cottage – it was my grandfather's small farm. There were three rooms, one to one side and one to the other. The kitchen was in the middle. There was a place above the two side rooms, and you had to have steps to get up there. Three or four of the boys used to sleep up there. There were three girls in the bed, myself and two of my sisters. Then there would be smaller ones in cots, and beds here and there. It was very crowded. We couldn't all have a meal at the same time. My mother and father would have theirs first, and two of us would sit with them. After dinner my father used to play his flute. He played the loveliest old tunes.
>
> We had oil lamps, and candles for the bedroom. Then you'd have to go out to the pump for a bucket of water. We often had to go three miles to a well to get a can of spring water as they usen't to like the pump water for drinking.
>
> At the back of our garden was a river. On a Monday I used to hate coming home from school, because my mother would be doing the washing. There would be a big bath of clothes and two buckets, one each side. We'd have to take them down to the river to rinse the clothes, then bring them back up again and hang them on lines or hedges to dry.

Modern facilities were scarce in rural houses. Even by 1946, only one farmhouse in five had any form of toilet, and only one in twenty had one indoors.[3] There was no electricity outside the major towns. Few country roads had proper surfaces – most were dirt roads. Turf was the main fuel, used for cooking and heating. The women of the house cooked food over the open hearth. The cottages were stone-built with small windows, making them smoky and dark inside, but warm enough when the turf was good and the thatch sound.

Molly: There was no such thing as coal at that time, just turf. It was an open hearth. There were hobs on each side, and you'd put a bit of a fire there and the oven on it, and you'd put in your cake of bread and bake it there. All the brown bread all the time! Often my mother would have two cakes of bread made in the morning before we got up for our breakfast, and she used to bake in the evening as well.

Everything was cooked on the fire. We had bacon and cabbage an awful lot, that's what everyone had. She'd take a piece of meat and put it in the iron pot, and the vegetables would be chopped up and put in and boiled as well. The potatoes too, everything was boiled. We used to keep two pigs as well, and my mother would boil for those two pigs in the morning after we'd had our meal. The pot over the fire was never empty.

In the spring, the pigs would be sold, and we'd buy what we needed to sow. We had a huge big garden, and my father grew everything we needed – carrots, parsnips, onions, cabbage and potatoes.

Molly married and had ten children of her own. She and her husband had a small house in a town, and she remembers two events which, at the time, seemed to be a wonderful improvement on her mother's lot:

I had to do all the washing in the house. The cold tap was out in the yard, and I had to heat all the water I wanted in a pot or a kettle. I remember you'd get a washboard at that time for 1/6d. It was made of tin, but it would wear out in no time and cut your fingers. One day I was at the shops and I saw this washboard, and it was made of glass. It was 3/6d, that was the price of it, and I had to wait a week or so until I could afford to buy it. They were only after coming in at that time, and it just shows you like. I've often told that story, I thought I was the queen bee the day I bought the glass washboard!

We were living in the same house when the electric light came. I suppose it was over forty years ago. Oh sure, I thought it was heaven on earth!

It is difficult to get a clear picture of women's role in the Ireland of the 1930s to 1950s. Personal memories, the occasional government report and the literature of the period all help, but there is a serious lack of anthropological and sociological data. One of the few studies of the time was Arensberg and Kimball's portrait of a rural community in Co. Clare in the 1930s.[4] Although their detailed descriptions of daily life are useful, their overall picture of people living satisfactory, well-defined lives within a stable peasant tradition has been criticised as over-romantic, as it ignored many unsatisfactory features of rural life – such as high emigration, the decline of smallholdings and the economic divisions within the community.[5] Ireland differed from other peasant cultures in Europe in that it did not have a stable unbroken tradition stretching back hundreds of years. After centuries of exploitation by foreign landlords, rural life had been violently and tragically disrupted by the great famine of 1845–8 and by lesser famines in other years up to the 1880s. Since the early years of the nineteenth century, the land had been unable to support all the children born on it. Emigration had begun before the great famine, increased greatly during it and continued at varying levels until the 1960s.

Prior to the famine, farms were generally subdivided for the children of the family. The average size of holdings therefore decreased, to the point where many grew barely enough potatoes to support a family. When the blight struck and the crop failed, starvation followed. The devastation was exacerbated by homelessness as landlords evicted tenants who could not pay the rent, and by the epidemics of infectious diseases that struck a weakened people. The population of Ireland dropped by almost a quarter between 1841 and 1851.[6] More than one and a half million people died of starvation or disease, or emigrated.

The famine wrought great changes in rural life. The landless labourers and cottiers were worst affected, and were virtually wiped out in some areas of the west. The farmer class, who either owned the land or had relatively secure tenancies, were better able to withstand the famine as they had poultry, cows and grain with which to supplement the diet of potatoes. The system of land inheritance favoured by the farmers became more firmly entrenched in the post-famine countryside.[7] This system brought with it particular patterns of marriage and family life – patterns which established the basic roles of women in rural Ireland well into the twentieth century.

The most urgent need was to stop the subdivision of land. Instead, farmers tried to maintain their standard of living from generation to generation by keeping their farms intact, and consolidating holdings wherever possible. This meant that only one son could inherit, and his marriage assumed a new importance. His wife would play an important part in preserving the family farm and ensuring the continuity of the father's line. Marriage increasingly became an economic transaction as the family's standard of living could only be maintained if the wife brought a dowry with her. Arranged marriages, which occurred among farmers before the famine, became more common in post-famine times. This was a change from the norm among the cottiers and labourers before the famine, when young people generally chose their own marriage partners. Although these classes increasingly adopted the behaviour patterns of the farmer class, non-arranged marriages persisted in some areas, particularly in the west, where sub-division of the land also continued to some extent after the famine.[8]

The famine also weakened women's economic position. The 1840s saw a dramatic drop in women's work as spinners of wool, cotton and linen.[9] On farms, women's work became less important with the shift from tillage to livestock in the countryside. Both these changes decreased women's economic contribution to the household and emphasised the importance of the dowry in marriage.

But a farmer could rarely provide a dowry for more than one daughter, and only one son could inherit the farm. As marriage became economically based, large numbers of men and women failed to marry at all, and many others who could find no place on the land were forced to emigrate.

Rural Ireland became characterised by its low marriage rate, late age of marriage, large numbers of single people and a high emigration rate. Each of these characteristics shaped and defined women's lives in particular ways.

Marriage

In post-famine farming families the father normally held the dominant position in the household. He was the one who made the decisions about the family and the farm and decided which son would inherit. Most fathers had very formal, authoritarian relationships with their children, particularly with their sons. At about the age of 7 a boy left his mother's knee and entered his father's sphere of work, but he stayed a 'boy' until his father agreed to pass on the farm to him, by which time he could be 40 or 50 years old. This led to the strange phenomenon, well-known in rural Ireland, of fully-grown men having no life of their own and being fully under their father's control. The 'boy' was also unable to marry until he inherited the farm, this being the reason for so many late marriages. As a result, many women married men much older than themselves. In half the marriages in the mid-1920s the bridegroom was at least ten years older than the bride.[10] This age difference in turn reinforced the dominant role of the husband and the subservience of the wife.

If an arranged marriage was wanted by the family, the parents looked for a suitable wife for the son who was to inherit the farm. The match was essentially an economic deal, designed to link two extended families with a bond of mutual obligations and to preserve the family farm. This tradition of arranged marriage was not confined to the countryside, but was followed to some extent by shopkeepers and tradesmen. In either case a suitable wife had to be found – someone who would be a good worker and bear healthy children. 'A good husband is a skilled farmer; a good wife is a skilled, willing household worker and auxiliary field hand', wrote Arensberg and Kimball. A farmer had explained to them the qualities to look for in a wife: 'If it wasn't for the woman the farmer wouldn't last, and when he is getting a wife for one of his sons, he should look to a house where there has been an industrious and intelligent woman, because she has taught her daughters to work and that is what is needed'.[11]

The two fathers negotiated the marriage agreement, sometimes aided by a matchmaker. If a deal looked possible, the prospective bride and groom met – often in a bar, or in someone's house, with relatives present. If they 'suited' the deal could go ahead.

Molly: I had a friend who worked in a shop, and on a Friday night the country people would be coming in and matchmaking. They would all be in, and drink coming into them, and we'd be in the kitchen chatting and playing cards and this would be going on in the bar next door. There would be such a girl coming in now, and they'd be making a match for her. They'd all go off and leave them to have a chat, the fellow and the girl themselves, and then the others would come back. They'd be chatting and talking about land. The families would regulate what the girl would have to do, what money she'd have and they might be bargaining over a few pounds like. Then they'd be shaking hands and going, and they might have to come back the following Friday to fix that up.

Then you'd hear [of] the wedding coming off. It all went by farm and work and money.

The bridegroom's father went to a solicitor and made the land over to his son; the girl's father made arrangements to pay the dowry. After the wedding the bride moved into her husband's house, and the old couple retired to the side-room of the cottage. The new wife had no possessions of her own. The dowry was paid by her father to her husband, and every knife and plate in the house belonged to him, and would eventually be passed on to her son.

Alice is now in her seventies and had an arranged marriage. She still lives with her husband in the farm cottage into which she moved on her wedding day:

My marriage was arranged by a cousin of mine. He said I would be suitable for the slaving! It was the custom for girls to marry farmers. I'd met Michael a few times at dances. There were no dance halls, only country crossroads where the girls and boys would meet on summer evenings, and dancing in the kitchens of country houses. Oh, we used to have great old times! Michael was living here himself with his brother and the father. I was charmed with myself for getting married. We had a party in our house after the wedding, a big do. Then we came up here from the crossroads with lighted candles and torches and we danced in the barn here below till morning. Most of the marriages were matches then.

Today, when expectations of marriage are so different, it is hard to understand what an arranged marriage was like. Alice says simply that she had to do as she was told. She felt lonely leaving home but came to live with nice people, and she accepted the work she had to do in the house and on the farm. Given the lack of data on the period, it can be helpful to look to literature to catch a glimpse of the feelings involved. In his novel *The Bogman*, Walter Macken describes the thoughts in a young man's mind as he ponders his marriage:

She could cook, couldn't she, and she had £250 in the bank as Barney stated and you could buy a new mowing-machine for that and a new plough and maybe another cow and they would be living on the fat of the land. Where was all the love business you read about in books long ago? He never saw any of it around Caherlo. They got married this way.

And later, after the wedding ceremony, he admits to himself that 'she embarrassed him. She shouldn't make this personal. It was a deal. She was all right, but the night frightened him. The long night home and then when they would be alone. Two strangers that were wedded for ever. He felt his knees quaking with panic'.[12]

For the woman, marriage meant leaving her own family and joining a strange household. In Maírtín Ó Cadhain's story, 'The Harelip', Nora is married to an older man on a farm many miles from her home. To her parents it is a good match, for their daughter has made a step upwards from their own small and rocky coastal farm to the richer land of the plains. But Nora herself feels 'tossed on a wave's crest at the caprice of God'.[13]

Have no regrets. You've made a good swap, lashings and leavings being your own mistress here on the level plain, in place of the rocks and the slave-labour. We'll send you an odd cargo of dulse, an odd bottle of poteen, and a bundle of nuts in the autumn.

Nora's heart missed a beat. She had forgotten until now that there was no dulse, no nuts, no poteen here.[14]

After the wedding, her relatives depart and she is left alone with this unknown man, her husband:

She took fright. Till now she hadn't thought of the bed. That dreary voice, assured, self-assertive, set up waves of repulsion in her, yet she recognised it as the voice of authority, not to be denied if he felt like bringing the thing to a head.[15]

As well as getting to know her husband, the new wife had to develop a working relationship with her parents-in-law. It could be difficult for the old mother to adjust to the new woman in her house, and tensions were inevitable. The younger woman had to prove herself by working hard and, above all, by having children. As one farmer explained, 'if the old people do not see evidence of increase of young, then the boy's father's people get angry and abuse her, but if they do, they do not let her do any work and are proud'.[16] A childless woman was an object of shame and derision. Nobody would have questioned the man's fertility. It was the woman's job to have children, and if she failed, she was no good. In some areas there was a tradition of 'country divorces', where a childless woman was sent back to her father's family. Her husband could not remarry as legal divorce was unobtainable, but he could pass on the farm to a brother, who could then marry and carry on the family line. Once again, the economic imperative of maintaining the farm overrode other considerations.

Traditional marriage has been described as 'co-operation without great physical closeness'.[17] A strict division of labour between men and women kept them apart for most of the time. The man tilled the fields and, if they lived near the coast, fished. The seasonal tasks were his – haymaking, harvesting cereal crops and cutting turf. The woman was responsible for the domestic economy. She took care of the young children, prepared food, provided clothing for the family and kept the house warm and in good order. She kept the poultry and pigs, and milked the cows.

Conrad Arensberg described the daily routine of a Co. Clare woman on a small farm in the 1930s.[18] The day began as she rekindled the turf fire and hung the kettle over it for breakfast. She served the men their breakfast of home-baked bread, eggs, milk and tea. All day she worked between the house and the farmyard, baking bread, tending animals and seeing to the children. There was turf to fetch for the fire and buckets of water to carry. For dinner she boiled potatoes, adding cabbage and bacon when she could. The men ate first, and the women and children ate afterwards. The chores continued through the afternoon with washing, mending and knitting to be fitted in. Supper was the next meal to prepare, along with feeding and milking the cows. After she had put the children to bed, there was often more baking or knitting to be done. According to an old country proverb, one woman in the house must always be working.

Siobhan was brought up in Co. Galway in the 1940s and remembers the role divisions in the family:

> My father looked after the livestock mostly. We were always there too, ready to help when it was needed. There were four girls and seven boys, and we always had to go out and help with the hay and the turf. But it makes me very cross, because thirty minutes or so before the meals we had to leave the field and go in and

ready the meals, whereas the lads were never asked to do these jobs at all. As a result they grew up hopeless. There was always someone there dancing attendance on them, getting their meals, washing and ironing, having their shoes polished. All these jobs were expected of the girls.

She remembers standing and serving the men before she and her sisters could eat:

> They ate at such a rate, it was non-stop cutting and buttering this home-made bread, which my mother would have baked in the early morning. When the table was empty we'd sit down and eat, and as soon as the table was cleared and the washing-up done we'd be out in the fields. It was non-stop.

The separation of male and female tasks was bolstered by folklore. It was unlucky if a man was present when a woman was churning butter, and bad luck to have a woman in a boat. As is so often the case, it was acceptable for a woman to help with men's work such as potato-picking and haymaking, but unthinkable for a man to help with hers. 'That a man should concern himself with a woman's work, such as the sale of eggs or the making of butter, is the subject of derisive laughter.'[19] This indicates that in rural life men's work was generally valued more highly than women's work.

Men and women were separated in many spheres of life other than their work. They sat in different parts of the Church during Mass, they went to town at different times and they often socialised separately. Women very rarely entered pubs. These were male territory, where men could gather and talk about farming and the weather and the state of the nation, undisturbed by their women-folk. Social contact between women mainly took place in the home.

A woman who married in the countryside lived out a closely defined role. Often in an arranged marriage, she was supposed to be subservient to her husband. Economically, and often emotionally, this subservience was real, though it was offset to some extent by the strength women developed through their responsibility for the children and the domestic economy. Also, in areas where seasonal migration was common, women would be left in charge of a farm for months at a time while the men were absent in England or Scotland. But generally the woman's tasks were clear-cut, and a farmer's wife was expected to fulfil her main roles of child-bearing and hard manual work around the house and farm. Some of the work might be shared with other female relatives if any lived in the house, and on larger farms the families would have been able to afford some domestic help; otherwise the wife carried out all the women's work herself.

Permanent celibacy

Many men and women in post-famine rural society never married at all. Until recently, Ireland had the highest proportion of single people in any European country. In the 1930s, 55 per cent of women and 74 per cent of men in the 25–34 age group were single. The corresponding rates for England and Wales at that time were 33 per cent for women and 35 per cent for men.[20] Even among people aged 45–54 in 1936, 34 per cent of men and 25 per cent of women were still unmarried.[21]

This exceptionally high proportion of single people persisted until the 1960s. Throughout the intervening decades, almost one in three men and one in four women never married. In his study of a west of Ireland parish in the 1960s, Hugh Brody found that of a total population of 436 people, eighty-seven were bachelors over the age of 35. The majority lived alone, while others lived with elderly parents or in sibling groups.[22] The picture is a familiar one. Even today, many rural parishes consist in large part of bachelors living alone – people who have been overtaken by time, living the old life in a new society and increasingly isolated.

What caused this excess of single people? Some commentators have looked to the puritanical nature of Irish Catholicism for an answer. The Catholic Church in Ireland is renowned for its preoccupation with sexual morality. It exalted celibacy as the highest form of human existence, and built on the Celtic tradition of penitence and asceticism in its support of a family system in which sexuality was strongly repressed.

Although the Church's attitude to sexuality has had a profound influence on Irish society, it is now widely accepted that Catholic morality did not on its own cause the curious social patterns of the countryside, but rather served to reinforce a system which developed out of economic necessity. As Robert Kennedy put it, 'the special character of present-day Irish Catholicism is the result, and not the cause, of a high proportion of single persons in the Irish population'.[23]

The desire for a good economic deal to accompany the marriage contract was so strong that it was often very difficult to find a suitable wife with a large enough dowry. A man could maintain his standard of living more easily by remaining single than by marrying and having children, unless his wife brought some compensating wealth with her. The need for a sexual partner and the desire to have children were subordinated to the need to preserve the family's living standard and social status. As most farming was at a subsistence level, many families had to struggle just to have enough to eat, and the memories of famine were all too vivid.

This basic economic reason for the low marriage rate is, however, complicated by other factors. By the time the chosen son was allowed to inherit the farm or business, and therefore ready to marry, he was often too old to do so easily. Frank O'Connor describes this in his story, 'The Impossible Marriage':

> His mother and he were both familiar with the situation in its simple form, common as it is in Ireland, and could have listed a score of families where a young man or woman 'walked out' for years before he or she was in a position to marry, too often to find themselves too old or tired for it.[24]

In the story, Jim is living with his elderly mother. She is very demanding of his attention and too jealous to allow him to marry:

> Jim had never been very shy with girls, but none of them he had met seemed to him to be half the woman his mother was, and, unknown to himself he was turning into a comfortable old bachelor who might or might not at the age of forty-five decide to establish a family of his own. His mother spoiled him, of course. . . But spoiling is a burden that the majority of men can carry a great deal of without undue handicap.[25]

Mothers in Ireland are renowned for their close relationships with their sons; tending to their needs, smothering them with affection and capturing them in a manipulative relationship of dependence and duty. It is a stereotype that has been exaggerated and for which women have been blamed unfairly, but it contains an element of truth. No doubt women in unromantic marriages found an outlet for their emotional feelings in their relationships with their sons.

Patrick Kavanagh's poem, 'The Great Hunger', is a savage indictment of rural life, and of the mother–son relationship, and points out the contrast between the ideal family and reality:

> Maguire was faithful to death:
> He stayed with his mother till she died
> At the age of ninety-one.
> She stayed too long,
> Wife and mother in one.
> When she died
> The knuckle-bones were cutting the skin of her son's backside
> And he was sixty five.[26]

The promise of marriage had been there, but the hope had died:

> Macguire grunts and spits
> Through a clay-wattle moustache and stares about him from
>   the height
> His dream changes again like the cloud-swung wind
> And he is not so sure now if his mother was right
> When she praised the man who made the field his bride.[27]

Even if a man was free and willing to marry, finding a wife could be difficult. Women migrated out of rural areas at such a rate that the ratio of men to women became very lopsided. There were more women in the towns and more men in the countryside. In 1936, for instance, for every 100 females there were 111 males in Connaught and 106 in Munster.[28] The situation was, of course, even more unbalanced for single people. Comparing men aged 25–9 with women aged 20–4, there were 112 men to every 100 women in rural areas, and for people aged 45–54 there was a staggering 185 men to every 100 women.[29]

Women in the countryside were faced with a dilemma. If they wanted to marry they could either stay on the farm and wait until the local bachelors became free to marry in the hope of being chosen, or they could leave home and take their chances with the rest in Dublin or abroad. The city life held many attractions and most women chose to go. A single woman had low status in the countryside, and faced a hard working life servicing the needs of the men in the household. Daughters were not tied to the farm by bonds of duty to the same extent as sons unless they were pressurised to stay and care for an ailing parent. Many young women left in their late teens and early twenties, and by the time the men were free to marry the women of their generation had gone.

In Dublin, the greater percentage of women meant that many of those who wanted to marry were denied the opportunity of doing so. But at least a single woman in the city could get a job and exert some degree of choice over her life. Yet even in Dublin jobs were scarce, and for many thousands of young women and men who could find in Ireland neither a job nor the chance to marry there was one remaining option – to take the emigrant boat.

Emigration

> Oh I pity the mother that rears up the child
> And likewise the father who labours and toils,
> To try and support them he will work night and day
> And when they are reared up they will go away.
>
> (traditional song)

By the mid-1920s, 43 per cent of Irish-born men and women were living overseas, over a million of them in the USA alone. Ireland was unique in the depths of the tragedy of its lost people. For most European countries the corresponding figure was about 5 per cent. After Ireland, the next highest was Norway with 15 per cent of its native people living abroad.[30]

Emigration was closely related to social class. Few people from large farms or professional backgrounds emigrated as they were more financially secure, and religious life was an option for the single. The majority of those on the boats to England and America were children from small farms or from unskilled and semi-skilled working-class homes. They were the sons who did not inherit, and the daughters for whom there was no place in the countryside. A woman from a middle-class family remembers that 'even to admit you had relatives in America was to go down socially'.

Up to 1950, with the exception of the war years, slightly more women than men emigrated. Their destinations were the big cities of the USA, Canada and Britain, where the majority found manual jobs. In the USA in the 1920s, four out of five Irish-born women workers were domestic servants, and the majority of the rest had semi-skilled jobs in factories.[31] Emigration from Ireland was largely 'a rural–urban movement which happened to cross international boundaries'.[32] Dublin could not offer women enough jobs. It was not a major manufacturing city, more a service and commercial centre, and at the same time as Ireland could not absorb all its young people, there was a growing demand for labour in many large industrial cities abroad.

Siobhan was brought up on a small farm and emigrated in 1948. 'At nineteen I went to America, to New Jersey. I had a sister there, and perhaps that decided me to go. Well, it was the understood thing then, there was nothing else in Ireland really. Only emigration. Very few did get jobs in Ireland.'

She was unusual as she came home again. Most emigrants stayed abroad and their sisters and brothers and cousins went out to join them. America exerted a strong pull on young people's minds, and American money from relatives helped many farming families to keep going. Audrey remembers it well from her childhood in Co. Mayo:

When I was growing up it was American culture all the time. The beautiful Christmas cards which used to arrive with glitter on them, and reindeers. I would have given anything to have got those. Then there were the clothes that used to come from America which were all frills and bows. And there were the magazines. I remember an advertisement for a fruit drink, with the perfect all-American family sitting on a beach. There was a kind of fantasy land about America. It was just across the water. New York was nearer than Dublin.

People in her village used dollars sent by relatives: 'It was the dollar that kept the west of Ireland afloat really. People had dollars and you could exchange them locally in the pubs and that. It was a usable currency'.

For many decades emigration had been an inevitable consequence of the practice of allowing only one son to stay on the farm.

People left in order to preserve the family farm, and sent money home to support the ones who had stayed in Ireland. But gradually, through the 1930s and 1940s, emigration became a preference rather than a necessity. At a time when politicians were praising family life in rural Ireland, when de Valera was exalting the countryside 'bright with cosy homesteads', the people of the west were streaming away, leaving the traditional way of life as fast as they could:

> 'It's a cruel life that takes you away from the land that God made you for.'
> 'Oh, what are you talking about, father?' said Michael irritably. 'Sure what did anybody ever get out of the land but poverty and hard work and potatoes and salt?'[33]

In this story by Liam O'Flaherty, the boy's sister is going to America too. 'Her mother's life loomed up before her eyes, a life of continual misery and suffering, hard work, birth pangs, sickness and again hard work and hunger and anxiety.' She knows what she is leaving, and as she thinks of her destination, the USA, her mind is full of confused thoughts 'of love and of foreign men and of clothes and of houses where there were more than three rooms and where people ate meat every day'.[34]

Hugh Brody wrote that by 1940, Ireland had developed its characteristic double nostalgia: 'Emigrants in Chicago sang heart-felt laments about home, while their younger brothers and sisters at home talked wistfully about the wonders and riches of America'.[35]

Emigration, like postponed marriage and the large number of single people, was largely the result of the economic order in the countryside in the post-famine period. It had a profound effect on women's lives – both on the thousands of women who left their country and on the generations of mothers who brought up their children only to see them disappear overseas.

Women's attitudes to rural life

What did women in traditional rural society feel about their role? Did they accept it, were they happy or unhappy, fulfilled or unfulfilled? It is difficult to know what questions to ask. Our values today are so different, our reference points so far removed from the boundaries of parish life. Is it fair to ask, from the standpoint of the 1980s, what women thought of their lives fifty years ago? Perhaps it is important to find out what we can. Although arranged marriages are a thing of the past, the values of traditional family life are still held up as ideals and lie at the root of many modern issues.

We have seen that emigration in this century increasingly reflected a rejection of the farming way of life, a rejection that may well have been more pronounced in women than in men. As early as 1911, George Russell had warned Irish society of the consequences of women's dissatisfaction:

> Today the starved soul of womanhood is crying out over the world for an intellectual life and for more chance of earning a living. If Ireland will not listen to this cry, its daughters will go on slipping silently away to other countries, as they have been doing – all the best of them, all the bravest, all those most mentally alive.[36]

It was not women who inherited the land, it was not women who felt the overriding importance of preserving patrilineal descent. There is no doubt that many women who have made the transition from rural to modern life look back on their own or their mother's lives and see little but grinding poverty, soul-destroying hard work and a total lack of personal choice.

Siobhan: If you ask people would they live their lives again, a lot of people say yes, but my mother wouldn't. She was working morning, noon and night. We lived in a two-bedroomed farmhouse. There were eleven children in two bedrooms.

As children we had oil lamps. Oil was rationed during the war and if your ration went before your next was due that was just too bad. We had no modern conveniences at all, not even cold running water. It all had to be drawn. Times were desperately hard. I remember my brothers going to school without shoes. It doesn't bear thinking about from those times to now. Everyone was in the same predicament, that is the reason we survived it, you see.

Molly: I look at all they have now, and I look back and think of all my mother had to do. She was on the go all the time as far as I remember. Only for that my father was good, we'd never have managed.

But what about women fifty years ago who had no modern standards by which to assess their lives? Until the 1940s the horizons of country life were generally very narrow. The daily tasks were predictable and routine, and people's lives were closely structured by religion. Few houses had radios or took newspapers, transport was limited and television not yet available. For many families the only contact with the wider world was the occasional letter from relatives in America. To gain some insight into the feelings of women in this closely circumscribed world we can once again turn to literature. In his vivid portrait of a woman in the west of Ireland in *The Road to Brightcity*, Máirtín Ó Cadhain describes the thoughts going through Bríd's mind as she walks nine miles to market with a butter creel on her back:

> There were dark areas slinking at the edge of her mind, and bitterness to sting her feelings, but to her conscious mind the drag and drudgery of life never seemed anything to grumble at. . . She was far from realising that man, not Providence, was answerable for the sea of troubles which confined her to struggle and skimp, sent her tramping every Saturday to Brightcity barefoot, left her worrying always, slaving all the time. . . Though she understood the ideas 'luck', 'bad luck', 'misfortune', well enough, she was unable to give any precise sense to the notions of 'pleasure', 'joy of life'. But she knew she was far from being easy in her mind, far indeed. What she would most like to complain of was that her peace of mind was shadowed by the unrelenting pressure of external life, dulling the daylight, so that her irritations of spirit were trying to break out in spurts of bitterness.[37]

She muses about the hardship of children and the agony of giving birth. 'Would she have another dead baby? God forbid. It would be the death of her. Yet welcome be the will of God.'[38]

Peig Sayers, too, accepted the will of God. Her stories of life on the Blasket Islands are internationally known as a beautiful portrayal of an island community, yet her own life was one of great hardship. After a period in service as a girl, she was married at seventeen. Her husband was sick for much of his life and died young. 'Since the time I was married I have never known a day that I was entirely happy.' She brought up her children to read and write, 'but there was no place for them in Ireland, and they have all gone to America but one, and soon he too will be gone, and I shall be alone in the end of my life. But it is God's will and the way of the world and we must not complain'.[39]

In his story 'Spring Sowing', Liam O'Flaherty writes of a woman's feelings about the hardship of her life: 'Then she thought of the journey home and the trouble of feeding the pigs, putting the fowls into their coops and getting the supper ready and a momentary flash of rebellion against the slavery of being a peasant's wife crossed her mind. But the feeling soon passes as she works with her husband on one of their few shared tasks, the spring sowing of potatoes:

> All her dissatisfaction and weariness vanished from Mary's mind with the delicious feeling of comfort that overcame her at having done this work with her husband. They had done it together. They had planted seeds in the earth. The next day and the next and all their lives, when spring came they would have to bend their backs and do it until their hands and bones got twisted with rheumatism. But night would always bring sleep and forgetfulness.[40]

We are left with a mixture of feelings. Attachment to the land is tinged with sadness; the satisfaction of a job well done is mixed with resentment against the hard nature of the work involved.

As we have seen, the system of land inheritance and marriage forced the majority of young people off the land. It was perhaps also inevitable that the commitment of both women and men to the land should decline rapidly once they started to compare their lot with outside standards. As this happened, women became less willing to participate in a way of life which offered them a clearly subordinate role. They knew that jobs, albeit low-paid ones, awaited them abroad, and as a result of campaigns for the emancipation of women in the USA and in Britain, the 'woman question' was a live issue in both countries and the status of women had begun to change. In Ireland, most feminist activity had been restricted to educated women in Dublin and had made little impact on rural life since independence.

In the 1940s the focus of emigration shifted from America to

Britain. Britain was nearer, people could travel to and fro, and they could make comparisons. A significant difference in opportunities for women in the two countries was apparent. By this time, the gap in living standards between Britain and Ireland was also very noticeable. In Ireland, most farming was still done with horses, and in Connacht only one farm in forty-five had a tractor in 1951. Only one in thirty people owned a car, only one in nine had a radio.[41] Rural electrification was under way, but incomplete. The standard of living on small farms had changed little since the turn of the century, a period of fifty years in which the material quality of life in Britain had improved dramatically.

By the early 1950s, rural life in Ireland was in a state of crisis. Emigration had reached epidemic proportions. The country was shocked when the 1956 Census revealed that almost 200 000 people had left in five years.[42] Young people were flocking to Britain. Of the generation born in the period 1932–41 only 60 per cent remained in Ireland by 1961.[43] A Government Commission on Emigration, which reported in 1956, had no doubt about why people were leaving:

> Emigration has been due to two fundamental causes – the absence of opportunities for making an adequate livelihood, and a growing desire for higher standards of living on the part of the community, particularly the rural community. . . In the past many people were content to remain assisting on their home farms for virtually nothing more than their subsistence – some hoping to inherit the farm, others in expectation of dowries. This way of life was accepted as inevitable, and emigration from farms was confined to those who were obliged to go through sheer necessity. Nowadays, fewer people are satisfied with a subsistence standard of living and they find an easy alternative in emigration.[44]

The Commission went on to note that 'particularly to the young mind, rural areas appear dull, drab, monotonous, backward and lonely'.[45] Ten years later, in a study of young people in a rural county, Damien Hannon found that only 5 per cent of girls were prepared to stay at home on the farm until marriage.[46]

In spite of the tendency of politicians to romanticise rural life, the problems of the social system in the countryside became all too clear to its inhabitants in the decades following independence. The high emigration rate, the low marriage rate and the declining number of small farms all indicated an unstable situation. During the 1950s and 1960s, traditional peasant farming was replaced by a smaller, more efficient agricultural workforce, relying on more mechanised methods of farming. In the early 1960s, Ireland began to industrialise, developing into a country where, for the first time, more people lived in towns than in the countryside and where an urban life-style became the norm. These economic and social developments caused many changes in women's lives, and brought new challenges to the ideals of family life established by both Church and State.

3 Of Housewives, Mothers and Mary

The system of marriage and family life which had dominated the post-famine countryside was transformed by changes in the rural economy. Rural life changed significantly as a result of the decline in traditional farming throughout the 1940s and 1950s and the policies of economic development initiated by the government in the early 1960s. When Damien Hannon and Louise Katsiaouni interviewed 400 farming families in the 1970s they found a great mixture of family 'styles'. One household might consist of a traditionally patriarchal family in which the father made all the decisions and was never seen cooking or putting the children to bed. Next door might be a farm of the same size where the husband and wife had a mutually supportive relationship and made decisions together. Overall they found that only one in three families conformed to the traditional model of the rural family. Between a quarter and a third of the families had a more 'modern' pattern of joint decision-making, some sharing of household and child-care tasks and a more open emotional relationship. The remaining families showed a variety of intermediate patterns. A particularly interesting finding of the study was a large variation in the wives' satisfaction with their husband's role. The results were a big 'thumbs down' to traditional marriage. Half the wives in this situation were dissatisfied, compared with only one in eight of the 'modern' wives.[1]

Many women who are now married to farmers worked in towns or abroad before their marriages. Many also have secondary education. They bring into their marriages the values and expectations acquired through urban living – a radically different situation from previous generations where a girl would remain on her parents' farm until a match was made for her. Hannon and Katsiaouni found, however, that the modern wives were still financially dependent on their husbands, and that few had jobs outside the farm. 'The end-point of change is not towards the modern liberated woman role, independent of her husband's provider role . . . but actually towards 'wifehood', 'motherhood' and even 'housewifely' role models assumed to be characteristic of the urban middle class.'[2]

The gap between the life-styles of rural and urban women has lessened considerably. The farmer's wife has been transformed into a housewife. She joins her urban counterpart in a role common to most industrialised parts of Western Europe and the USA.

From farmer's wife to housewife

With the mechanisation of agriculture the emphasis shifted away from neighbourhood co-operation towards individual achievement. Great differences emerged in living standards between neighbours on similar-sized farms as the old system of mutual aid split up and families went their separate ways. Today, variations in conditions are very obvious in rural areas. In particular, rural prosperity has not been evenly distributed throughout the country. The West is still relatively much poorer than the east, but even in the east there are still significant pockets of rural poverty.

As the population of rural areas continued to decrease, the average size of holdings increased as small farms were amalgamated. With the gradual development of more modern farming methods, earnings from the sale of crops and stock increased, and the rural economy took on a healthier aspect. As a result, the disposable income of farming families rose, enabling them to buy more consumer goods. This process was facilitated by the introduction of the mass media into the countryside. During the 1950s radios became commonplace, and television arrived shortly afterwards. Radio and TV programmes brought images of urban life and advertisements for the latest consumer goods into remote rural kitchens. The isolation of the countryside was gone. Women and men could now evaluate their own way of life with reference to middle-class urban standards. The comparison showed up the material deficiencies of life on a small farm, and developed expectations of a more comfortable existence.

In the late 1960s and throughout the 1970s, the flow of people out of the countryside was reversed for the first time in over a century. Former emigrants returned, and country villages near large towns began to be used as dormitory areas for people with city jobs. Many of these brought with them the standards to which they had become accustomed in England or in Dublin, and were impatient with the lack of central heating and telephones in rural homes. They either built new houses or renovated old ones, changing them out of all recognition.

The modernisation of farms and the penetration of urban ways into the countryside changed women's work on the farm and in the home. As subsistence farming gave way to market-oriented production, the farmhouse budget became increasingly cash-based. Previously, farming families had provided most of their own needs, with shopping confined to tea, sugar, flour and the occasional pair of shoes or special piece of clothing. With more money available women bought more food and clothes instead of making them. White sliced loaves appeared instead of the traditional soda bread and children increasingly wore cheap imported clothes from chain stores. Hannon and Katsiaouni found that in half the farming families they interviewed the wife did very little traditional subsistence activity such as baking, knitting and making children's clothes.[3] The new emphasis on economic production also meant that the cows and chickens, normally looked after by the woman, were either dispensed with or were up-graded into commercially viable units, in which case they often became men's work instead of women's work. Women's traditional role on farms was disappearing fast.

Some women maintained their involvement in the farm by taking on a new role – that of secretary and administrator. On a modern farm there are letters to write, accounts to keep, tax forms and loan applications to see to. Where the woman has taken over this work she has kept a foothold in the management of the farm and may be an equal partner in decision-making.

In other families women have withdrawn altogether from farm work. The men have taken over all the outside work and the responsibility for managing the business. In this case, as her productive role has ceased, the woman has become more like an urban housewife than a traditional farm woman. She has retreated into the kitchen. Her home has changed too, into a place more easily recognised by her urban sisters. In the 1950s and 1960s rural homes became a market for consumer goods for the first time. The open hearth was replaced by a solid fuel range, and later by a cooker. Dirt floors gave way to linoleum and then to carpets. The arrival of electricity in the countryside enabled women to buy small electrical gadgets, and graduate if they wished to fridges, freezers and washing-machines.

Siobhan lived through this period of change, having been reared on a small farm. By the mid-1950s, things were beginning to improve:

> It was obvious they were going to keep improving, and people were getting more enlightened as regards everything, but particularly farming. There was more money by this time and we had got the electricity. We were getting the odd little bit of electrical equipment – the electric iron and electric kettle, which was a great thing in those days. There was a little electric ring, not a cooker as such, and a battery radio.

She married a farmer in 1963. Her husband still had a horse at the time they married, though most of the farm work was done by tractor. Siobhan welcomes the difference between her own life and her mother's, which was dominated by poverty and endless work. 'Most farming families nowadays have a certain amount of financial security. Things were very good for farmers for the past ten years. That little bit of security is very important. I think it gives you a lot of self-esteem.' They have been able, for instance, to afford to send two of their children to university, whereas their own parents could barely manage to put their children through secondary school.

She helps her husband on the farm only at certain times of the year. 'During the summer I am very much involved. I'm outside most of the time and especially during the turf season. I love the bog, particularly footing the turf.' She does all the housework and cooking, and unlike many of her contemporaries she has many traditional skills – she bakes and sews and grows vegetables. But like many urban wives, she often felt lonely and isolated when the children were growing up:

When you are rearing a family, you have to reduce yourself to their age group. Then as they're growing up – maybe it is your own fault – you don't go out and mix as much. You are too involved in the family. You lose out. The longer you are at home the more confidence you lose.

As a housewife with young children in search of outside company, Siobhan joined her local branch of the Irish Countrywoman's Association:

It was an outlet for me. It got me out of the house and it got us talking about our children. I'd feel that nobody had the same problems as I had with my children, whereas everybody had the same problems. It's amazing how much a thing like that lightens your load if you are worried about something. It did so much for me in those years when the children were small.

The isolation of women in their homes, especially with young children, is a familiar feature of Western industrial society, and something which is now common in the countryside as well as in the towns. With the change from traditional farming life, the home has ceased to be the place where men and women, with their separate tasks, collectively produce what the family needs to survive. The work has become individualised and the neighbours do not help each other as much as they used to as each family is intent on developing their own farm. There are fewer neighbours anyway, as the farming population has decreased so rapidly. The family on the farm, like its urban counterpart, has tended to become a smaller, nuclear unit of parents and children, removed from the extended family of grandparents, cousins and aunts. Within this nuclear family, the wife is often cut off from contact with relatives and neighbours. As she is now confined to the domestic sphere, far more of her time is spent with only her children for company, instead of with her mother and mother-in-law, sisters and neighbouring wives. Maura compares her mother's life to her own:

There was a great closeness, there was no television on the road and they had a great support system, helping each other with their babies. We've been living where we do for two years and we hardly know the people round us. It isn't like the place where I grew up where we were running into people's houses all the time and the doors were always open. We are much more closed off.

In both town and countryside, the home has ceased to be the central focus of productive activity and social life. Instead of working around the house and farm, the men and older children travel away from home to their jobs. Instead of neighbourly visiting, house-dances and story-telling round the fire, people seek social entertainment away from the house in pubs and discos, evening classes and clubs. This removal of activity from the home leaves the housewife alone, often with an uncomfortable feeling that whatever is real and important is happening 'out there'.

Most of a housewife's daily routine is governed by other people's needs. She cooks and cleans for her husband and children. Mealtimes are organised to fit in with school and her husband's job. When they have finished their day's work she is still at hers – available, active, doing all the things they need done. If her husband gets a transfer or a new job, she will uproot herself and move with him. She experiences the familiar problems of the suburban world in which the woman's main focus in life is her children and her house, where she is all-too-often understimulated and she feels undervalued by society.

In the early 1960s, Alexander Humphries looked at the family lives of the 'New Dubliners' – people whose parents had lived in rural homes and who were themselves part of the growing urban population.[4] He found that few urban wives participated in activities which produced income of any kind. Their husbands were the breadwinners and they were full-time housewives. Compared with their own mothers the wives had taken on a greater share of domestic labour and a greater degree of responsibility for the socialisation of the children. The husbands were simply not there to help, and in particular did not take charge of the older boys as their own fathers would have done. So the women did more, but it was evident to Humphries that 'the wife's status has not increased correspondingly, and that the status of the Dublin family is rated principally on the husband's occupational position, income and factors attending on these, while the wife's contribution tends to receive less acknowledgement'.[5]

Yet the woman's work is as essential to her husband's employer, and to the economy of the country, as her mother's was to the farm.

Women service the male workforce, ensuring they are properly fed and clothed and have a warm home to come back to where they can relax before the next day's work. But the housewife's work has a low status. It is invisible. Each woman works within the confines of her own home, unseen by others. She does not clock in or out, but is on duty twenty-four hours a day. When Ann Oakley interviewed housewives in Britain she found that their average working week was 77 hours. Some women were working 100 hours or more per week and none worked less than forty-eight.[6] Modern conveniences have not reduced these hours as much as one might think. Modern cookers and mixers may make food preparation easier, but cooking is far more complicated than it used to be. People today expect more elaborate meals than boiled potatoes and brown bread. Perhaps automatic washing-machines are one of the few real time-savers, though adults and children have far more clothes than they used to have, and expect them to be cleaner and washed more often.

The advent of modern household conveniences has been accompanied by the widespread acceptance of the standards of modern consumer-based living – whiter-than-white shirts, three-piece suites and fitted carpets, central heating, fitted kitchens and carefully chosen colour schemes. Most women today would be horrified at the thought of living in a traditional cottage where chickens pecked at the dirt floor and an occasional coat of whitewash was the only decoration.

Maintaining modern standards involves a great deal of work. Yet housework is rarely seen as real work. There is no tangible product. Tidiness and cleanliness are temporary, meals are consumed as soon as they are prepared. The chores are endlessly repeated, day after day, week after week. And most of the work is boring. There is little to give a woman a sense of achievement or purpose. Humphries found that Dublin housewives in the 1960s said marriage was 'a drag', and tried to prolong their working lives outside the home.[7]

When asked, 'What do you do?' many women still answer, 'I'm only a housewife.' The use of the word 'only' reveals how effectively the low status of the housewife has been internalised in women's minds. But most women are housewives because they are mothers. It is motherhood that they regard as the valuable part of the job. Looking after and bringing up children is important work. The problem for many women is that it is impossible to separate the housework from looking after the children, and against their better judgement the housework seems to dominate their time. The majority of the day is spent cleaning-up, washing and preparing meals, not in playing with the children.

It is an uncomfortable situation for a woman. She has chosen to stay at home yet she resents being there. She feels the drudgery of endless cleaning but she can't see a way out of it. She wants to enjoy her children but the boring daily routine makes her irritable and tired. With her day full of baby talk and with very limited contact with other adults she wonders why she feels depressed and unable to cope. But she chose to be there – if she cannot cope she feels it must be her fault. If she complains she feels guilty. The pain is pushed inside, and may be numbed with pills or alcohol. The majority of tranquillisers, sleeping pills and anti-depressants prescribed each year are taken by women.[8]

In Ireland, as in other countries, women began to question the role of the housewife as part of the wider debate about women that surfaced in the 1970s. Why should it be the woman who does all the housework just because she is a mother? Why can't men do housework? Equality, as someone said, begins at home. As a result of these debates women demanded that their husbands and lovers take on a fairer share of the housework.

Tracy: My mother's view of marriage was that she was there to look after her husband and us to the best of her ability. My father did lots of building stuff in the house, and occasionally on a Sunday morning he would give us breakfast, but he never did the washing up or anything like that. Whereas Sean cooks, and I wouldn't say he does as much as I do because he has got a full-time job, but he certainly does a lot more than a lot of men. That's very important to me. I haven't got this far in order to spend my time cooking and washing dishes. It's a necessary evil, that's all, not my job as such.

Carole is another woman with clear ideas of how housework should be shared if she marries – again a very different view from that of her own parents:

My mother took on all the responsibility for the household duties and the children. My father would come in at half past six and his tea would be on the table. He would do whatever chores had to be done that evening and that was it. Even now, if he sits down to his meal and there isn't salt on the table he will not get up and get it himself, no way. He will expect it to be handed to him. I don't like it at all.

If I marry, it would have to be a sharing role, particularly if we were both working. He should share the housework and the outside work or whatever. I would be very adamant about that, particularly in relation to children.

The difference between Carole and her sister Annie is revealing. Annie is married, has three children and does all the domestic work herself. Her husband does none at all:

Recently they were in our house, Annie was outside and the baby wanted his nappy changed, so her husband ran outside and dropped him into her arms and said 'There, he needs changing'. I was very annoyed that she should allow him to do that, but it doesn't seem to affect her the way it affects me. She is happy looking after the children and doing the household chores.

I think it is because Annie married so young. She was the eldest of the family. She lived at home all her life before she got married. She didn't have the same opportunities that I had. I think college had a very strong impact on me. I was more open to developing different ideas because there was such interaction between people, and an interaction of ideas. Also the fact that I left home and was no longer under the influence of my parents. I was an independent person, and whatever I did was up to me, and I had to make my own decisions. I think that has been the reason for the incredible difference between us.

Exposure to other ways of living may raise a woman's expectations, and lead her to question many of the assumptions she was brought up with, particularly assumptions about the proper role for women. There are, however, still severe limits on the extent to which couples can evenly divide household tasks. While housework and motherhood remain very closely linked it is difficult for a woman to reorganise the domestic work without reassessing her role as a mother. If she tries to get out of the housework she is vulnerable to the accusation of neglecting the children. To explore the reasons for this we need to turn our attention to motherhood and all that it involves.

Motherhood

The Church presents motherhood as a vocation, as the greatest calling for women apart from religious life. When visiting Ireland in 1979, Pope John Paul II called on women to remember their true role in life: 'May Irish mothers, young women and girls not listen to those who tell them that working at a secular job, succeeding in a secular profession, is more important than the vocation of giving life and caring for this life as a mother'.[9] He went on to say that the future of the Church and of humanity 'depends in great part on parents and the family life that they build in their homes'. The word was 'parents', but it was clear that the Pope was calling on women to shoulder the main responsibility for the quality of family life.

Not every woman was happy with this message from the Pope, coming as it did at the end of a decade of change for women. Elizabeth, a practising Catholic, reacted strongly to the speech:

> He destroyed any concept I ever had of accepting the Church as it stands today because to say that women are tied to a situation when men aren't doesn't make any sense to me. As far as he is concerned women should stay at home and mind their own business and take care of the children while men can go out and get the jobs. I don't accept that moral teaching at all. The reason is, it is made by men. No woman was ever asked what she wanted.

The image of the Catholic mother is very strong. She is glorified as a myth and woven into the ideal of the Catholic family. Mother is the spiritual and emotional foundation for the family, the source of love and affection and of moral values. It is to her that members of the family can turn when in trouble or distress. There is some truth in this image in that mothers have traditionally been the dominant figures in their families' emotional lives, providing strong role-models for their daughters and sometimes having over-dependent relationships with their sons. But the idealised Catholic mother is more than this. She is also expected to protect and forgive her children, and display the virtues of humility, gentleness and mercy.

It is an ideal which is clearly modelled on the image of Mary as mother of Jesus.

Audrey remembers this ideal from school: 'The religious theme was that every woman was trying to imitate the Virgin Mary. That was basically a sacrificial model and it permeated its way into the culture. Women were supposed to sacrifice themselves – that was the order of the day.'

And how does she feel about this model now, as a mother of two teenage children? 'I don't think it is a very good way of life. I don't do it now. Because at the end of the day you are no good to anybody if you are a martyr. I think if I had fallen into the mould I would probably be on ten Librium a day, and be having a casual nervous breakdown or be an alcoholic.'

Yet to other women the Virgin Mary is very important as a female presence in a male Church, as a woman who understands, who was herself a mother.

Elizabeth: I relate to her because she was a mother, and I am a mother. I get a great deal of strength from her. She suffered, she knew what it was to be human. She may not have had a choice but she lived and she watched him growing up. When my daughter ran away to England, if I hadn't had that faith I'd have lost my mind.

Carmel: Mary was my friend. I used to like putting flowers on the altar for her as a kid. I liked her, and I still do. I figured that if she had a kid she knew what it was all about. One day when everything was going wrong and my son was being impossible, I went into Church and sat there and said, 'You had a child, how in the name of God did you manage?' I just sat there, and when I came out it was like I'd been talking to a friend and I'd got something off my chest.

The symbolic importance of Mary as a mother is complex. Women both love and hate what she represents. As a mother, she provides a human face in the Church. She is a source of comfort, and protects sinners from the wrath of God. Yet hers was an essentially submissive motherhood. The power to conceive was not hers to control as she wished. She was visited by the Holy Ghost and submitted to the role of carrying the Son of God. 'Be it unto me according to thy word.' A woman who obeyed without question, a channel for a male God to create his son. And when he was born, she did not celebrate her power to give birth, to create and nurture new life, but denied herself and worshipped her son. As Simone de Beauvoir writes: 'She will be glorified only in accepting the subordinate role assigned to her. "I am the servant of the Lord." For the first time in human history the mother kneels before her son; she freely accepts her inferiority'.[10]

This image of Mary contains the origin of the stereotype of the traditional Irish mother as a woman overdevoted to her sons, protecting them and serving them, rearing them to believe they are more important than she is. And as Mary was merciful, her son could not refuse his mother. A mother can manipulate the bond with her son to tie him to her and make him emotionally dependent on her, unable to free himself to love another woman.

In *Alone of All her Sex*, Marina Warner notes that the Mary cult is strongest in those countries in which the symbol of the 'subject housewife' is strongest, and where 'women are expected to be, and are, men's devoted wives and mothers'.[11] The countries to which she refers are Ireland, Spain, Portugal, Italy and Belgium. Undoubtedly the glorification of sacrificial motherhood is still very strong in Ireland. It is under threat, as many women now refuse to live their lives according to the Church-prescribed pattern. But in addition to the social and economic factors that maintain the ideal by tying women to the home, idealised motherhood has a powerful emotional weapon on its side – guilt. Guilt if you go out to work, guilt if you buy yourself a new pair of shoes when the children need clothes, guilt when you feel inadequate as a mother, guilt if your unmarried daughter becomes pregnant. Guilt is the private, hidden legacy of Catholicism even in women who have long since relinquished their faith.

The replacement of traditional rural life with a predominantly urban pattern has altered the relationship between mothers and their children. When the father is away at work all day he cannot take the older boys with him as he would have done on the farm. It is now mother, not father, who takes most of the responsibility for them. As the nuclear family becomes the norm, children are increasingly cared for by their mothers alone, often in isolation from other families. As the woman's sphere of work shrinks from farm and village to her own kitchen, she is pushed into closer

contact with her children. There is a big contrast between the role of
the modern housewife and mother in sole charge of her children all
day long and the situation described by Elizabeth, who was brought
up in Co. Wicklow in the 1940s:

> The thing I remember about the Wicklow hills was the neighbour-
> hood and the neighbours, because you were everybody's child. It
> was not only your mother telling you what to do, everybody was
> telling you what to do! They were an extremely close-knit
> community. Most of them were farmers. We were never short of
> affection and kindness. We grew up with a lot of love around us,
> never realising that it wasn't parental love – it was a general
> kindness and concern for everybody around the neighbours.

With large families – and twelve or fifteen children was not
uncommon – it was in any case physically impossible for mothers to
be with all their children all the time. Now, a greater degree of
individual contact is possible as families are generally much smaller.
This extra closeness has its disadvantages, as it can increase the
problems of the isolated housewife who feels imprisoned in the
house with her young children. It is as if motherhood has been
downgraded through becoming indistinguishable from house-
wifery. Like other aspects of a woman's work in the home,
mothering has been individualised, made private and invisible.

On the other hand, smaller families, and the extra contact
between parents and children that these allow, can bring closer and
more rewarding relationships. Audrey, for example, describes the
difference between herself and her mother in these terms:

> She would have other people to look after the children while she
> did all the cooking, whereas now the cooking I do is minimal
> really and I would spend more time with the children. I feel I
> missed out on that a lot as a child. I mean the times we had
> conversations are milestones that I remember. But that was the
> way everybody was brought up. People spent very little time with
> their children. People had far too many children for a start, and
> they were seen as an inevitability of marriage. There was no
> parenting, apart from disciplining or whatever. I would say I am
> more sharing, and more supportive of my children than they
> were.

The majority of married women in Ireland are still full-time housewives and mothers, though this is changing rapidly. Although only 16 per cent of married women work outside the home, this figure has tripled since the early 1960s.[12] Motherhood is now taking up a smaller proportion of women's lives. Women today tend to marry younger and have fewer children. Although Ireland still has a significantly higher birth rate than any other EEC country,[13] the gap has narrowed due to falling fertility rates during the 1960s and 1970s. Between 1971 and 1979 the birth rate for married women aged 15–34 dropped by 20–25 per cent. For older women, the decrease was even sharper – 33 per cent for women aged 35–9 and 40 per cent for those aged 40–4.[14] In other words, women are having fewer children, and having them earlier in their marriages.

Clare has one child and says, 'I couldn't cope with another.' And her mother?

> My mother had eleven children, and I was the second eldest. She had her first child when she was 30 and her last child at 45. There is only a year or two between every one of us, and the one and only time there was a two-year gap she had twins. It's incredible. She didn't mind the pregnancies, but she was in fear of actually having babies. She dreaded childbirth.

It is little wonder that many women were quick to take up artificial contraception as soon as it became available. They did so in spite of the Church's attitude to having children, namely that 'Christian couples should co-operate with the Creator in having them because they are the supreme gift of marriage'.[15] This teaching is, of course, fundamentally opposed to the feminist notion of a woman's right to control her fertility. Women campaigned vigorously for contraceptive rights because without this control, a woman cannot make real choices about other areas of her life.

During the 1960s the Pill beame widespread in most European countries, Catholic ones included. Ireland was no exception. Contraception was illegal, but the Pill was available on prescription as a cycle-regulator. As one woman commented, 'we must have the highest rate of irregular periods in the world!'. The Pill helped to accelerate the decline in fertility, and to quote the demographer Brendan Walsh, 'there is no evidence that the Papal Encyclical of

1968 [against contraception] arrested or reversed the downward trend in higher order births in Ireland'.[16]

Changing fertility patterns have brought women's lives in Ireland more in line with those of women in the rest of Western Europe. The overall trend is towards small families, born relatively early in the mother's life, so that full-time motherhood is over by the time a woman is in her thirties or forties. This can create problems for women who have become used to basing their view of themselves on their role as a mother, as their identity changes suddenly when the children leave home. For other women this transition is a positive step as they are then free to pursue activities of their own, one option being to seek to re-enter the labour force.

In the traditional role of the mother in Ireland there was no question of her having a job outside the home when her children were small. The introduction of maternity leave in 1981 (in the Maternity Protection of Employees Act) was something of a triumph over this tradition. The Act gave a woman the right to take fourteen weeks maternity leave, during which she is paid 80 per cent of her normal earnings, followed by four weeks unpaid leave. She can then return to her former job if she so wishes. The Act gives a shorter period of leave than corresponding legislation in other EEC countries, and there is no provision for paternity leave, but is a significant advance on the situation only a decade previously when the marriage bar was still in operation in many jobs. Inevitably, the legislation by itself is not enough. In a society where there are very limited child-care facilities and few husbands prepared to be fathers-at-home, the option to return to work after maternity leave can only be taken by a few – either women who are forced back to work through economic necessity or higher-paid women who can afford to pay a child-minder of their choice. And in a culture where the ideology of devoted motherhood is so strong it can be very hard for women to resolve the conflict between their own needs and those of their children.

Maura is facing a classic dilemma. At the time of interview she was pregnant with her second child and trying to decide whether to give up her job as a teacher. She already has one child, and returned to work after taking maternity leave:

When I had my son, I thought 'How am I going to leave him and go back to work?' It was just a miraculous change in my life. I've been back at work for a year now and it has worked out fairly well. But you have to sort of detach yourself from the whole mother thing. You have to hand over your child. It is difficult. I am just coping at the moment. I have 22 hours teaching with thirty-three kids in each class, changing over every 40 minutes. I am just absolutely stretched when I am there.

Although her husband shares a lot of the work in the house, she feels the strain of the routine. 'Especially getting up in the morning and getting him fed and changed without trying to rush him, which I often am doing. It is not how I want to live my life, but at the same time if I gave up my job, apart from the fact that I need the money, how would I be at home all day?'

With her second child on the way, she must make a decision. 'It feels like all or nothing.' On the one hand, she gets a great deal out of her work and does not want to stop:

It is a private area of my own life, a sort of validation of myself. A kind of confirmation of myself, of my ability. I enjoy working with other people and I feel very equal to them. I feel efficient and competent and capable and all those good things. I also love my subject and I like to impart that. Whereas at home – I have seen this happen to a lot of women who give up work – your world becomes much more narrow, and I would be afraid of losing confidence in myself.

On the other hand, she feels she is missing out on motherhood:

My mother couldn't send me anywhere, it was part of mothering to be there. I mean, why do you have a child? Do you have a child so that someone else can look after it? I haven't worked it out. It is a jumble in my mind.

Maura's dilemma is faced by many women. At the moment society views work according to the male norm of a 40-hour working week for an uninterrupted working lifetime. Motherhood is seen as a full-time occupation for women at home. The two concepts are commonly regarded as mutually exclusive. Men have jobs, mothers stay at home. A woman must either be that mother at home, or she must adopt the male life-style of a full-time job and struggle to find enough time for her family. As Maura says, it is an all-or-nothing choice. So the dilemma will continue for women until there is a more flexible set of options open to them and to men, including more child-care facilities, more opportunities for part-time work and job–sharing, longer maternity and paternity leave and a greater willingness by husbands to share parenthood in a meaning-ful way. These changes will not come about until the existing stereotype of the perfect mother is replaced by a more balanced picture which recognises the needs of the mother as well as those of the child.

Motherhood without marriage

In January 1984 a tragedy occurred in the small town of Granard in Co. Longford. A 15-year-old schoolgirl called Ann Lovett left her parents' house and went up to the Grotto Of Our Lady which overlooks the town. She was in labour. Alone, and exposed to the winter weather, she gave birth to a baby boy. Both she and the baby died shortly afterwards. No-one in the town, apart from one friend, admitted knowing that she was pregnant. A Sunday newspaper broke the story, which generated a storm of controversy. Why had Ann been unable to tell anyone she was pregnant? Had her parents and teachers really not noticed? What about the father of the child? What kind of personal anguish must she have suffered during the pregnancy? How could such a thing happen in 1984?

Ann Lovett's pregnancy had a particularly tragic outcome, but she was not an isolated case. 1642 unmarried teenage women had babies in 1982. Of these, seventy-five were aged 15 or under.[17] Ann Lovett's death focused attention yet again on the atmosphere of shame, guilt, secrecy and punishment which surrounds women who are pregnant outside marriage. As a group of women from Kilbarack in Dublin wrote to the *Sunday Tribune*: 'We demand that Ann Lovett's death be not in vain. That her death, and that of her baby, will raise the consciousness of a society which supposedly venerates motherhood within marriage, yet denigrates it outside marriage'.[18]

Motherhood outside marriage is denigrated because it involves sex outside marriage. It is seen by Church leaders and politicians as a threat to family life and the institution of marriage. Within marriage, motherhood is desirable, necessary, a vocation. Outside marriage it is shameful, sinful and an object of charity. Many mothers must have gasped in sheer disbelief at the statement by the Irish bishops in 1975 that 'our esteem for marriage must never lead us to adopt a harsh or rejecting attitude towards the unmarried mother. . . We say with confidence that any intending mother will receive in this country a quality of care and compassion equal to that to be found anywhere'.[19] Reality betrays the myth. The treatment of women who become pregnant outside marriage is one of the scandals of Irish social history.

A single woman who finds herself pregnant can do one of several things. If she wants to terminate the pregnancy she must go to England for an abortion in a private clinic. If she decides to go through with the pregnancy, she has three main options. She can marry the father and legitimise the child, she can give up the baby for adoption or she can keep the baby and live as a single parent. In a recent survey of 250 pregnant single women, Doctors Rynne and Lacey found that 26.4 per cent opted for abortion, 25.5 per cent decided to marry the father and 28.6 per cent put their children up for adoption. Of the remainder, 11.4 per cent decided to keep the baby and either marry or live with the father and 8.2 per cent opted to live as single parents.[20]

Two of these options – terminating the pregnancy and living as a single parent – have only recently become realistic for most women. Prior to 1967, when the abortion law in Britain was liberalised, termination was very difficult to arrange. Abortion is illegal in Ireland and even today few doctors will risk carrying out a termination even where the woman's life is threatened. There is some evidence that backstreet abortion used to be available as fifty-eight cases of illegal abortion were investigated by the Guardai between 1926 and 1974.[21] Most of these cases came to light because women became ill or died as the result of the abortion, suggesting that significant numbers of successful abortions were carried out. Even so, attempting to get an abortion was undoubtedly a difficult, expensive and very risky undertaking. The majority of women had little choice but to take the pregnancy to term and either marry the father or give up the baby for adoption.

In the latter case, secrecy was at a premium. Even if parents were told, knowledge of the pregnancy had to be kept from neighbours for it would bring shame and dishonour on the family. As a result, few women had their babies at home. They invented aunts in Dublin or jobs in London and left home, often not to return. Many took the boat to England to have their babies there anonymously. Others went to mother-and-baby homes in Dublin or a distant town. Today, there are schemes which place pregnant girls with families living a suitable distance away from home with whom they stay until their babies are born. The existence of such schemes indicates the degree of secrecy which still surrounds many pregnancies outside marriage.

Most mother-and-baby homes were run by religious orders. The regimes were frequently harsh and disciplinarian. The prospective mothers scrubbed floors and worked in laundries and were kept in no doubt as to the shameful nature of their condition. A few homes are still open. Síle decided to go to one in 1979 because it was so difficult at home when she was pregnant. Her parents made her run upstairs when the neighbours called and she did not go out and see her friends. Both parents came with her for the journey to the home. 'How green we must have seemed, asking the conductor to put us off at the right stop. It was written all over our faces – the country trio, the farmer and his wife and their young daughter with a bump.'

The home was not at all as she had expected:

We had a vision of a comforting, friendly place, of people saying, 'Come in, come in, sit back and relax and get it over with'. But we walked into this massive red-brick prison of a place, the gate clanged and Daddy took off as fast as his legs could carry him! Mammy and I walked like snails up this big driveway and rang the bell, and a nun showed us in.

There were about forty of us sleeping in one room. It was done up in cubicles with curtains so you could hear every move in the next bed. It was all big high barred windows and freezing cold. It was horrific after coming from home.

In most mother-and-baby homes it was an automatic procedure for women to give up their children as soon as they were born. Until the 1960s it was not uncommon for women who had been disowned by their families and had found refuge in a convent home to stay on as poorly-paid workers for the nuns, institutionalised and cut off from their former lives. Otherwise, once their babies were born, women were expected to leave the home and get on with their lives as if nothing had happened.

It is hard to imagine the emotional trauma involved in living through an unwanted pregnancy, giving birth, giving away the baby and then having to pretend the whole thing never happened. It is undoubtedly the source of life-long psychological scarring for some women, yet it seems to have been largely ignored. It is a problem that is conveniently hidden in individual women's emotions. The children are visible. They are wanted and loved by the families who adopt them, but their mothers remain shadowy, unidentified figures, their feelings unrecorded.

Marriage too is often a problematic way out of an unplanned pregnancy. It is fine if the couple had intended to marry anyway, but potentially disastrous if it is a decision forced on them by their parents. It is well established that marital breakdown is more likely when the partners are young and when the woman is pregnant at the time of marriage. The Church has recognised this problem and now discourages young people from seeing marriage as a convenient way out of an embarrassing pregnancy. In many cases marriage is in any case out of the question because the partners do not want to marry, or because the pregnancy is the result of a casual affair, or of rape or incest.

For those choosing to keep the child and live as a single parent there were, and still are, considerable practical difficulties as well as the problem of living in an unsympathetic society. The child suffers too as it is officially illegitimate, a status which denies it certain rights, notably the right to a share of the father's estate. A state welfare allowance for unmarried mothers was not introduced until 1973. Before that date women were dependent on charity or their families, or had to find a job, with all the difficulties that implied about arranging child-care and combining single parenting with employment. Inevitably, women with young children tended to find themselves in the lowest paid, most menial jobs.

Throughout the 1970s the percentage of unmarried women keeping their babies steadily increased. The illegitimate birth rate rose from 2.7 per cent of all births in 1970 to 4.6 per cent in 1975, but the proportion of these babies given up for adoption dropped dramatically from 82.7 per cent in 1970 to 27.7 per cent in 1979.[22] With the rise of the women's movement in the early 1970s several self-help groups for single parents were formed. The largest of these was Cherish, which was founded in 1972 and has had a considerable impact on attitudes to single women with children. Cherish has kept a high public profile, breaking the aura of secrecy and shame, and has campaigned for better financial and social rights for single parents and their children. One of the founders recalls the time when Cherish began:

> My memory is of a group of us literally huddled together for protection from the world outside. There was nowhere else to go to share feelings and experiences. It was great to share the joys of being a mother. Cherish was mainly about sharing the joys then. There were lots of people who wanted to hear about your problems – they assumed you were one big problem – they didn't think you were entitled to any pleasure in parenting. I stopped apologising and lost the feeling of fear and embarrassment when I took my son for a walk.[23]

The experience of having a child when single was another area of women's lives to come out into the open in the 1970s. Some improvements were won as a result of various campaigns. The state introduced the unmarried mother's allowance and politicians gradually accepted the need to abolish the status of illegitimacy. Women became more assertive in making their own choices when faced with an unexpected pregnancy. But there is still a long way to go before Irish society values motherhood equally both inside and outside marriage. The allowance enables women to live, but at a poverty level. It can be cut off at any time if the social welfare officers suspect a woman of cohabiting. Single parents are frequently discriminated against when trying to obtain housing and employment, and meet hostile attitudes from many people. The effect of this hostility is to put an enormous strain on unmarried women who discover they are pregnant. In their Dublin survey, Doctors Rynne and Lacey found that 42 per cent of the single women who had had babies had not told their mothers of their pregnancy. Of those who had, three-quarters said their mother's reaction was of shock or disappointment. After the initial reaction, however, 95 per cent of the mothers did help and support their daughters.[24] It is most probable that fear of a hostile reaction prevents many young women, like Ann Lovett, from telling anyone of their condition.

Síle had her son when she was 19. She is the eldest daughter of a farming family in the west of Ireland. She was working in a local town and living in a flat there when she became pregnant by her American boy-friend. When she was six months pregnant, her mother found out. By this stage Síle had left her job and had no money so she agreed to go home with her mother. Her boy-friend had gone back to America. 'When I told him I was at home he said, "Aren't your parents wonderful?" and that was the last I heard from him.'

After having her baby in the mother and baby home, Síle resisted the pressure to give him up for adoption. Her mother, the nuns in the home and her social worker all advised adoption, but she was determined to take the child and manage on her own. She now lives in a flat with her son on the unmarried mother's allowance of £47 a week. The boy is at school and she is thinking of finding a job. She is acutely aware of many people's judgemental attitudes toward her as an unmarried mother:

If you dress badly it's 'You think she would tidy herself up a bit', if you dress anyways nice you are 'looking for it'. We are not an 'in' thing with the politicians so they won't bother with us. All these unmarried mothers, poor things. If Seamus has an accident it is through my carelessness. If I'm out at night, they think he's left on his own.

How would she like it to be?

I'd like people to see that we are totally normal. You can examine me, I am flesh and blood. I look after my child well. He is not battered. He is totally normal although he is illegitimate – and that is a word that should be banned. The difficulty is getting across to people that we are normal – it is just that something happened. We do not whore around afterwards, neither do we turn into bad man-haters. We are not poor unfortunate idiots, we are mothers.

4   Marriage: A New Partnership?

In arranged marriages the relationship between husband and wife was the least important part of the partnership. Marriage was primarily an economic contract which served the needs of farmers and fitted in with the political ideology of the self-sufficient state based on family units. After a match was made, people hoped the marriage would 'take'. If it did not, the couple had little choice but to stay together anyway. For better or for worse, the permanence of marriage was part of the contract. Women were expected to accept their husbands whether they loved or battered them, whether they treated them well or drank the family into poverty.

In traditional marriage a woman's main emotional bond was not with her husband but with her children. She often also continued close relationships with her own relatives, particularly with her brothers and sisters. An anthropologist in Co. Kerry reported a conversation which illustrates the way in which siblings were often more important than spouses:

> Another widow woman during her life history addressed herself from time to time to an enlarged and yellowed photo of a young man over her fireplace. 'Is that your husband?', I finally asked, and the old woman laughed incredulously. 'My husband! No, dearie, my husband was never so fine and handsome a man as that. Up there is my brother, Brendan Fitz, God rest his soul, he died a policeman on duty in New York.'[1]

The function of marriage changed with the decline in traditional rural life. In the towns there was less need for children to

wait for marriage until they were 30 or 40 years old as the boys
were not in a position to inherit a farm and the girls no longer
needed a dowry. Young women and men could get a job and
become financially independent as soon as they finished their
education. As a result, the average age of marriage dropped from
its unusually high level in the first part of the century. Between
1945 and 1975 it reduced from 33 to 27 years for men and from 28
to 24 years for women. In 1945, only one in three brides was less
than 25 years old. By the mid-1970s the proportion had risen to
two out of three.[2] Marriage also became more popular. The
marriage rate increased up to the mid-1970s, reducing the difference between Ireland and other European countries and bringing
to an end the characteristic Irish pattern of large numbers of
single people in the population.

In the 1970s, changing expectations of marriage were closely
linked with changes in the status of women. As women forced
many issues out into the open, problems associated with marriage
were high on the agenda. The campaign for a better deal for
deserted wives, the opening of refuges for battered women and
the attempts to legalise contraception all turned public attention
on to marriage, and particularly on to the enormous gap between
the ideal of the Catholic family and women's actual experience of
marriage and family life. In women's groups and in the media
women spoke about their personal situations. The picture that
emerged was not a pretty one. The public was forced to accept
that women were battered, that rape within marriage was a
reality. Women brought out the pain of desertion and their sense
of desperation at having too many children. They also articulated
the desire to live their own lives and have an identity other than
being this man's wife or that child's mother.

Many women rejected the idea of marriage altogether, choosing
instead to live with a partner outside marriage, to come out as
lesbian or to remain single:

Kate: My mother is only now beginning to accept the fact that I'm
not going to get married. Well, I might meet a fellow and fall
madly in love, but I'm not anxious or desperate mad to get
married. This attitude that you have to get married is something I
have to battle against. I always found I was too independent. I did
a few lines with men, but they always petered out because they

tried to tie me down. I prefer to be in control of my own life and to be able to decide for myself that tomorrow I'm going to do this, or even in six weeks time I'm going to do that. Since about 16 I've had that attitude. If it happens, it happens, but I've no intention of going out there and looking for a man.

This same reassessment of marriage was taking place in Britain and the USA, in all countries where the new wave of feminism was causing women to question their lives. It was, perhaps, both a more dramatic and more painful process in Ireland where the ideology of the family had such a strong hold, and where the Church and political leaders perpetuated the myth that Ireland somehow had fewer problems and was less sinful than elsewhere.

The women's movement exploded this myth and focused attention on women's right to be equal partners in marriage. A new ideal of marriage emerged; an ideal which can be found in the manuals for marriage guidance counselling and pre-marriage courses and, to some extent, in the changing expectations of young people. A love-bond between a man and a woman is now accepted as the normal basis of the marriage relationship. According to this new ideal, marriage is partnership and friendship as well as love. It should be the source of an emotionally fulfilling relationship and of mutual love and understanding. Neither partner is subordinated. Both recognise and respect each other's needs. As Carole, a young single woman, put it:

I have strong feelings about how I would like the relationship, such as having very open communication, and working hard at it. I would like to think that we could be great friends, relating everyday experiences and problems, sharing a life together. I think if I marry it would have to be someone with an awful lot of respect for me and my ideas, and I would have a lot for respect for his ideas as well.

In its pastoral work the Church acknowledges elements of this new view of marriage. One priest wrote 'we are rapidly moving away from seeing married life as an impersonal contract with rights and duties to seeing it as a relationship in which partners help and heal each other and grow as persons'. He added 'the bond between them is an inner bond of love rather than an outer bond of law'.[3]

This new emphasis has altered many people's views of the permanence of marriage. If the relationship breaks down, the couple involved are not likely to feel that there is much in their marriage worth preserving. Most modern marriages last only as long as the partners relate to each other in a way that is worthwile and satisfying. The old view that people should stay together for the sake of the children carries less weight as people realise that children can be as disturbed by a tense or violent atmosphere as by an actual separation.

The modern ideal recognises that problems arise in any relationship and need to be worked through. Both partners should be open and honest about their feelings, confronting difficulties as they arise and finding mutually acceptable solutions. A relationship in which both parties are committed to open and constructive communication is preferred to one based on manipulation, aggression or withdrawl from feelings.

This process of dealing with conflict was not so necessary in traditional marriage where roles were clearly defined and where the bond between the partners was rather different. Now, people expect to talk about their relationships; they are encouraged by everyone from marriage guidance counsellors to social workers to look at how they feel, to explore their personal needs and to learn to communicate with each other.

Many women see a big difference between themselves and their parents in the way in which they conduct their relationships.

Audrey: I would never have married the same kind of man as my father because it would have been too much of a strain. My mother's relationship had that kind of bowing subservience to him. The relationship was almost like a game, a manipulative game. You got things because you rolled your eyes in a certain way, and you behaved in a certain way. It was what I would refer to as the black-satin-knickers strategy! I don't have that kind of relationship at all. I saw myself when I married as an equal, totally equal if not better! If there are rows we have them straight out, not the kind of tension-filled scenes which would go on in my parents' home.

Tracy: I'm sure at times my mother felt like walking out on the lot of us. But that would never be expressed in any way. I remember her saying to me once, 'You never heard your father or myself fighting, did you?' Things like that didn't go on, you didn't fight, it wasn't part of how things should be. That's a big difference between us because I fight a lot. I would say I express myself a lot more than she did.

Both these women believe they have formed more equal and satisfying marriage relationships than their own parents did. Part of the change is the way in which they deal with conflict with their husbands. In traditional marriage silence and withdrawl were common ways of coping with disagreements and hurts. Individuals had little scope to express their feelings. Big boys don't cry. A good child is a silent child. Tears are a sign of weakness. Touching was rarely acceptable and sexual feelings were expected to be firmly controlled. Women had some outlet for emotional expression in their relationships with their children, whereas men often suffered a greater degree of repression of their feelings. Liam O'Flaherty caught the mood in his story, 'Going into Exile', where father and son stand together outside the cottage the night before the boy leaves for America: 'Each hungered to embrace the other, to cry, to beat the air, to scream with excess of sorrow. But they stood silent and sombre, like nature about them, hugging their woe'.[4]

The mother, too, holds back her tears until the last moment. Not until the children are leaving does she let go. 'She burst into wild tears, wailing: "My children, oh, my children, far over the sea you will be carried from me, your mother." And she began to rock herself and she threw her apron over her head.' As a woman, it was acceptable for her to keen for the loss of her children, whereas her husband had to stay controlled throughout the parting.[5]

It is little wonder that so many people who were brought up in this tradition, especially men, find it difficult to acknowledge their feelings. But without this acknowledgement conflict resolution remains a problem as both partners will tend to bury their anger or irritation instead of bringing it out into the open.

A familiar escape route for men is alcohol. As the Irish bishops wrote in *Human Life is Sacred*, 'excessive drinking is without question one of the greatest sources of marital unhappiness and breakdown in Ireland'.[6] Elizabeth's story of her marriage is a case in point. She fell in love with her husband the night she met him and married him shortly afterwards when she was 22. 'The happiest months of my life were when we were newly married', she recalls. But before long the problems began to show. 'He was eleven years older than I but he is still not emotionally equal and never will be. He is a drunk. He has a personality problem that he covers with drink. He was always a heavy drinker.' Elizabeth can see how the conflict between them arose and steadily worsened:

> I need people, I need to be involved with people. I need affection, I need to give it and receive it. I didn't even get that slightly in my marriage. He was someone with no concept of human relations. He wants affection, but he doesn't understand what he wants and has no idea of how to give it back.

After seven years, during which she had three children, she left him. Her health was deteriorating and a neurologist told her she would have to change her life-style. 'I was so tired by that stage, so physically and emotionally worn out. I wasn't prepared to cope with it any longer.'

For Elizabeth, as for many women in similar situations, the decision to leave was not easy. She could see the tragedy in her husband's life and yet had to accept that she could not solve it. 'I still love the man I married and the man I lived with for those first months, but that man is buried, totally buried. It took me an awful long time to find out and to put myself on an even keel about it.'

It is not uncommon for a woman to marry someone whom she regards as older and more mature than herself only to find after a while that it is she who has the greater emotional maturity. In most cases it is the woman who carries the main responsibility for the emotional well-being of the whole family. Mother is the person expected to soothe and care for everyone else. It is part of women's traditional role to do so. The role has its positive aspects in that it helps women to learn about the emotional side of life and to develop a deep understanding of human relationships. Add to that the experience of childbirth and the demands of looking after young children and it is not surprising that women tend to go through more emotional change than their husbands. Men's involvement with the caring, affective world is often peripheral. Their traditional role takes them away from it through its emphasis on the external world of work and activity instead of the more internal world of feelings and reflection. So an imbalance between husband and wife develops, and it becomes harder for men to engage in the process of sorting out a relationship. The emotional arena has a long-standing 'feminine' label on it, and many men cannot allow themselves to enter such a place. Taught all their lives to repress the feminine part of themselves, they have lost touch with their feelings and are fearful of what might happen if they allowed that shadowy, forgotten area out into the light again.

If the emotional side of woman's traditional role has some advantages for her, other aspects of it do not. The low status of women's work as housewives and mothers is reflected at an emotional level in marriage. A woman's role as an equal partner in marriage is undermined when her husband and the world about her judge housework to be trivial and child-rearing easy. A man who sees his wife as an equal when they are both working can find his view of her changing when she is confined to the home. He is actively involved in the 'real' world of work; she is separated from that world. Her daily reality is created more by children than by adults and she appears to live a narrow, circumscribed existence. His perception of her, and her perception of herself, is devalued. Her self-esteem drops as she feels at a disadvantage when she tries to talk things over with him.

As extended families declined and smaller nuclear households became the norm, women began to rely more on their relationships with their husbands for emotional fulfilment. Women today have fewer sisters and brothers, parents and neighbours at hand to turn to for day-to-day support and companionship. Instead, they may expect their husbands to fill the gap. The danger in the modern ideal of marriage is not that a woman should expect a man to offer friendship, companionship and support as well as love but that she should look to him as the *only* source of all these. The isolation of the nuclear family can thrust a woman into over-dependence on her marriage relationship. She is then very vulnerable. When stress arises it feels more intense and more threatening. She may develop anxiety about her marriage and fears that her husband will leave her. If the feelings are turned inwards they can start a vicious circle. Anxiety increases self-doubt, which in turn reinforces her sense of powerlessness. The inequalities in the wider society have come to roots at the most intimate level, in the complex bond between a woman and a man.

The open communication required by the modern ideal of

marriage can only take place effectively between two people who have a fairly clear concept of themselves and who see each other as equal human beings. Irish society differs little from other Western countries in the barriers it erects in the way of this ideal. The social and emotional problems arising out of the nuclear family and the separation of men's and women's worlds are common to most industrialised capitalist nations. Ireland also shares with these countries the tradition of sex-stereotyping of children at school – another major source of inequality in later life.

Men and women are not brought up to see each other as equal human beings. Even when young people mix freely in their social lives and in their education, the discriminatory attitudes they see in adults and in the media impinge on their attitudes to one another and colour them with false assumptions and twisted expectations. When single-sex schools are the norm, as in Ireland, the problem is heightened by the physical absence of the other sex. In girls' minds both positive and negative views of boys become exaggerated through dealing with images and stereotypes rather than real people. Men are all too easily either romanticised as superior beings or despised as brutes with uncontrollable sexual urges.

These stereotyped views of men are reinforced by magazine stories and romantic fiction. Heroes are predictably handsome, taller than the woman, well-mannered and skilled in the art of love-making; men to look up to and love with a selfless dedication. Audrey remembers being immersed in this kind of fiction as an adolescent:

> Our models were straight out of Victorian novels. The heroines were all meek and mild and went through a lot of vicissitudes in life before falling in love with the right guy. They were totally romantic novels, and we were living in a kind of dream fantasy world. We all made eyes at the window-cleaner and the altar-boys but we never met any men.
>
> When I first had boy-friends later it was incredibly hard. You were expecting all sorts of gallant behaviour from these guys, who promptly jumped on you in the back seat of the car on the way home from the hop, and you didn't know where you were.

> *Tracy*: I had no friends that were boys. When I was about 12 I went into a friend's house when her brother was there with his

friends, and I remember walking into the kitchen with a magazine that I'd bought. I held the magazine rigid in front of me and kept my eyes down in it because I couldn't handle being there. I was so embarrassed I didn't know what to do. That is so stupid when I think of it now. I would hate that situation to arise for my children, and I would do everything I could to avoid sending them to a single-sex school.

The distortion is as great in boys' views of girls. Girls are stupid, 'silly eejuts', soft. Later on they become dangerous, desirable, tempting – anything but equal human beings. Three dominant images colour men's view of women: images of the virgin, the whore and the mother. They appear in stories, songs and religious imagery as well as in schoolboys' fantasies. They cause problems in a relationship when the man sees the woman as a combination of images instead of seeing her clearly as herself. The three images are by no means exclusive to Ireland. Their power is, however, heightened by the dominant sexual ethic in Irish society and by the high degree of separation of the sexes in childhood. Without everyday knowledge of girls as friends boys have little experience with which to counteract the stereotypes.

The virgin is the pure, chaste image of woman. She is innocent, with an intense passive goodness. She is unattainable, removed from base sex, and can save men from the sinfulness of their sexuality. Her virginity makes her vulnerable, but she also has power in her ability to purify and forgive. The image clearly reflects the virginal aspects of Mary and some of the saints. The virgin is untroubled by the problems of the body; menstruation and bodily functions do not exist for her. Her image can be found in many songs:

> The pale moon was rising above the green mountain,
> The sun was declining beneath the blue sea,
> When I strayed with my love to the pure crystal fountain
> That stands in the beautiful Vale of Tralee.
> She was lovely and fair as the rose of the summer
> Yet was not her beauty alone that won me,
> Oh no, 'twas the truth in her eye ever dawning,
> That made me love Mary, The Rose of Tralee.
>
> (traditional song)

Everything is pale and pure, she was lovely and fair with truth in her eye. In the next verse, 'Mary all smiling sat list'ning to me'. She has an ethereal quality, and men who come in contact with her are purified and refreshed.

The whore is the contrast to the virgin. She represents the dark, sensual side of woman, a source of temptation and sexual pleasure for men. The whore is also the source of sin, an image to be both feared and desired. She has power over men. She is the siren who lured men to their death, the mythical female warrior with teeth in her vagina. She is the woman in pornography, the object of lust. The whore is a symbol of the female sexuality that is feared by celibate men. In the words of Marina Warner, 'the foundations of the ethic of sexual chastity are laid in fear and loathing of the female body's function, in identification of evil with the flesh and flesh with woman'.[7] Lust destroys the soul as death rots the body, and woman as whore is to blame. Because of her, woman is not to be trusted as she can disguise herself to deceive men. The whore is also the witch:

> Oh did you not hear of Kate Kearney,
> She lives on the banks of Killarney,
> From the glance of her eye, shun danger and fly,
> For fatal's the glance of Kate Kearney.
>
> Tho' she looks so bewitchingly simple,
> Yet there is mischief in every dimple,
> And who dares inhale her sigh's spicy gale
> Must die by the breath of Kate Kearney.
>
> (traditional song)

The virgin is almost bodyless, but the whore is all flesh. She is the fluid feminine, with power in her physical being. 'Love has pitched his mansion in the place of excrement', wrote W. B. Yeats in a poem.[8]

The images of whore and virgin sometimes alternate, especially when repression causes sexual feelings to burst out as one or the other extreme. In *Portrait of the Artist as a Young Man*, James Joyce describes how the woman in the hero's mind changes from one to the other:

A figure that had seemed to him by day demure and innocent came towards him by night through the winding darkness of sleep, her face transfigured by a lecherous cunning, her eyes bright with a brutish joy. Only the morning pained him with its dim memory of dark orgiastic riot, its keen and humiliating sense of transgression.[9]

And after he has given way to lust, he is drawn back to the purifying image of the Virgin Mary:

His sin, which had covered him from the sight of God, had led him nearer to the refuge of sinners. Her eyes seemed to regard him with mild pity; her holiness, a strange light glowing faintly upon her frail flesh, did not humiliate the sinner who approached her. If ever he was impelled to cast sin from him and to repent the impulse that moved him it was the wish to be her knight.[10]

The image of the whore is also used to justify male power. Men's use of physical brutality, forcing woman into submission, is the response to the whore's supposed sexual power over them. Rape is an act of violent domination using sex as a weapon. It is an expression of hatred and fear of women. Men use the word 'whore' as an insult. It is a label that defiles the female sexuality which makes men feel threatened because they do not understand it.

If the virgin and the whore represent the two opposite ends of the sexual dimension in men's minds, the mother image is somewhat different. She is the symbol of security and warmth, someone who nourishes both body and soul. In loving a woman as mother, a man can retain something of his childishness. His love is not contaminated by all the complexities of sexuality. Her love for him is profound and lasting; it reassures him and boosts his self-image.

The mother is Mary in her other aspect, as the mother who worshipped her son. As both mother and virgin, Mary represents the impossible ideal, the mother who bore a son but who was untainted by sex. And she reveals another aspect of the mother-image – she is defined in relation to a male child, not a daughter. Mother is the woman who nurtures and services men.

This role of the mother is also symbolised in images of Mother Ireland. The country is the mother whose sons were prepared to sacrifice themselves for her, as in Patrick Pearse's poem, 'The Mother':

> I do not grudge them; Lord, I do not grudge
> My two strong sons that I have seen go out
> To break their strength and die, they and a few,
> In bloody protest for a glorious thing. . .[11]

In all the imagery and symbolism that distorts men's and women's views of each other it is easy to lose sight of the possibility of an adult, mature relationship between two people. A man whose attitude to a woman is distorted because he worships her as a virgin, despises her as whore or seeks in her a mother-substitute is not the equal partner demanded by the modern ideal of marriage. The three images damage relationships by reducing the rounded humanity of an individual woman into one or more stereotypes. They prevent men from seeing women as fully equal and provide a false justification for aspects of their behaviour towards them.

Marriage as institution

Although the love bond between a man and a woman is now the normal basis for marriage, being married involves much more than a relationship. Marriage is also a contract governed by the laws of both Church and State. 'The institution of marriage', said an early feminist pamphlet, 'is something invented to preserve male superiority and a system of female chattels'. In a section entitled 'Five Good Reasons to Live in Sin', the pamphlet, *Change or Chains?*, summarised the ways in which the institution of marriage constrained and disadvantaged women.[12] The date was 1971, and the first reason was that if a woman lived 'in sin' rather than married she could keep her job. A marriage bar was still operated by the Civil Service and some other employers.

Second, the tax system discriminated against married women by taxing them more heavily than single women. The third reason for living in sin was to preserve the right to open a bank account or borrow on hire-purchase. Once a woman was married, finance companies required her husband's signature on all transactions. (Her signature, of course, was not required on his documents.) The fourth reason was that once married there was no escape, and if a woman left her husband she was presumed to have deserted him and lost any rights to the house or to his money. Last, 'if you live in sin you don't submit to the insult that society offers women who marry – the status of property. An adult and equal relationship is something two people forge together'.[13]

This was the crucial distinction. By living in sin a couple could develop the kind of relationship they wanted while removing themselves from the institutional weight of rules and regulations with which society surrounded marriage, and especially wives.

This is still the case, and a problem for the modern ideal of marriage. In reality there is a large contradiction between the ideal of the marriage *relationship* and the constraints imposed by the *institution* of marriage. According to the notion of the ideal relationship, wife and husband are equal partners. In reality the State assumes that a woman is dependent on her husband. In the ideal relationship, both partners have equal rights as human beings. In reality the Church expects a woman to put the needs of her husband and children above her own.

Church view of marriage

Church and State maintain the institution of marriage in different ways. To the Church marriage is the cornerstone of Catholic society, holy and indissoluble. The Irish bishops are quite clear about their views: 'Whatever weakens marriage weakens society and endangers the future of civilisation'.[14] Their emphasis is not so much on the relationship between husband and wife, but on the creation of a loving family for the children: 'Marriage and marriage alone is the true expression of love and the normal condition for the emotional security and maturity of children'.[15] They do not make clear how this fits in with the need for 'understanding' for unmarried mothers. Living in sin is not acceptable because it is as its name implies – sinful. To the Catholic Church marriage is the only proper place for sex, and even then only if it is meant for the procreation of children: 'Sexual intercourse, ordained towards procreation, is the maximum expression on the physical level of the communion of love of the married. Divorced from this context of reciprocal gift . . . [it] is a moral disorder'.[16]

The Church sees pre-marital and extra-marital sex, contraception and divorce as threats to the institution of marriage, and hence to the stability of society. Marriage has a symbolic importance too:

'Christ is the Bridegroom; the Church is his bride'.[17] And as Christ is the head of the Church, so the bridegroom becomes the head of the family. As the Church serves and honours him, so a wife is supposed to serve and minister to her husband.

Traditionally, the Church's view of the model wife was of someone, like Mary, who was submissive, and who put her own needs in second place. Motherhood was her vocation and the central role in her life, and she willingly accepted as many children as God sent. It was a view that reinforced the subordinate status of the wife, and which fitted in with the economic order in the countryside. Today, the Church officially holds a more enlightened view:

> There is . . . in modern times a timely movement towards equality between the sexes, and a greater and overdue recognition of the rights of women within marriage and the home, and also in society. There is a better understanding of marriage as a partnership between equal persons, in which each looks to the other for personal fulfilment, rather than for financial security.[18]

But do the other teachings of the Church support this view in practice?

In *Human Life is Sacred*, the Irish bishops spoke of the subordination of 'I' to 'We' in marriage. This is achieved by 'mutual consideration and concern' and 'control of one's selfish impulses'.[19] Both husband and wife should make continuous efforts to overcome their selfishness. But in reality, it is more often the woman who compromises, who gives in and who sacrifices her own needs. To be fair, the bishops do acknowledge this problem. The following comments about men are not from a feminist publication but from the Hierarchy itself: 'Their tenderness and thoughtfulness sometimes end with the honeymoon. Irish married men can remain bachelors at heart, happiest in male company outside the home and not trying to build even a friendship, much less a loving marriage, with their wives'.[20]

But the bishops fail to make the connection between men's attitudes to women and the stereotypes that are rooted in religious imagery – an imagery whose message is that women should be virgins and then mothers and never whores. Men's attitudes are affected also by the ideology of the family to which the Church subscribes, which gives men a breadwinning, leadership role and women a restricted, home-based existence. Even more seriously, the Church does not wish to acknowledge how women's inferior status in marriage is reinforced when contraception and abortion are regarded as sinful and when divorce is unobtainable. If a woman cannot control her fertility it is hard for her to feel sufficiently in control of other aspects of her life. A woman who is in perpetual fear of becoming pregnant will find it difficult to relax and enjoy the 'communion of love' of the married.

Even though the Church in its pastoral work supports some aspects of the modern ideal of marriage, certain of its teachings prescribe a role for women that contradicts the notions of equality implicit in the ideal.

State view of marriage

The State is committed, through the Constitution, to protect marriage and the basis of family life. Many aspects of the law, and of State services such as the social welfare scheme, reflect this adherence to the family.

Some areas of State regulation have improved since *Change or Chains?* was published. Prior to 1970 the assumption that a woman was financially dependent on her husband was so ingrained that even a wife deserted by her husband was entitled to no State benefit. Now she can claim the Deserted Wife's benefit or allowance, though the qualifying conditions are strict. This is, however, no recognition of a woman's right to be financially independent as the allowance will be withdrawn if she is found to be cohabiting with another man.

The law governing maintenance of spouses and children after marital breakdown has been improved, and a woman can now apply for a barring order to keep her violent husband out of the home. The Family Home Protection Act of 1976 prevents either spouse from selling the house and its contents without the consent of the other. This is an important protection for separated and deserted women who want to stay in the family home.

The marriage bar at work has gone, and the Employment Equality Act brought some measure of legal protection against discrimination in employment.

In spite of these changes the State still reinforces the subordinate role of women in marriage in several ways. A wife's domicile is legally that of her husband, even if they are separated and live in different countries. There is no legal recognition of rape within marriage. A man can sexually assault or rape a woman simply because she is his wife.[21] Financially, direct discrimination in the tax system has gone, but the revenue commissioners will assess a wife with her husband unless she specifies otherwise. The social welfare system still discriminates openly against married women, in their eligibility for unemployment benefit and assistance, for injury and disability benefits and for some aspects of free medical treatment (though this situation is due to be changed to bring Ireland in line with EEC standards).

But perhaps the most serious way in which both Church and State uphold the institution of marriage is their mutually agreed ban on divorce. This was written into the 1937 constitution and is still in force.[22]

The campaign for divorce in Ireland is an important issue for women. It can be argued that women are particularly disadvantaged by the absence of divorce. Men in unsatisfactory marriages have the traditional option of going to England, where they can obtain a divorce after a period of residence. It is harder for women to leave a bad situation. Many are tied to their homes by children or by financial dependence on their husbands. If they take the children and go, they are likely to face great difficulties in finding suitable housing and arranging some sort of financial support from either the State or their husbands. Some women are desperate enough to leave, as the persistent crowding of the refuges for battered women demonstrates. Others can see no way out of relationships that have gone seriously wrong and feel trapped in their own homes. In the words of the AIM group for family law reform:

> too many Irishwomen choose to muddle through life with low grade relationships; wives who are taken for granted, or positively disadvantaged by their role of wife and mother, and though they become bitter and resentful over the years, never confide or seek help from others.[23]

On the other hand, the increase in the number of married women with jobs outside the home and the changes in the status of women have meant that fewer women are prepared to put up with a bad marriage and that more women are in a position to support themselves financially. This has contributed to an important shift of opinion away from the traditional view of marriage and towards a greater understanding of marriage problems.

The true extent of marital breakdown in Ireland is unknown. There are no official statistics on the numbers of separated or divorced persons (the latter being those who have obtained a divorce abroad). An oft-quoted figure is the Divorce Action Group's estimate of 70 000 people whose marriages have broken down.[24] This is approximately 6 per cent of all marriages, or one in seventeen. As this gives Ireland by far the lowest rate of marital breakdown in Europe, it is likely to be a conservative figure. It probably conceals the many marriages in which the relationship has broken down but where the couple continue to live under the same roof because they cannot agree to a separation agreement or they feel, for various reasons, that they must keep up the pretence of a marriage. The AIM group goes so far as to suggest that unhappy homes 'account for around 40 per cent of all those rated as married'.[25]

Various other statistics related to marital breakdown are rising annually. A state allowance for deserted wives was introduced in 1970. By 1976 almost 5000 women were in receipt of the allowance or the associated benefit, and the number has continued to rise annually.[26] As eligibility rules are tight, the total does not give a true picture of the number of wives on their own. But the increase suggests either that more marriages are in difficulty or, more likely, that people are increasingly prepared to acknowledge their marital problems and seek a solution to them. The name of the allowance is revealing, as it reflects a wife-as-victim attitude towards women in broken marriages. The campaign for the allowance managed to swing public opinion behind the need to help the supposedly innocent wives who were deserted by their selfish husbands. It created little awareness of the fact that many marital problems are based on a breakdown in the relationship that is felt by both partners. In many cases it was in fact the wife who forced the matter to a head, as women were becoming more assertive over their desire for satisfactory marriages.

A related statistic is the excess of married women over married men recorded at every Census. The men are presumably living abroad, and though some of them are still in thriving marriages the excess includes the many women whose husbands have found their own solutions to marriages they no longer wanted.

The numbers (mostly women) applying to District Courts for maintenance orders for the support of themselves or their children increased tenfold in the 1970s. The increase in applications reflects the rise in numbers of separations, though maintenance continues to be a problematic area because of the difficulty of finding the man in some cases and the problem of those who default on their payments.

Because of the limited legal solutions to marital breakdown – notably the absence of divorce – many couples resolve their problems without recourse to the State. Instead, they make private arrangements for separation and maintenance. As the lawyer William Duncan notes, 'the cases actually coming to the notice of the courts, marriage tribunals, social welfare officials and legal advice centres represent the tip of an iceberg whose submerged dimensions are unknown'.[27]

At present, the various solutions offered by the Church and State are messy and unsatisfactory. The Catholic Church is totally opposed to divorce, but it does annul a small number of marriages each year. An annulment is a declaration by the Church that the marriage is deemed not to have existed. It is granted in certain cases of non-consummation or where the character of one party is such that they lacked the capacity to assume the responsibilities of marriage. Up to 1000 couples per year apply for an annulment, but only a small percentage of these are successful. The proceedings are long and costly and often emotionally painful. An annulment does not give the civil right to remarry. As a result, a person granted a Church annulment who then remarries in a Church is technically bigamous in the eyes of the State. The State turns a blind eye to this fact, but recent governments have allowed the anomaly to continue.

It is likely that many couples apply for an annulment because they want the right to remarry, which in other countries they would obtain through divorce. But annulment is no substitute for divorce. Elizabeth divorced her husband while they were living in the USA, and is adamant that she wanted a divorce rather than an annulment:

Divorce is absolutely necessary. The annulment is a ridiculous concept to me as you cannot nullify something which exists. I cannot say my marriage never happened, which is what an annulment asks you to do. Divorce is much more acceptable than annulment because you are rending asunder a marriage that cannot work while accepting that it exists.

The State offers no scheme which offers people the two things they usually want – an end to their existing marriage contract and the right to remarry. Civil annulment is a possibility but the conditions are tight and only a handful of petitions are granted each year. A form of judicial separation is an option to those who can afford a High Court hearing, but again very few cases are heard and the order confers no right to remarry. Most couples whose marriages break down are left permanently suspended in a half-married, half-unmarried limbo, with a tangle of family law and social welfare regulations to fight their way through as they try to rebuild their lives in some dignified fashion.

Norma is in a fairly common situation. Her marriage ended when her husband went off with someone else. Their son was 2 years old at the time. She now lives with her boy-friend, but cannot marry him:

I don't feel that I'm really recognised. I am labelled 'single parent', but I've also got the label of a married woman on me. I can't get divorced and I can't remarry. I'd like to see us given some sort of status. Even filling out forms, you come to the part on marital status and the choice is married, single or widowed. There is no 'divorced' or 'separated' on forms. It makes me very angry. I normally strike the whole lot out and write 'separated' down. Because we have to be counted if we want to get anywhere.

She is particularly hurt by her parents' lack of understanding of her position. They hold traditional views about the permanence of marriage and cannot accept that her husband has gone for good:

So much has happened to me that my parents would never have dreamed of. I don't think they will ever cope with the split-up of my marriage. They are very bitter towards my husband. I am still married as far as they are concerned. Even though it didn't work out that is the way I stay. Another relationship isn't on with them. It means that I just keep quiet about my private life. I don't tell them anything.

Once again the problem is obscured, hidden from public view and buried within the individual. Norma knows what solution she wants: 'I would get a divorce if I could. I would like to see divorce being made available – not readily available, but I would definitely like to see it come in because there is a need for it'.

To Clare, another woman who is separated from her husband, the absence of divorce is 'an absolute scandal'. 'It is like so much in Ireland. Because you don't have a divorce law you don't have definite statistics on numbers who are separated. They are creating this Catholic Ireland image, this great country, and yet you've got such misery underneath it all.'

In order to introduce a divorce law, a two-stage process is required. The government must first hold a referendum to remove the constitutional ban on divorce, after which appropriate legislation can be introduced into the Dáil. Opinion polls suggest that such a referendum would probably be passed. A poll carried out for the *Irish Times* in February 1985 found that 70 per cent of the respondents thought that divorce should be permitted in certain circumstances. The commonest reason given for divorce was irretrievable marital breakdown, followed by violence, hardship, drink and children's suffering. Only 46 per cent, however, said they would vote to remove the constitutional ban on divorce, with 45 per cent saying they would vote to keep it. The discrepancy in these results seems to indicate a degree of suspicion amongst some of the electorate about what kind of divorce law might be brought in once the constitutional ban was removed.

The division of opinion in the poll followed the traditional – progressive split that is familiar from campaigns on other social issues. Support for divorce was strongest amongst younger, urban and middle-class groups. People over 65 years old and those living in rural areas had the highest rates of opposition to divorce in any circumstances.[28]

Although support for the introduction of divorce legislation is growing, opposition to any form of divorce is still strong within the Catholic Church and among groups which aim to defend traditional morality. The Church's opposition to divorce is based on two main arguments. On doctrinal grounds the Church 'cannot allow divorce and freedom to marry anew without violating divine law and the clear teaching of Christ'.[29] The Church also argues that divorce undermines the stability of marriage. 'Where marriages are being dissolved by civil law they tend to fail in that society with ever increasing ease, and divorce does indeed become a social plague.'[30] Opponents of divorce often use the argument that divorce laws lead to more marital breakdown. In his introductory statement on behalf of the bishops to the New Ireland Forum, Bishop Cahal Daly made this point, and said that since the liberalisation of the divorce law in Northern Ireland the number of divorces had increased threefold.[31]

Two assumptions underlying this argument can be challenged. There is an implicit assumption that because something gets on the statute book everyone will want it. It is as if people cannot be trusted to adhere to their own moral convictions, and the law is required to protect them from themselves. Professor John A. Murphy calls this attitude a 'subtle form of lingering episcopal paternalism'.[32]

The more serious assumption is that divorce laws actually cause marital breakdown. There is little evidence to support this view. As William Duncan so graphically puts it in *The Case for Divorce*, to deny divorce in an attempt to prevent marriages breaking down is like forbidding funerals in the hope of eradicating the problem of death.[33] Divorce is generally sought by people whose marriage relationships are over, and who wish to be free of the contractual aspects of the marriage. To quote William Duncan again, 'there is no evidence that divorce laws, whether liberal or strict, have by themselves any appreciable impact on marital stability. The causes of marital breakdown appear to have much deeper roots in social and economic changes. Indeed, the introduction and reform of divorce laws seem to have followed rather than initiated social change'.[34] If the reform of divorce laws normally follows social change then it is entirely predictable that the campaign for divorce in Ireland should gather momentum in the early 1980s, following a decade in which attitudes to marriage and to women's rights changed so significantly. People's expectations of the marriage relationship have altered rapidly, but the institutional framework has lagged behind. The debate about divorce centres on the question whether the relationship or the contract is the most important aspect of marriage. To those who see the contract as more important, marriage is for ever. To those who favour the relationship, permanence cannot be guaranteed and divorce is a human right that should be available to all.

The arguments for and against divorce also revolve around the notion of the family. The traditional Catholic view that divorce undermines marriage and family life – the view enshrined in the Constitution – is based on a rigid view of the family as a unit created by a permanent contract between husband and wife. Supporters of divorce, on the other hand, hold more diverse views about what constitutes a family. Many would argue that remarriages, separated parents with children and unmarried parents are all valid families. There should be no discrimination against them by either Church or State, as what really matters is the quality of the relationships within the home, not whether the family corresponds to a set formula. In this sense, the support for the campaign for divorce reflects changing attitudes towards morality in general as well as towards marriage itself. The success or otherwise of the campaign will be an indication of the power of these changed attitudes against the traditional Catholic ideology of the family and the institutions which support it.

5   Sexuality I: A Matter of Choice

All women are sexually oppressed in Ireland. We are oppressed because we have little chance to understand and define our sexuality on our own terms, or to express it in ways we have freely chosen. (Women's Right To Choose Campaign, Dublin, 1984.[1])

Sexual intercourse, ordained towards procreation, is the maximum expression on the physical level of the communion of love of the married. Divorced from this context of reciprocal gift. . . [it] is a moral disorder.' (Sacred Congregation for Catholic Education, Rome, 1983).[2]

The women's movement has, from the start, campaigned for every woman's right to define her own sexuality and make choices about her own body. A woman's sexuality is part of her self. She cannot accept herself fully, cannot feel positive and loving and confident in herself, unless she accepts her body and feels in control of it. One essential aspect of this is fertility control:

We recognise that control of our fertility is one of the most basic of our human rights and without this control we will never be able to achieve the other aims of feminism, i.e. the right to enjoy our sexuality independently of our reproductive role, the right to work outside the home, to make choices of careers and partners.[3]

The Catholic Church too recognises the importance of sexuality: 'Sexuality is a fundamental component of personality, one of its modes of being, of manifestation, of communicating with others, of feeling, of expressing and living human love'.[4] Both the Church and the women's movement condemn the abuse of sexuality in the form of male violence in rape, incest and pornography. But there the similarity in approach between feminists and the Church ends. From a traditional Catholic viewpoint the free expression of sexuality is potentially dangerous. The Church tends to include sex with other evils, such as drugs and the pursuit of materialism, which tempt people away from the Christian way of life. It sees only two valid ways for Christians to express their sexuality – through chastity and through the procreation of children in marriage. It specifically denounces the feminist aim of separating sex and reproduction. Feminists support a woman's right to choose her sexual partners, whereas the Church says she can have only one – her husband.

Above all, the Church is in conflict with the women's movement over the latter's attempts to promote an open, creative and self-determined female sexuality. For centuries, male clergy have sought to repress and control female sexuality, condemning it as the province of the whore. Sexual woman was a threat to their chastity, a source of temptation to be pushed away and denounced.

The weight of this traditional fear and distrust of sexuality, especially women's sexuality, has undoubtedly contributed to the general repression of sexual behaviour in Ireland. It dovetailed neatly with the requirements of farmers in the post-famine countryside, where strict control of individual sexuality was necessary to preserve the rural family system. And if women were to be confined to the home as mothers and denied a wider role in society, then a strict moral code was required to support this form of the family. A narrow view of sexuality was therefore perpetuated in independent Ireland, as Church and State worked hand in hand to enshrine Catholic morality in the 1937 Constitution.

Both feminists and traditional Catholics see the connection between sexual behaviour and the wider social order. Feminists argue that without a free choice in sexual matters, women cannot make real choices in other aspects of their lives. Traditionalists say this is a threat to the family, and that women can only have limited choices because many forms of behaviour are immoral and wrong. The feminist view clearly *is* a threat to the family – to the traditional family which prescribes a restricted role for women.

Enormous changes in sexual behaviour and attitudes have taken place in Ireland in the past twenty years. But the issues involved are still highly controversial. In 1983, when the economy of the Republic was in grave difficulty and unemployment was rising at an unprecedented rate, the political issue of the year was the (success-ful) campaign by anti-abortion groups to amend the Constitution to prohibit abortion – which was already illegal. It is over issues to do with sexuality that the conflict between traditional and progressive forces in Irish society can be seen most clearly.

Sex education – necessary or dangerous?

Two recent surveys have confirmed that large numbers of young Irish women are ignorant of many basic facts about their own bodies. In Dublin, two doctors interviewed 112 single girls under the age of 18 who had babies at St James' Hospital. Sixty-two of them had no knowledge of their own fertility and its relation to the menstrual cycle, and twelve had only a rough idea.[5] A similar survey by Dr Andrew Rynne and Dr Liam Lacey of 249 unmarried mothers found that 28 per cent of them had had nothing explained to them about their periods and were therefore unlikely to have any real understanding of the physiology of reproduction. The researchers were struck by:

> the appalling amount of misinformation and naivety that landed these otherwise responsible young women with an extra-marital pregnancy. . . . The picture is overwhelmingly that of a group with no, or only a very sketchy, knowledge of sexuality, reproduction and birth control.

They concluded that there is a clear and urgent need for pro-grammes of life education in schools.[6]

Misinformation and ignorance are not confined to unmarried mothers but are common to most young women. Few young people receive comprehensive sex education in the form of the necessary information and a chance to discuss the related areas of relation-ships, morality and health. The following experiences are not untypical.

Carole (aged 28): We got sex education from priests. It was a giggling matter. No one took it seriously and you didn't really ask the questions you wanted to know. You felt foolish, silly. My parents never mentioned sex to me. I was waiting for them to take me aside one day or give me a book to read, but that never occurred. There was no mention of it at all.

I think most people find out from friends. But you gather it in such a way that even with friends you are afraid to ask too many questions in case they think that you don't know. So you pick up pieces and stay quiet about the areas that you don't know about.

Clare (aged 32): Sex education? Oh no, we had none of that at all. When I was in sixth year, someone came and gave us a talk. I don't remember anything. It was just before we left school, in the same lecture as how to prepare for an interview.

My father used to keep books he didn't want us to read on top of the wardrobe. I would take his book in one hand and the dictionary in the other and I learned a lot of things like that. But I didn't really know an awful lot until I started nursing.

Some women found that their schooling mystified sex, and wrapped it up in a dark cloak of morality:

Audrey (aged 48): During the retreat the priest would address the sixth class about sex. We all waited with baited breath for this class! I think it was something to do with French kisses. I remember being told about this girl who dressed up one night and went to a sinful dance hall, and it just so happened that was the night it went up in flames and she went to roast in hell for all eternity, and was it worth it? We were all wondering what she did. That was never said, she was just in 'an occasion of sin', and that was sufficient, and she went to hell. But that was really all the sex education we got.

Maura (aged 30): My mother didn't give me any information at all about sex. I was given a book called *My Dear Daughter*. I remember being ill with the flu and trying to figure it all out – all these concepts like transubstantiation. It was all metaphysical sex, blessed virgins and all, and I really didn't have a clue what was going on.

Anne is now in her forties and received no sex education at all, only moral training:

> We were told everything was wrong but we were not told why it was wrong. At Catechism class the sister would start talking about what was in her mind and it was about sex but sex was never mentioned. It was about giving men our bodies, that they would only use us. We hadn't a clue what the woman was talking about. All we were doing was watching the clock, thinking would she let us out for lunch?

As a result, Anne grew up profoundly ignorant of sexual matters, as she discovered to her cost when she married:

> I went into marriage with my eyes closed, really and truly. Whatever knowledge there was, my husband had it. I am married twenty-four years and if I said this to teenagers today they wouldn't believe me, but I went into hospital in 1960 to have my first daughter and I did not know how that child was going to be born. Up until the last few minutes before she was born I thought she was going to come out of my tummy. I didn't know how. It's incredible, but it's true. With my children I talk about it out in the open, because I swore what happened to me would never happen to them.

Women who receive little sex education from either parents or school tend to end up with a very patchy knowledge, much of which may be wrong. Misinformation is perhaps even more dangerous than ignorance. Young women can get pregnant because they have completely muddled ideas about the safe period or about contraceptives and how they work. Susan, for instance, is a young woman who became pregnant at the age of 19 because neither she nor her boy-friend used contraception. She was scared to go on the pill because a friend had told her that if she conceived when taking the pill the child would be handicapped. She eventually acquired some sex education in rather unusual circumstances – while serving a prison sentence. Two teachers came in to run sessions on science with the women prisoners:

> They were doing stuff on how you get pregnant, on the man's body and the woman's body. Actually I think that was the only

education I got on sex. When I saw the pictures and everything was explained I learned an awful lot, especially about periods – if you have sex before a period or after it and when you can actually get pregnant. I didn't know that before.

Many parents, perhaps because of their own upbringing, find it difficult to discuss sex with their children. Schools fare little better. The Department of Education has issued no guidelines on sex education, though it is currently looking into the matter. Schools vary widely, from the occasional one in which sex education is fully integrated into the curriculum to others in which it is not taught at all. In most, sex education is covered by outside 'experts' who are brought in for one or two sessions, or is given an hour or so in biology or religion classes. In general, boys probably get even less sex education than girls.

In the wake of Ann Lovett's death Health Boards were flooded with calls from teachers and parents asking for information about teaching materials on sex education for schools and how they could introduce them. When such a tragedy occurs public opinion becomes more sympathetic to those who call for more information about sexuality to be made available to young people. But the public memory is short, and soon the voices of conservatism became louder again: 'if you tell them about it they'll only experiment'; 'it is wrong to inform unmarried people about contraception beause it is wrong for them to use it'; 'a stricter moral education is what is needed, not sex education'. And so the ignorance, and the suffering it causes, continues.

The Church plays a major role in this area. It has a strong influence on the school curriculum, both through the nuns and brothers in teaching-posts and through the priests who sit on school management committees. The Church is firmly committed to imparting information on sex only in the context of moral education. This can be very useful if the moral issues are presented as topics for discussion, but all too often young people experience such moral education as a rigid set of rules about sexual behaviour – rules that reflect the Church's moral code. 'Sexual relations outside marriage are sinful',[7] masturbation is a 'grave moral disorder',[8] homosexuality is 'a problem' which must be received with understanding but which is never morally justified.[9]

The Irish bishops made clear in *Human Life is Sacred* that 'the authentic Christian teaching on the morality of sex has not fundamentally changed and will not change'.[10] In 1983 the Vatican reiterated these points in *Educational Guidance in Human Love*, a document about sex education. The document confirms the importance of marriage as the basis of family life and the only proper place for sexual intercourse.[11] But is the Church really talking about *sex* education or about something different?

> In order for the value of sexuality to reach its full potential, *education for chastity* is absolutely essential, for it is a virtue that develops a person's authentic maturity and makes him or her capable of respecting and fostering the 'nuptial meaning' of the body.[12]

To achieve this, self-control is advocated, as are the virtues of modesty and temperance. In addition, the document refers to the urgent necessity of transmitting to the young the Church's ban on artificial birth control.

Education Guidance in Human Love mystifies sexuality even further. It does not say how 'education for chastity' is likely to help future Ann Lovetts or help young people to take a mature view of sexual relationships. It tends to reinforce the traditional Catholic view of the body as a source of temptation and sin, to be dealt with through rigid control and self-denial.

> *Audrey*: I was taught to see my body as something that had to be covered up, and was slightly unclean. The emphasis was that the greatest vocation in life was to be called by God to be a nun. Everything after that was secondary anyway. Sexuality was very suppressed. It was dirty. And when you are talking about the west of Ireland, it was an extraordinary sexuality. I don't think sex was ever really supposed to happen.

Sex certainly wasn't supposed to happen on your own, with someone of the same sex, or outside marriage. Even within marriage lust was a sin. Once again we return to the symbolic importance of the Virgin Mary for women, for she was a woman who became a mother without having sex at all. She did not menstruate and she remained a virgin through childbirth. She is eternally pure and ethereal, a woman untouched by the demands of her physical body. Yet most women find that their bodies are forced into their consciousness daily. During the years of menstruation a woman's physiology is never static. It changes continually as her cycle moves from ovulation to the pre-menstrual phase to bleeding. Her weight fluctuates, her mood changes. Menarche is a major transition in her life, and menopause another. If she bears children, pregnancy and childbirth bring a myriad of other changes. All these bodily events are real and immediate and have strong effects on every woman's social and emotional life. Yet they are barely acknowledged in either the virginal image of the pure Catholic girl or in the ideal of the devoted mother. Mary experienced none of the physical events common to all women. She is presented as a static figure, whereas women experience life as a series of cycles.

Many of the female saints reinforce the ideals of purity and virginity. Maria Goretti is one example. She was a young Italian girl who was canonised for defending her virginity to death. She resisted a man who tried to rape her, and he murdered her with a stiletto. Pope Pius XII beatified her by public decree in 1947, saying that 'Italian girls especially, in the fair flower of their youth should raise their eyes to Heaven and gaze upon this shining example of maidenly virtue which rose from the midst of wickedness as a light shines in the darkness'.[13]

Clare remembers the story from childhood:

> I remember at school these travelling players came and did a play about Maria Goretti. You didn't see the man touch her in the play. It wasn't until years later I realised he'd tried to rape her, but of course we didn't see that at school as it would have been too explicit.

And her reaction to it?

> The thing that really annoys me is that everything we were told about women was that they are pure, they are virgins. Also this thing with celibacy – to me that makes sex dirty or underhand. You have the priests up in the pulpit telling people how to live their lives. It infuriates me.

It is at puberty, when girls start to menstruate and are aware of new sexual feelings, that many start to feel confused about their bodies in relation to their religion. In her childhood Tricia remembers the sweetness of the saints and the stories of the smell of lilies where they walked, and felt happy with her religious beliefs. But at puberty, she became aware of problems: 'Lust appeared as a major sin. Sexual thoughts were nasty, dirty and we had to pray for them to go away. We had to confess impure thoughts.' When her periods started, she felt 'a mess'. 'I felt removed from the cool, virginal figure of Mary who didn't seem to have a body at all, in one sense.' In Mass, her confused feelings often resulted in sexual images of Christ – perhaps, she thinks, because he was set up as an object of love.

Adolescent confusion is nothing new. In Ireland the sexual aspect of it is exacerbated by single-sex education. After twelve or more years of segregated education it is inevitable that girls and boys will experience some difficulty in relating naturally to each other, especially when sexual repression fosters an unhealthy combination of fear and fascination for the opposite sex. It is often particularly difficult for young men and women to make ordinary friendships. When Tracy, for instance, found that her first boy-friend became a valued companion, she remembers that 'it was a real breakthrough for me to realise that boys were actually people'.

Carole is 28 years old and is still trying to decide what to accept and what to reject of the Catholic morality with which she was brought up:

> I'm not a very willing person when it comes to sex. I feel very, very inhibited. Basically because it is outside marriage. I suppose it is the fear of becoming pregnant, plus the fact that it has been drummed into me for so long that it isn't the right thing to do. I find it very hard to shake that off, and in many respects I'm not trying to shake it off. I think it is a good thing in some respects. I'm glad that I have a strict moral code myself.

Women who have chosen to reject the teaching on the sinfulness of sex outside marriage often have to deal with the inevitable guilt:

> *Clare*: Oh the guilt, it is an awful thing. When I started sleeping with fellows I felt guilty. I only did it out of curiosity, to see what it was like. I was 19. I didn't enjoy it, it was awful. It took me a while

before I met somebody who I liked and who I enjoyed sex with. To really let myself go took years.

Audrey: I remember losing my virginity. It was hilarious. It was in Belfast – we were staying in the house of some friends of his. There were holy pictures all over the place, and I remember he came into my room and we got into bed. I can remember losing my virginity and immediately overhead was the picture of the sacred heart and the neon light! How I got my sex life sorted out after that I don't know. All my old values came back. I felt terribly, terribly guilty about it. I had let down the whole side. I had gone and done something that had totally cast me out of something that was very important for me to belong to.

Tracy was relatively unusual in that she managed to escape the guilt. She went to university in Dubin in the mid-1970s and found a more open attitude to sex:

When I went to college I met Mike and I just decided I wanted to sleep with him. I went along to my brother's wife, who was quite liberated, and she told me of a doctor who would prescribe the pill. So I got the prescription and went ahead. For people in college it was probably fairly commonplace, because the opportunity was there. It was a much more acceptable thing to do. I never felt bad about it or anything.

The more open sexuality advocated by feminists is often confused with promiscuity because the argument is misunderstood. Defining one's own sexuality does not necessarily mean having many sexual partners, but means being free to choose the dimensions of one's own sexual activity. Tricia, for example, describes how she sorted out the confusion for herself:

I used to find it difficult to say no to sexual encounters I didn't want. In the 1970s there was the idea that sex was amazing and wonderful and that everyone had to be sexually available to everyone else. I thought it was prudishness on my part which made me feel revolted by that, and it was being in the women's movement that made me realise that you have a perfect right to decide who you want as your sexual partners, and that you don't have to be sexually available.

Many parents are now bringing up their children to have a more open, confident approach to their own bodies. This is not simply a matter of sex education, but is an attempt to integrate the children's physical being with their emotional and intellectual development, rather than separating and distrusting everything to do with the body.

Attitudes to sexual matters have liberalised considerably in the past few years, in that previously taboo topics such as sexual relationships, bodies and contraception are now openly discussed. But the continuing high profile given by the media to stories to do with sexuality indicates that many of the issues are still unresolved. One such area is the question of sexual choice.

Sexual choice

It is not easy to be anything other than heterosexual in Ireland. Lesbians, gay men and bisexuals experience a great deal of discrimination. Sexual relations between men are still illegal. The Catholic Church views homosexuality as a 'problem' which 'impedes the person's acquisition of sexual maturity'. The Vatican's document *Educational Guidance in Human Love* confirms the Church view that homosexual acts are morally wrong. Although it suggests that priests should treat homosexuals sympathetically, their sexuality is seen as deviant. There is little understanding in the Church that lesbian and gay relationships can form a loving and satisfying way of life:

> Pastorally, these homosexuals must be received with understanding and supported in the hope of overcoming their personal difficulties and their social mal-adaptation. Their culpability will be judged with prudence; but no pastoral method can be used which, holding that these acts conform to the condition of these persons, accord them a moral justification.[14]

The Irish bishops, while being careful not to condemn people with a 'homosexual orientation', deny that gay people have a valid sexuality: 'The truth of the language of sexuality is missing in homosexual acts and sexual relations between people of the same sex. . . deliberate homosexual acts are objectively and gravely immoral'.[15] The bishops regard chastity as the only moral option for gay people.

The oppression of gay women and men in Irish society is an extreme form of the general disapproval of non-marital sexual relations. Women who love other women are rejecting the role of wife and mother that society holds out to them. Both Church and State therefore accuse lesbians of undermining 'normal' family life. The right for lesbians to express their sexuality is therefore an important part of the general feminist demand that all women should be free to control their own bodies and define their own sexuality.

Many lesbians in Ireland remain invisible because of the discrimination they are likely to face if people know about their sexuality. A lesbian who comes out has to face the threat of rejection by her family and friends. She may lose her job, especially if she works with children. If she is married and leaves her husband she may lose custody of her children.

In Dublin and some larger towns lesbian and gay groups such as Liberation for Irish Lesbians and the National Gay Federation have been set up to campaign for gay rights and to provide a degree of support and social life. In rural areas and in smaller towns lesbians are often very isolated, having little contact with other gay women and facing a greater degree of ostracism if they come out. Mary lives in a town in the west of Ireland:

> I think it occured to me at the age of 22 that I was a lesbian. I think I always knew there was something different. I remember the relief at school when someone whispered that word 'lesbian'. I was 14 and I hadn't heard it before. I was desperately in love with the vice-principal at school, and when I left at 18 I still wasn't being very honest about myself.

For Mary, the late teenage years were ones of depression. She felt isolated and had no one to talk to:

> We had to suppress so much, I would imagine there is a strong link between depression and that. If you are putting that much

energy into *not* being what you are, if you deny a part of yourself and all kinds of feelings you have, it must have a very bad effect on you as a human being.

She avoided going out with boys as much as possible:

One of the reasons that I was terrified of people inviting me to parties was because they might *know*. About six months with a boy was the longest I could tolerate, and I was really relieved when it was finished. I just found it so uninteresting. I wasn't with someone of my own kin or anything. There was no feeling really. Whereas with women there were a lot more emotions involved.

When she realised she was a lesbian, she tried to summon up the courage to contact a gay group. On a visit to Dublin she found the address of a group in a magazine. 'I remember I was actually extremely depressed, and the only way I allowed myself to go to that address was to ring up the Samaritans and blurt it out there, and let them tell me to do it. It was a childish way of doing it, but. . .' She made contact, joined in a social night and met a woman with whom she fell in love. But back home in the west life was not so easy. Her parents still do not know that she is a lesbian. None of her friends with whom she grew up are gay, though she has come out to most of them:

When my feelings were in a state that I was going to burst I told a few friends. People really surprise you. One I thought was very strait-laced was very cool about it all. I have one real old buddy who is really Catholic and as far as she is concerned it is not on. So I certainly don't have what you might call a lot of supportive friends.
Lesbians seem to be invisible. I'm not saying it isn't changing. It must be changing with every year. I know more women who are gay. There would have been a time when I felt I was the only lesbian in town. We are very much ignored. You realise that men don't accept us. They won't accept that we don't rely on men for our emotional, sexual and other needs. It is quite a blow to their ego, I think. They are quite taken aback.

It is awkward to have open relationships in a small town. There are very few other lesbians to whom to look for support and friendship, and Mary says she has not yet fully come to terms with her sexuality and how to integrate it with the rest of her life – a difficult task given prevailing attitudes to lesbians. To keep in contact with other lesbians, she goes to Dublin for weekends, where she has friends in the lesbian feminist community:

I didn't think of the link between lesbianism and feminism at first. A lesbian conference I went to was a big eye-opener. It was in 1978, a beautiful sunny weekend, and it was so loving, it was really very special. It was a nice experience to have and I am pleased I experienced it in Ireland at that time. Then I had to go back home of course and pretend that it hadn't happened. But my feminism grew out of that. It feels like the most natural way to develop. There are so many other things that happen, say about rape, the exploitation of women in the media . . . you can't help being a feminist if you are someone who believes in equality and fair play.

What would she like to see changed? She would like to see lesbians become more active and form groups all over Ireland, not just in Dublin:

We are crippled in such a way that we can't organise. There must be something about the repressive Catholic thing that stops us. There must be a lot of guilt. The thing I would like to see most is just women feeling good about themselves. Just women being a bit bolder and defying society and saying, 'Blast you lot, we are just going to get on with our lives!'

Tricia is another woman who has learnt to acknowledge her attraction to other women, though she regards herself as bisexual rather than lesbian:

Accepting the side of myself that is into women sexually was quite difficult. I suppose because it is counter-cultural. I didn't know any lesbian women when I was growing up. It is there, it is part of myself. Perhaps it is not the strongest part of my sexuality, but recognising that it was there was very good, though painful at times.

  It seemed so much less complicated relating sexually to women than to men. I would have problems all right but it didn't seem so gamesy or as difficult as it does with men sometimes. Also it was so much easier to be affectionate to women than to men because it wasn't rebuffed in the same ways. Affection in relationships with men can be so tied up with sex – constant sexual activity rather than seeing it as a whole spectrum of feeling and touching.

I went through about six months trying to make up my mind whether I was a lesbian. I was very much at sea because it is quite difficult to know how you see yourself. The conclusion I came to was that in fact I was bisexual and that it was more the individual person that I'd be involved with rather than thinking of myself as heterosexual or gay. It seemed to me that was a choice I could make as well as any other choice.

Celibacy

When discussing sexual choice, another option to be considered is celibacy. Celibacy has a long history in Ireland. It has been a dominant feature of religious life from the ascetic practices of the Celts through the early Irish monks to the present day. Also, permanent celibacy was the fate of the many ordinary men and women who failed to find marriage partners as a result of the strict family system in the post-famine countryside. For these bachelors and spinsters the morality of the day ensured that being unmarried meant doing without sexual partners of any kind.

As the marriage rate increased during the 1960s and 1970s, the proportion of single people in the population declined. As a result of changing sexual mores and a loosening of traditional Catholic morality it is no longer possible to make a simple equation between being single and being celibate. Probably the only non-religious people who could realistically be categorised as celibate today are older, unmarried men and women and younger people who choose not to have sexual relationships for a period of time.

Nuns, brothers and priests are the most prominent groups of people for whom celibacy is a chosen way of life. Traditionally, the Church viewed chastity as the highest form of human existence. Through denying the body and the desires of the flesh, men and women could concentrate on spiritual matters and strive towards purity and grace. Celibacy was equated with an almost asexual state in which an individual suppressed all aspects of his or her sexuality and struggled to deny all sexual feelings. It was a view that reinforced the repression of sexuality, especially in women, who were regarded as symbols of the evil forces of nature.

Although the Church no longer officially regards celibacy as a superior state, it comes perilously close to it on occasions. According to *Educational Guidance In Human Love*, celibacy is 'the supreme form of that self-giving that constitutes the very meaning of human sexuality'.[16] And rather than lower the status of the celibate life, Pope John Paul II has sought to elevate marriage to the same level by advocating 'conjugal chastity' – a periodic abstention from sex by married couples.[17]

Since the Second Vatican Council of the Catholic Church took place in the 1960s, the necessity for priests to be celibate has been brought into question, and the understanding of religious celibacy has changed significantly. As popular psychology brought to public attention the emotional and social problems caused by severe sexual repression, the traditional view of celibacy began to seem at best unhealthy and at worst positively harmful. A distinction had to be made between *sexuality*, meaning an aspect of every individual's physical and emotional being, and the sexual *act*. Only then could a different concept of celibacy emerge. The modern view of celibacy is as an informed choice rather than a vow to be obeyed without question. In religious life it should be seen as a mature decision by a person who acknowledges his or her own sexuality.

Sr Maria: It is part of our humanness to become aware of our sexuality. My sexuality is controlled but not repressed. I have to be fully aware of myself as a woman with my feelings, my desires, my need for experiencing love and tenderness and how I am going to have those needs met other than in married life or in an explicitly sexual relationship. That is what I have to work out in my life. I would say I have grown in my capacity to do that. One of the things that is being stressed now in the area of celibacy is that you grow in your understanding of it and your commitment to it.

It is only recently that celibacy in religious life has been seen in this way. When Sr Maria entered a convent in the 1950s, celibacy was barely discussed and there was little support for nuns who found it problematic.

When we were training to be sisters we were told that the vow of obedience would be very hard and the vow of poverty would be very difficult, but don't worry about the vow of chastity, it will be the least of your problems. The whole theology of sexuality as a positive thing was something that had yet to be articulated.

In practice, the vow of chastity proved to be by far the most difficult for Sr Maria. As a young nun she was sent abroad to teach. A young priest was working in the same school and they fell in love, an experience which, she says, 'blew to pieces all the legislation on morality that had been handed to me'. For several years they struggled to sort out their relationship, trying to decide whether to leave religious life and get married or to stay and work it through. This was in the years following the Second Vatican Council when for a time it seemed possible that the strict ruling on celibacy for the priesthood might be relaxed. But once the Vatican confirmed there was no question of celibacy becoming optional, a decision had to be made:

We just decided we couldn't look at the relationship any more as possibly ending in marriage. The commitment to the Church was very important to both of us, and we were not quite prepared to abandon our ministries in order to get married. There was an incredible amount of pain and suffering in all that. Because of the struggle we had, when we made the decision in the relationship we became more creative working together in our ministries. I think when you have suffered at a deep level and come through it you are closer in a deep way. We both worked very well with couples in relationship, and while we didn't draw on our experience overtly with them, the fact is they would often say 'I can't imagine how you two understand so well'!

Having come through the experience, how does she feel about celibacy now?

People ask me why nuns can't marry. The very essence of our commitment as religious women is the vow of chastity – setting us free to be more present to a greater number of people in the sense of really loving them without the reciprocal support of a marriage relationship. Eventually you begin to feel you are freer to develop a relationship with the world about you precisely because you haven't got an exclusive relationship with which to be preoccupied.

Often a woman says to me, 'How can you be so alive and warm and not have problems as a nun with your relationships?' And I say that yes, I do have problems. For example, if I am sitting on a committee with a man and I feel attracted to him and I know he likes me, I have to make a conscious choice what I am going to do about that. I know what my feelings are, knowing myself as a woman, and I know these feelings are quite natural and that there is nothing wrong with them. I am grateful really for the singlemindedness that my consecrated celibacy gives me.

Sr Kathleen also fell in love, an experience she does not regret. It was, she says, her awakening after a number of grey years during which she had felt confused and rather trapped in religious life:

He was very good for me, he brought me out from what I'd settled into. I began to be enthusiastic about life again. But I had fierce problems with my sexuality because I couldn't cope with that side of the relationship. Always before I quelled my feelings, but now somehow I said I'm not going to, I'm going to enjoy this. But I was also wondering how I could love him and still be a sister. I really didn't meet anybody who helped me for three years. Then I met a lovely priest, who was so sane and sensible and did more for my sexual formation in one week than had been done in all the years before that. It was realising that anything human was OK, and what's wrong with loving somebody? Isn't that what it's all about? He said what a marvellous thing it was if celibate people could support each other in love.

But Sr Kathleen and her friend still struggled with how far they could express their love physically. What exactly did celibacy mean, and where should they draw the line? They decided to take the risk of at least some physical expression, and Sr Kathleen describes herself as 'celibate but not very chaste'! The questions about celibacy have continued to engage her:

My idea was that celibacy was remaining unmarried so that I would be free to give myself to a lot of people, rather than making a commitment to one. But when he moved away a few years ago, I was thrown back on myself and the emptiness inside made me wonder about it again. I just couldn't tell you about all the inner turmoil and the wondering, and being totally lost. I think now I'm faced in the right direction. I've read and read, I've taken every book on celibacy from every convent bookshelf and every bookshop. I would say that the essence of celibacy for me is not being unmarried, though that is important, but some kind of relationship with God and Christ, some kind of an inner love out of which I can love others. I'm not saying I am quite defined about this love, and I feel embarrassed and vulnerable talking about it. I hope now I will be able to love people, and that any love I have for one person will be deep, but not exclusive. That is what I'm working on at the moment.

Sr Teresa is in her fifties and, like many nuns, has found her view of celibacy changing over the years. She used to see celibacy as something to do with the genital area, and now understands it in terms of relationships. 'I would see myself being chaste if I relate authentically to people, if I don't use people and I respect their dignity and integrity.' She too sees chastity as fundamental to religious life. On a practical level, she feels she would not be free to move around and work in different countries if she had a husband or children. Emotionally and spiritually, she concurs with the modern view of celibacy as something one grows to accept and understand:

I think I accepted it initially, like you accept marriage, and it is not until you have lived into it that you see the implications of it, the restrictions and the joys. I knew I would get crises, same as in marriage you get crises, and the choices you make as a result of these crises determine what you are going to do. So it is something you choose and rechoose, and I find that the rechoosing is done for different reasons.

To these nuns, celibacy is a state they have chosen. Other women might question the possibility of a genuinely free choice within the strict doctrines of the Catholic Church. Sexuality is now acknowledged by the Church, but a celibate person is still not expected to express his or her sexuality in any active way with another person.

A matter of choice

Although a more open attitude towards celibacy reflects a more general rethinking on sexuality within the Church, there remain many areas in which the Church is strongly opposed to the feminist notion of choice. 'Choice' is a key word in the feminist approach to sexuality. But a realistic choice cannot be made without good information. The moves towards improving sex education and providing counselling services for pregnant women have therefore developed alongside campaigns for contraception and freedom of sexual expression. In the women's movement the links between the different aspects of sexuality are recognised, as they are by the moral Right, who oppose any liberalisation in the whole area of sex and sexuality. The last few years have seen a significant change of attitudes to sexual matters and a rejection of many aspects of repressive sexual morality, especially by young people. Because of the links between sexual morality and the ideology of the family, these changes have not been accomplished smoothly but have raised major public debates. In particular, contraception and abortion are two issues that have generated a great deal of controversy. The next chapter looks at these issues and the questions they have raised about the role of women in relation to the family and traditional Catholic morality.

6 Sexuality II: Contraception and Abortion

The headline in the *Irish Times* read as follows: 'Contraceptive Campaign Set Up'. The date was not, as one might expect, in the mid-1960s, but in March 1984.[1] Contraception is still a live issue in Ireland. In spite of the changes of the 1970s, the pill and other forms of artificial birth control are not readily available to everyone who wants them. Unlike most other European countries, in which campaigns for birth control started up to sixty years ago, it is only in the past fifteen years that contraception has been discussed openly in Ireland. Before that time it was a taboo subject, part of the misty area of sexuality which was private, unspeakable, tinged with sin.

Clare's story is an example of the difference between Ireland and its closest neighbour, England. As a student nurse she went to train in London in the early 1970s and was astonished at the open attitude to contraception which she found there:

I couldn't believe what I saw in the nurses' changing room – empty pill packets in the dustbin! They were taking them out of their handbags and just putting them in the rubbish. I couldn't believe it, because there was no way that would happen here with single girls. It was a huge thing for me to see at that time, it really was.

In Ireland contraception was not only taboo, it was illegal. The notorious Censorship of Publications Act of 1929 made it an offence to publish, sell or distribute literature advocating birth control. In 1935 the Criminal Law Amendment Act banned the sale and importation of contraceptives. Both Acts were part of the process of enshrining the Catholic moral code into the law of the newly-independent Irish State, and remained virtually unchallenged until the late 1960s. From then on things moved rapidly. Individuals and organisations increasingly ignored the law or found ways of getting round it. The first family planning clinic opened in Dublin in 1969. It could not sell contraceptives so clients were asked for donations. A decade later there were five clinics in Dublin and one each in Cork, Limerick, Galway, Bray and Navan – all openly flouting the law by selling contraceptives to anyone who wanted them.

As the pill became available in the mid-1960s it could not be used legally for contraceptive purposes but it could be prescribed as a cycle-regulator. By 1978 the Irish Medical Association estimated that 48 000 women were using the pill.[2] Women were ignoring the Church's opposition to contraception because they found that the rhythm method was not sufficiently reliable, and they wanted to use the safer methods now available. Anne, for instance, has used the pill since her seventh child was born, and says that she would not have had as many children had she known about it earlier:

> I don't know how many I would have had, but I most certainly wouldn't have had seven, because the majority of them were accidents. You weren't even told about the safe period in those days. Then they said you were allowed this ovulation thermometer. I tried that, but with the kids roaring and babies crying in the morning I hadn't time to look at a thermometer! But I certainly would have used something down-to-earth like the pill. Since my youngest was born I got a bit of sense and learned about it, which I didn't have time to do before, and nobody told you anyway years ago.

The demand for freely available contraception was an inevitable product of the women's movement. The separation of sex and procreation, made possible through contraception, enables women to control their fertility by deciding if and when to have children. Without some control over her fertility, a women finds it difficult to control other aspects of her life.

One of the most imaginative and well-remembered actions in support of the demand for contraception was the Contraceptive Train to Belfast in May 1971. Women aimed to challenge the law against the importation of contraceptives and to show up the hypocrisy of the situation in the Republic when contraceptives were freely available in the North. One Saturday, forty-seven women took over two carriages on the Dublin-to-Belfast train. When they arrived in Belfast they headed for chemist shops and bought large quantites of whatever contraceptives they could find. When the train arrived back in Dublin that evening the women brandished condoms and creams at the Customs officials, who decided against a confrontation and waved them through, to cheers from the crowd that had turned out in support.

In the same year, and on two subsequent occasions, independent Senators made unsuccessful attempts to introduce a Bill to legalise the importation and sale of contraceptives. Then in 1973, the McGee judgement in the Supreme Court relaxed the law by ruling that a married couple's right to privacy included the right to import contraceptives for their own use. Mrs McGee already had four children and had been told by her doctor that another pregnancy would put her life at risk. She could not take the pill, and decided to import a contraceptive jelly to use with a diaphragm. The Customs authorities confiscated it. Mrs McGee, backed by the Irish Family Planning Association, took a case to the High Court on the grounds that the 1935 Act was unconstitutional as it violated a married couple's right to privacy. The High Court Judge dismissed Mrs McGee's case, but her appeal to the Supreme Court was successful.

After the McGee judgement it was clear that the contraceptive laws would have to be changed. It was only a matter of time. But another six years of vacillation and confusion passed before new legislation was finally enacted by the Dáil. The Health (Family Planning) Act came into force in 1979. It had been steered through the Dáil by Charles Haughey, then Minister for Health, who described the proposals in a famous phrase he must have regretted since as 'an Irish solution to an Irish problem'. The Act was a very feeble piece of legislation. It legalised the sale of contraceptives only to those with a doctor's prescription. It was designed to restrict contraception to married couples, as prescriptions were only allowed for medical reasons or bona fide family planning. A further major limitation of the Act was that it allowed doctors, nurses and chemists to opt out of the scheme if they held conscientious objections to contraception.

The Bill had been opposed by the Labour Party and by the feminist-led Contraceptive Action Programme because it did not go far enough. Opposition had also come from conservative groups such as the Family League and the Knights of St Columbanus who were committed to the preservation of the Catholic family and who vehemently opposed any liberalising measures.

The Catholic Church steered a somewhat less extreme course. The bishops' statements of 1973 and 1978 made an important concession. The Hierarchy acknowledged that although contraception was against their moral teaching it did not follow that the State was bound to prohibit it: 'There are many things which the Catholic Church holds to be morally wrong and no one has ever suggested, least of all the Church herself, that they should be prohibited by the State'.[3]

The door was open for a change in the law without a major confrontation between Church and State. The delay in passing a bill and the narrow scope of the resulting legislation have been blamed as much on the 'faint-heartedness of Irish politicians'[4] as on the Church.

The Church has not, however, modified its view that contraceptives are morally wrong. The bishops do not only object to artificial forms of birth control on the grounds that they contravene God's plan. They also blame many of the ills of modern society on the 'contraceptive mentality':

> Societies in which contraceptives have become generally accepted and widely used have experienced a lowering of standards in sexual morality. Marital infidelity has increased. The stability of the family has been weakened. A whole new attitude towards sexual relationships has developed. Promiscuity has tended to increase. Legalisation of abortion has usually followed.[5]

In this statement the bishops make the elementary sociological error of assuming a causative relationship where a correlation has been observed. It is an observable fact that a new attitude to sexual relationships developed at the same time as contraceptive use increased. But it is quite illogical to assume that contraceptives caused the change. The bishops advance no evidence to back up their assertion. A moment's reflection suggests the causative relationship is most likely to be the other way round. The demand for contraceptives is essentially a demand from women. It is one aspect of the changing status of women, reflecting the fact that from the 1960s onwards women increasingly questioned their roles and sought a greater degree of choice in many areas of their lives – the choice of whether or not to marry, what type of job they did and, most important, how many children they had. This in turn wrought changes in prevailing attitudes to marriage and sexual relationships. It resulted in a more open discussion of sexuality and a demand for the means for women to control their fertility. The increase in the use of contraceptives was the result of wider changes in society rather than the cause of them.

In 1985, an amendment was made to the family planning legislation to allow the sale of non-medical contraceptives to anyone over the age of 18. The arguments about cause and effect were heard once again. The Archbishop of Dublin, Dr McNamara, predicted that the liberalisation of the law on contraception would promote moral decline, venereal disease, and a sharp increase in teenage pregnancies, illegitimate births and abortions. He said that the proposed legislation would be 'an invitation to youth to turn from the paths of self-discipline and to engage in pre-marital sexual activity with the aid of contraceptives'.[6] Those in favour of the bill argued that prohibiting contraceptives does not make people less inclined to have sex. The reality was that many young people were sexually active in any case, and the easy availability of contraceptives was essential in order to avoid the trauma of unwanted pregnancies.

Survey data suggests that significant numbers of young people embark on sexual activity without proper knowledge of, or access to, contraception. In their study of unmarried mothers in Dublin, Drs Rynne and Lacey found that 56 per cent of their respondents had never received any instruction on contraception.[7] In addition, 73 per cent had never used any form of contraception prior to becoming pregnant, even though over half of those surveyed were having intercourse frequently or regularly with their partners.[8] Without some protection against pregnancy women are playing what has been termed 'Irish roulette'. Nuala is one such woman:

> The first time I had any experience of sex I felt guilty and afraid as to the consequences. Waiting for the end of the month thinking will I, won't I? And then the relief! But I was a coward too in another way in that I wouldn't go and get contraception. I was

afraid to ask a doctor for it. I was afraid I would have been refused it because I wasn't married.

Even when a family planning clinic is nearby, many young women are afraid to go in because they are not married:

Clare: In the family planning clinic where I work about 50 per cent of the women who come in are single. When I first started going to a clinic to get the pill they used to call everyone 'Mrs' no matter what you were. I remember thinking, oh God, will they ask me questions about whether I intend getting married or have I got a regular boyfriend, because I didn't have any of these things.

Over the past decade the availability of contraceptives has improved somewhat, especially for single people. The improvement is in spite of the law rather than because of it, and owes much to the efforts of the Irish Family Planning Association and various campaigning groups. But availability is still very patchy. Many women, especially in rural areas, have great difficulty in obtaining contraception. With no clinic nearby, even condoms can be difficult to obtain. The family doctor may not approve, the local chemist may refuse to stock them. People have to get supplies by mail order, travel miles to a clinic, or do without. In Dublin and large towns there are more clinics, but for women relying on doctors the situation is still highly unsatisfactory. As well as the fact that the doctor may object to supplying contraceptives, the lack of medical training in the whole area of the family planning makes many women wonder whether they are getting full information on the best method to use and on possible side-effects. Women with money have less problem getting what they want – it is working-class women who suffer most. Audrey, now in her forties, is one woman who is angry that the law is a barrier only to those without wealth or influence:

In the 1960s everybody I knew was on the pill. Why? Because the system is so rotten. They were going to good gynaecologists, guys who have been handing out the pill for fifteen years. Now to this day you have doctors who other women attend, and they won't give women the pill because they disapprove of it. It might be an hour waiting for a bus to see the nearest other doctor, and the woman might have ten kids. Now where is the justice in all that?

The prevailing judgemental attitudes to contraceptives undoubtedly prevent some women from seeking protection from pregnancy. Going on the pill or having a diaphragm fitted is a significant step for a woman. It means accepting that she is sexually active. Many women, especially young single women, do not want to admit to themselves that they are. They play out society's hypocrisy in their own minds, persuading themselves that it is not really sex because they only do it occasionally or when they have had a few drinks. They do not dare to think about getting pregnant because that would confirm the reality of what they are doing.

A related problem is that if a girl goes on the pill, she may fear that her boy-friend will think her calculating or loose, so she hangs on to her falsely innocent self-image instead of taking responsibility for her own actions. By using contraception, a woman is claiming some degree of control over her own body. She is making a decision to have sex without wanting to get pregnant, and is therefore making a choice about her own life. Some husbands, boy-friends and priests undoubtedly dislike contraception for this reason, even if they do not admit it. Contraception denies a man the proof of his virility, and denies the Church part of its power over women. On the other hand, certain men welcome contraception and expect the women to use it as it absolves them of the responsibility of the possible consequences of a sexual relationship. It is likely that some women stop themselves from using contraception because they sense this opposition and do not feel assertive enough to take a step towards self-determination.

Medical practice generally still follows the Church's teaching in its prohibition on the related area of sterilisation 'whether of man or woman, whether permanent or temporary'.[9] The Irish bishops are adamant on the issue:

> Any form of sterilisation, whose direct and immediate and intended effect is to render the sexual faculty incapable of procreation, is direct sterilisation, and as such is absolutely forbidden according to the doctrine of the Church. Catholic hospitals may not provide facilities for such operations. Catholic medical personnel may not co-operate with them.[10]

As a result, very few hospitals in the Republic will perform tubal ligations for women on a regular basis, and the waiting lists are long.

Only where a women's life is in grave danger will most hospital managements even discuss the possibility of giving permission for sterilisation. Apart from one private clinic now offering this service, the only alternative is to go to England for a private operation. As both options are costly, the operation is only a realistic choice for women who can afford it. For women who cannot, the door is closed. No sterilisation. This is another case where women are denied choice by doctors and the Church.

Abortion

If contraception was the moral issue of the 1970s, abortion became the issue of the early 1980s. In September 1983, as a result of a referendum, the Constitution of the Republic was amended to include an article establishing the right-to-life of the foetus. In three short years, abortion had evolved from a near-taboo subject into an issue that dominated moral discussion and political debate. It is useful to look at the development of abortion as an issue as it reveals a great deal about the religious, social and political forces at work in Irish society – all of which have a profound effect on women's lives.

The decade of debate generated by the women's movement in Ireland differed from that in most other European countries and the USA in one significant respect. There was an almost total absence of demands for abortion rights. The need for abortion was discussed in some feminist groups but it did not surface as a public campaign. In Britain, by way of contrast, the defence of abortion rights was a prominent issue throughout the 1970s. Parliament liberalised the British abortion law in 1967, and in subsequent years a number of elected members introduced bills which attempted to restrict the new rights. Feminists set up a national campaign under the slogan of 'A Woman's Right To Choose' and, with other groups, mounted an effective series of campaigns to defend the 1967 Act. In Ireland during the same period all available energy went into the contraceptive campaign. The possibility of de-criminalising abortion seemed, and still seems, light-years away.

In Britain and the USA feminists linked the demand for free, legal abortion with the demand for contraception, as both issues were part of a wider campaign for a woman's right to control her fertility. In Ireland, women took great trouble to separate the two issues. There were good reasons for doing so. The Church and other groups opposed to contraception frequently raised the spectre of abortion as an evil that was likely to follow if contraception was legalised. As the Irish bishops wrote, 'it is significant that many of those who have been most prominent in campaigns for contraception are also found among the leading advocates of abortion'.[11] Given the close association between the two issues elsewhere, there was some truth in this assertion, but in Ireland women argued that it was not the case. The public opposition to abortion was so strong that any link would have jeopardised the campaign for contraception. An opinion poll carried out among lay Catholics in 1977 found that 74 per cent of respondents agreed that abortion was always wrong. A further 21 per cent agreed that it was generally wrong, leaving a mere 5 per cent who thought otherwise.[12] Even in the women's movement, people were frequently divided over the morality of abortion. The view that abortion is killing a baby and that the foetus has the right to life from the moment of conception – the view held by the Catholic Church – was strongly supported by the majority of the population.

In 1980 a small group of feminists in Dublin started a Women's Right to Choose group to discuss what to do about the lack of abortion facilities in Ireland. They established the Irish Pregnancy Counselling Centre, one of the first centres prepared to discuss abortion as an option for pregnant women. The Centre offered non-directive counselling and referred women who wanted terminations to private clinics in England.[13] Also in 1980, members of the British anti-abortion organisation, the Society for the Protection of the Unborn Child, arrived in Ireland to help to establish an Irish SPUC. This new group joined forces with various doctors and groups concerned with maintaining traditional values and came up with the idea of a constitutional amendment against abortion.

At first sight it may seem odd that SPUC and the Pro Life Amendment Campaign (PLAC) had such success in making an issue out of abortion in a country where it was already illegal and where the majority of the population thought abortion was morally wrong. A closer look at the context makes the reasons clearer. Although abortion was not available in Ireland it was relatively easily obtained across the water in England. British abortion statistics showed that the number of women giving Irish addresses was rising each year. In 1977, the year in which 95 per cent of those questioned in an opinion poll said that abortion was wrong, 2183 women giving Irish addresses had abortions in England.[14] This represented an increase of 21 per cent over the previous year, and numbers have continued to rise annually. It is likely that the true figures are at least double the official ones as many Irish women are reluctant to give their home addresses.

Many women having terminations in England go alone, having obtained the address of a clinic on the grapevine, but anti-abortion groups were particularly aggrieved about the abortion referral services offered by the Irish Pregnancy Counselling Centre and the Well Woman Centre in Dublin. Such services were not illegal. The law in Ireland could not prevent women going abroad for abortions.

But the steady stream of women going to England for terminations was only one concern of the moral Right. Their campaign was not against abortion alone, but against the general liberalisation of Irish society. The amendment campaign was, to a large extent, a battle between progressive and traditional forces. PLAC was an organised backlash against a decade of liberalisation. It was an attempt to re-establish the old values. The campaign against abortion was a vehicle for reiterating the wickedness of sexual permissiveness and the importance of Catholic morality.

When Pope John Paul II visited Ireland in 1979 he called on Irish people to hold true to the old faith, to reject materialist values and to return to things of the spirit. He saw Ireland at a turning-point. 'Your country seems in a sense to be living again the temptations of Christ. Ireland is being asked to prefer the "kingdoms of the world and their splendour" to the kingdom of God . . . Now is the time of testing for Ireland. This generation is once more a generation of decision.'[15] He recalled the major role which Ireland had played in the conversion of Europe to Christianity and called on the Irish today to recover their historical destiny as a people prepared to show their Christianity to the world. One way of doing this was to maintain the ban on abortion, as the Pope made clear in his homily at Limerick: 'May Ireland never weaken in her witness, before Europe and before the whole world, to the dignity and sacredness of all human life, from conception until death'.[16]

Anti-abortion groups believed that an amendment to the Constitution would provide an opportunity for this 'witness' to the sacredness of life 'from conception'. In 1981, there was no large-scale campaign to legalise abortion, only the Women's Right to

Choose Group in Dublin, but in the future there might be such a campaign. In proposing the amendment, PLAC wanted to prevent any future attempt to legalise abortion. It seemed a safe issue, as abortion was one area in which traditional values had not been seriously challenged.

Many groups associated with the moral Right were eager to join the campaign. PLAC claimed it was non-sectarian, though no fewer than five of the eleven groups associated with it had the word 'Catholic' in their names – groups such as the Irish Catholic Doctors' Guild and the Catholic Young Men's Society. Also involved was the Council for Social Concern, an umbrella organisation for traditional groups such as the League for Decency and the Family League that had been prominent in the campaign against contraception. The Council for Social Concern operated out of the same address as the Knights of St Columbanus, a secret organisation of mainly elderly Catholic men who promote anti-liberal values. At a lecture to the Knights in 1978, a Professor had said that 'Ireland stands alone in her fight to defend the Judeo-Christian moral code of sexual behaviour and the sanctity of life'. The Knights were also linked to another PLAC organisation, the Responsible Society.[17]

PLAC encompassed a formidable collection of groups dedicated to the preservation of traditional Catholic values. Their proposed wording for the amendment was as follows: 'The State recognises the absolute right to life of every unborn child from conception and accordingly guarantees to respect and protect such right by law'. This was later amended to include the equal right-to-life of the mother. The only exceptions were to be those already allowed by the Catholic Church, that is, where a woman has an ectopic pregnancy or cancer of the uterus and the foetus has to be removed as part of an operation to save her life.

At first, PLAC made rapid headway. A general election was in the offing and within days of PLAC going public both the Toiseach, Charles Haughey, and the leader of the opposition Fine Gael party, Garrett Fitzgerald, had agreed in principle to the proposed amendment. Garrett Fitzgerald was later to regret his haste. Seventeen months later, as Toiseach, he recommended a 'No' vote in the referendum after an unsuccessful attempt to change the wording.

The great majority of priests backed the amendment, and many advocated a 'Yes' vote from the pulpit. A statement from the Catholic bishops did acknowledge the right of each person to vote according to conscience, and recognised that not all those opposed to the amendment were in favour of abortion. But the bishops also made clear their own support for the amendment: 'We are convinced that a clear majority in favour of the amendment will greatly contribute to the continued protection of the unborn human life in the laws of the country'.[18] A decisive 'Yes' vote would, they believed, constitute the witness for which the Pope had called at Limerick.

Although the amendment was passed in the referendum in 1983, PLAC's campaign backfired in many ways. When the Anti-Amendment Campaign was launched at a meeting in Liberty Hall in Dublin, 3000 people turned up. By then, the implications of the proposed amendment were becoming clearer and opposition was growing in many quarters. The feminist pro-choice voice was audible, but it was by no means the loudest. Many anti-amendment people were also anti-abortion. Their opposition was based on the potentially damaging social, medical and legal effects of the amendment. Many family doctors and the Irish Family Planning Association were anti-amendment on the grounds that it could make certain forms of contraception unconstitutional and would interfere with existing medical practice. The Protestant Churches, the Jewish community and many individuals were against the amendment because of its sectarian nature. It was an attempt to write the teaching of the Catholic Church into the Constitution, thereby reversing the process of creating a genuinely pluralist state in Ireland. Another side to this argument was that the amendment would further hinder progress towards Irish unity by making the Constitution even more unacceptable to Northern Protestants. Many lawyers also joined the campaign, arguing that the whole thing was unnecessary, badly worded and a misuse of the Constitution. The anti-amendment campaign became a focus for a wide variety of progressive, liberal and feminist interests, all of which were united in their opposition to the authoritarianism of the moral right and in their desire to stop Ireland taking a step backwards away from pluralism.

The campaign turned out to be anything but the walk-over for which PLAC had hoped. Instead, it developed into an extraordinarily divisive issue. Doctors, lawyers, politicians, journalists, trade unionists, students and even farmers were bitterly divided on the question. With the bitterness and emotion came some unpleasant aspects of the campaign. Several politicians associated with the anti-amendment stance were subjected to obscene phone calls and offensive letters; people handing out leaflets on the streets were verbally abused by pro-amendment supporters who accused them of being baby-murderers and killers.

The amendment also divided woman from woman. Women formed a significant part of the grass-roots support of PLAC and SPUC. On the other hand, many women – not only feminists – were deeply worried about the amendment. The dominant image of the campaign was of middle-aged men arguing with each other, using words like 'zygote', 'implantation' and 'foetus' with little or no reference to the women's bodies to which they were related. The arguments about medical terminology and constitutional law were remote from the realities of women's lives, and especially remote from the complex emotions involved in unwanted pregnancies and the decision to have an abortion. Nell McCafferty effectively voiced women's anger in an article:

> The PLAC poster, advocating support for the amendment, shows a baby. The mother of the baby is not shown. The PLAC tee-shirt shows a foetus in the womb. The woman has been removed. Separation of woman and womb has now been achieved. The womb's the thing. We have been wiped out. We are the disappeared. We are not to be trusted. Our wombs have been kicked right out of us. No woman can be trusted with a womb of her own.[19]

The questions raised by the amendment were much wider than the single issue of the morality of abortion. Also at issue was the degree of male control over women's bodies and women's lives. The following quotation illustrates this. It is from a 44-year-old woman who has reservations about abortion but who was strongly anti-amendment:

> My view about abortion would be a very deep-rooted one that a person has a right to be born. On another level, at this stage in my life I would not force my views on anybody. That happens to be my personal view, but I believe in a society where everyone has

free choice. My opposition to the amendment was because it was about political manipulation. It was about a weak government, it was about politicians who just use women. It was the hypocrisy. People have a public face and a private face. And in a sense it was all about power, and where women's position in society really was. Men were making choices about women's sexuality, which for me just wasn't on. I just couldn't accept that any man has the right to make decisions for me, my body and my sexuality.

For some women the issue was even more personal. Clare has had an abortion herself:

The way people were talking about women who have had abortions was unbelievable. I felt they didn't know, they hadn't any personal experience of abortion for themselves or from someone they knew, because otherwise they couldn't have spoken so glibly and called us murderers the way they did. I felt angry with them and also sad for myself. I accept that there were genuine people involved, but I felt angry because it is all very well for them telling people to keep their children, and that they would get this support and that support. But where is the support when the baby is born? Are they going to get them a house?

Pro-amendment groups stressed the need to support unmarried mothers and their children, but many women opposed to the amendment were cynical about this commitment, pointing out the close links between PLAC's views and the generally judgemental attitudes of the moral Right towards sexuality.

The amendment reinforced the power of doctors, politicians and priests over women's bodies. They were attempting to take back the control that the changes of the 1970s had gradually prised away from them. The attempt was only partially successful. The campaign had brought abortion out of the closet. It was now openly discussed and people began to question many previously unchallenged assumptions about its immorality. Another result of the campaign was that virtually every young woman in Ireland now knew how to get an abortion. Statistics on the number of women going to England for abortions were widely quoted, and the condemnation in PLAC literature of abortion referral centres served only to advertise their services. In addition, feminists and like-minded people who had worked together against the amendment had formed links that survived the campaign itself. Groups and networks existed which could become active again in the event of a further erosion of women's rights.

The results of the referendum gave an interesting picture of opinion in the country. Overall, the 'Yes' vote was 66 per cent, the 'No' vote 33 per cent. The turnout was very low at just over 50 per cent. The 'No' vote was highest in Dublin and the large towns, and four Dublin constituencies and Dun Laoghaire returned a majority of 'No' votes. The 'No' vote was lowest in the rural areas, particularly in the west. Mayo East, Roscommon, the two Donegal constituencies and Kerry South recorded the highest 'Yes' votes – over 80 per cent in each case. A poll published in the *Irish Times* shortly before the referendum predicted the result very accurately and gave a breakdown of opinion by age and occupation. The conservatism of the farming community was confirmed by a ratio of 91:9 in favour of the amendment, whereas in the highest socio-economic group the ratio was 58:42. Support for the amendment was also strong in the older age groups. In contrast to this, support was lowest in those aged 25–34, where 58 per cent were in favour and 42 per cent against.[20] The poll results were in accordance with the general trend for older people, particularly in rural areas, to accept traditional values and for the younger, more urban population to be most strongly critical of those values.

The amendment did little to help pregnant women or to alleviate the pressures on unmarried women. It reinforced rather than helped the degree of antagonism towards women who have abortions. It is probably true to say that having an abortion is more traumatic for many Irish women than for their sisters from elsewhere. The journey to England is long and tiring (unless she can afford to take the plane) and lonely if she goes by herself. The boat trip and operation are expensive. Above all, a woman from Ireland often carries the burden of secrecy. She will probably have concealed the purpose of her journey from parents and friends, and may have no one to whom to talk about it when she returns home. As a social worker from London who counsels Irish women seeking abortions told the *Irish Times*:

They come rigidly committed to secrecy. Their predominant emotion is that nobody must ever know. . . We are very concerned about the fact that they won't get any aftercare here [in Ireland], medical or psychological. They just slip back into their lives here, unable to reveal or confide what they have been through and that, I think, must be an unbearable pressure.[21]

Who are the women who seek abortions? In 1983, Open Door Counselling published the results of a survey of the first 202 women who attended their centre in Dublin, 98 per cent of whom decided to go to England for terminations. The report concluded that 'the decision to seek an abortion is not lightly taken nor is there any one type of woman who seeks an abortion'. The majority were in their twenties and single, though one in five was married. Their occupations ranged from clerical and service workers to home-makers, professional workers and students. 75 per cent of the women were not using any method of contraception at the time they became pregnant, and 36 per cent had never used contraception at all.[22]

The survey also revealed the hidden nature of unwanted pregnancies. Only one in four of the women told anyone in their families about their pregnancy, and only one in three told a friend. Two-thirds told their partners, about half of whom were supportive in some way. 'It would seem,' the report concluded, 'that the majority of women felt unable to tell either friend or family about their pregnancy. This is surely a poor reflection on the supposedly compassionate and caring nature of Irish society.'[23]

Open Door describe the many factors which compel a woman to seek an abortion. All felt negative about their pregnancies. Younger women felt unprepared to have a child, especially where they had little support. Others feared hurting their parents, or were in an unstable relationship. Some were worried about the effects of the pregnancy on their health. The factors involved are complex, and women usually make the decision because of a number of pressures.

Clare is 32, and went to England to have an abortion when she was 30. She did not go through a referral agency but obtained the address of a clinic from a friend. She phoned for an appointment and went alone. Like many Irish women she travelled in secrecy to a strange clinic in a foreign town, with no pre-abortion counselling and no support afterwards except from one or two close friends. 'It was a terribly lonely time. I got the boat over, then took the train from Holyhead to London, and then the tube to the clinic. It was awful, it was very traumatic.'

Had it been a hard decision? 'Well, it wasn't, considering the circumstances I was in. I was living in a two-roomed cottage with no bathroom or toilet, on my own with my daughter. I was living on £42 a week, the deserted wives' allowance.' She and her husband had parted the year before when her daughter was a toddler. 'It was a complete fiasco of a marriage. It should never have taken place. There's nothing you can say about it.' She finds it difficult bringing up the child on her own, though her husband takes her on alternate weekends. She got pregnant again by mistake during a brief relationship. 'When I told him he said, "I've got enough problems of my own without worrying about yours." I never saw him again.'

She felt that abortion was the only option. 'I felt as if I couldn't cope with it at all. I felt there was nothing else I could do, that my whole life was ruined. Apart from the personal feelings about it, I felt I just couldn't face my family and the whole social thing about having a child on my own.' But it was not an easy decision, because she believed abortion was killing, in a sense. 'I felt it very much. But I felt it was my life or the child's life.'

PLAC hoped that the passing of the constitutional amendment on abortion would close debate on the issue. It has not done so. Women's Right to Choose groups are still active in Dublin, and many of the issues raised by the campaign are still being discussed in medical, legal and feminist circles. The number of women going to England for abortions continues to rise. A total of 3677 women giving addresses in the Republic had their pregnancies terminated in Britain in 1983.[24] It is undoubtedly true that easy access to termination facilities in Britain is one reason why there has been little demand for abortion facilities in Ireland. For how long this will continue to be the case is a matter of speculation.

The abortion amendment had the effect of bringing another issue of sexual morality out into the open. The rapid growth of the anti-amendment campaign, and the fact that it encompassed such a wide range of feminist and liberal groups, showed that many people were no longer prepared to accept traditional Catholic values in the Constitution or as the basis of social legislation. In spite of the Church's encouragement to people to vote only half the electorate turned out on the day, suggesting that the Church could not influence the public as easily as it could in the past. Above all, the amendment campaign revealed the deep split between traditional and progressive approaches to questions of morality. The traditional view has changed little over the years, whereas the progressive view has developed rapidly in recent time, due in no small measure to the activities of the women's movement. As feminists have shown, virtually all matters to do with sexuality are women's issues, and society's approach to them is a good indicator of how that society treats women in general.

7   Girls in School

Josie: You'd think some of our teachers were living in the seventeenth century. 'What do you want to be, dear? A waitress, or maybe a dancer?' And you say, 'An astronaut'. 'An astronaut! Oh my goodness, you must be cracked!' I'd love to be an astronaut.

Joan: One of the girls in my class wanted to be a farmer and Miss M. nearly had hysterics! She was talking to us one day about getting married, saying, 'Wouldn't you like to get married when you leave school?' We were saying, 'No thank you very much'. And she said, 'Why not? Don't you know the greatest thing in life is to cook your husband a nice dinner and put it down for him?'

Maeve: When we started school some of the nuns were saying, 'You should take domestic science because you want to be able to put a good meal in front of your husband'. We said that boys in school should be doing domestic science so that they can put a good meal in front of us!

Josie, Maeve and Joan are in their second year in a convent secondary school. The reputation of the school is generally good, and local people believe that it provides a sound academic education for its pupils. But how sex-stereotyped are the teachers' expectations of the girls? How broadly-based is the curriculum? Does the school equip girls for living and working in the 1980s? Even a superficial glance reveals some worrying features. Pupils must choose in their first term between domestic science and science, so a proportion of girls go right through secondary education without having studied any science at all. Technical and

123

mechanical subjects are not available. No computing skills are taught, except for an introductory course in Leaving-Certificate year. A significant proportion of the staff hold old-fashioned views about the appropriate jobs and roles for women in society. The school is probably fairly typical, providing the kind of education thought to be suitable for girls.

Educational issues have long been of interest to feminists. The schooling a girl receives is crucial to her later life in many ways. The values handed down to her will influence her views; the way in which teachers encourage or discourage her various interests and ideas may vitally affect her confidence and her ambitions; the subjects she is taught will govern her access, or lack of access, to different fields of employment.

Despite its importance, there is no legal prohibition on sex discrimination in education in Ireland, and little systematic research into the area. The only major study, *Schooling and Sex Roles*,[1] was commissioned by the Employment Equality Agency to look at the provision and allocation of subjects in schools and the extent to which girls and boys differ in their choice of subjects. The study particularly concentrated on the role of education as a preparation for working life. It details the ways in which schooling influences later occupational choice and how girls are disadvantaged by their limited subject choices and poor self-images.

But to understand the influence of schooling on girls we need to look at the general aims of the educational system as well as the details of the curriculum. The New Curriculum, introduced into National Schools in 1971, is quite specific about the wider function of schooling:

> The educational system is a mechanism by which one generation transmits to the next the basic elements of the ever-increasing fund of human knowledge, the common culture of the society, the social habits, customs and national attitudes on which the health and cohesion of the society depend, and its religion, morality and ethics which in a fundamental sense determine the essential quality of society and of the people who constitute it.[2]

Some degree of transmission of cultural and social norms is obviously necessary to enable children to grow up as well-balanced members of society. But as far as girls are concerned, warning bells ring when one reads phrases such as 'national attitudes' and 'morality and ethics which . . . determine the essential quality of society'. For if these define a role for women which is both narrow and subordinate, the educational process will have a built-in disadvantage for girls.

To what extent is this the case? To answer this question we need to look not only at the subjects in school, but also at the 'hidden curriculum' – the attitudes towards women in the ethos of the school, the expectations teachers have for girls and the sort of self-image they encourage their pupils to develop. As the education system has changed so much in the past fifteen years it is helpful to look at the period up to the late 1960s before discussing present trends.

The National (primary) schools were, and still are, denominational. They were under the management of the parish priest or, in the case of Church of Ireland schools, the local parish. The school managers appointed the teachers and supervised the curriculum. The majority of post-primary schools were run by religious orders of nuns or brothers, with a smaller number of state-run vocational schools that offered more technical subjects. Children normally stayed in primary school until the age of 14 and transferred to secondary school if their parents could afford the fees. Many could not. Educational attainment was, and still is, strongly class-related. A relatively high proportion of middle-class children obtained second-level and third-level education, whereas few children from working-class families or small farms proceeded beyond primary school. A recent survey found that one in three adults had left school before the age of 14.[3]

Ireland is unique in the degree to which the clergy control education. The State provides the necessary finance but until very recently had little control over the content of education. This was carefully controlled by the Catholic Church. The Department of Education accorded with the Church view that the primary responsibility for children's education lay with the parents. In practice, this meant that the State had little influence once the parents had decided to send their children to a Catholic school.

The denominational nature of education was not confined to schools but was carried into third-level education. Catholic teachers were trained in Catholic colleges of education, and as J. J. Lee comments, 'there was litte danger of any deviation from prevailing orthodoxy among minds drilled in those institutions'.[4] In addition, the constituent colleges of the National University of Ireland catered for Catholic students and the Hierarchy banned young Catholics from attending the mainly Protestant Trinity College in Dublin.

The acquiescent attitude of the government to religious control of education was summed up by General Mulcahy, Minister for Education from 1948 to 1951, and from 1954 to 1957. He said that the State 'accepts that the foundation and crown of youth's entire training is religion. It is the desire that its teachers, syllabuses and textbooks in every branch be informed by the spirit underlying this concept of education, and it is determined to see that such facilities as ecclesiastical authorities consider proper shall be provided in the school for the carrying on of the work of religious education'.[5]

As late as 1960 this view was confirmed in a report from the Council for Education. The report stated that the dominant purpose of secondary schools was 'the inculcation of religious ideals and values'. 'This central influence', the report went on, 'which gives unity and harmony to all the subjects of the curriculum, is outside the purview of the State which supervises the secular subjects only.'[6] Today, this reads as an extraordinarily complacent document. It contains no indication of the challenge to existing methods of schooling which was to come. The authors talk of 'the paramount educative value of this historic religious purpose in the schools' and of 'the advantages our pupils have compared with others in modern times'.[7] And when describing the values of the religious orders running the schools, the report rather smugly comments that 'in Ireland, fortunately, there is no need to dwell on the importance of such values'.[8]

In such an environment pupils had little opportunity to question the religious ethos that permeated every aspect of school life. They were rarely allowed to ask questions in any case, given the strictly disciplinarian approach to education with its lecture-based teaching, rote learning and liberal use of corporal punishment. Until the late 1960s schools adhered to the nineteenth-century view that children are naturally unruly and badly behaved and that the role of education is to turn them into civilised adults through discipline and strict control. Teachers were trained to adopt this approach, and as a large proportion of National school teachers were the children of farmers and shopkeepers they were 'by reason of background and social experience . . . the stern agents of authoritarian social, cultural and religious control'.[9]

The curriculum was formal and narrow, based as it was on the traditional arts and religion. In National schools, nearly half the working week was devoted to the English and Irish languages, the rest being taken up with mathematics, religion and other subjects. For secondary schools, the 1960 report on the curriculum stressed the humanist subjects of theology, philosophy, literature and history. The authors expressed reservations about science as it was an intellectual discipline not concerned with morality! They did acknowledge that scientific studies could lead to 'a knowledge of the creator',[10] though they decided against recommending science as a compulsory subject. In 1957, when the report was being written, only 18 per cent of girls and 64 per cent of boys took science for their Intermediate Certificates.[11] Most girls took domestic science instead. In another complacent moment, the authors of the report stated that 'the desirability of providing instruction in domestic science for girls following a secondary school course is so obvious it does not require to be stressed'.[12]

The experience of women who attended school in the 1940s and 1950s reflects the rigid concept of education that dominated the period. Talking to women about those years, the strongest memories are of strict routines, punishment and very formal teaching. Anne, for example, was a reluctant pupil in a rural National school in Co. Mayo during the 1950s:

School was terrible. I dreaded walking into that school. I can still see the stone steps that led up to the classes and I still hate them. Isn't it awful? I envied the brainy ones who could get on with their lessons as it was a struggle for me to do so. And then you didn't get any help in those days unless you copied off someone else. It was fear the whole way through. There was nothing but fear, fear of the nuns. All the things we weren't supposed to do – we weren't supposed to knit on a Sunday and we got beaten if we didn't go to Mass on a Sunday morning. No matter what we did it wasn't right.

She also has strong memories of the class-snobbery of the teachers. 'My father worked in a shop and my friend's father was a carpenter. The other girls' fathers were posher, and the snobby element was there. They got away with murder and we got murdered for it!'

For Brid, a middle-class girl who went to a Dublin convent school, the physical conditions were better but the attitudes she encountered were much the same:

> The idea was to break you and remake you in their mould, and if they couldn't they would get rid of you. Their mould was rather like a nun – subservient, everything for the love of God. Offer everything up, never question anything. They were so rigid, so bigoted.

The cruelty she experienced at the hands of the nuns is indicative of the depth of ignorance about child-development that was common to teachers at that time. She vividly remembers one punishment:

> They knew I was afraid of the dark, and I fell innocently into a trap. A nun came into this little room. There was no bed, just a chair in it, and she came in and stood on the chair and took out the bulb – it was daylight – and locked the door. It got darker and darker. I was left there all night screaming my head off and trying to get out. I had no skin left on my hands. How they could do that I'll never know. That was the kind of cruelty. It was a lovely building, we had a lovely dormitory, but they didn't have a heart or a soul between them.

Audrey went to a convent boarding school in the late 1940s:

> It was big, cold and draughty and we were always hungry. It was vast and I remember being terribly lonely. I hated it. Some of the nuns would delight in telling you that you were depraved, that you might be possessed, that no good would come of you, that you were damned from the start. It was a total put-down and it left an incredible mark. I mean it wasn't until I left the country that I began to see it from a distance. It was a total relief to be able to say 'My God, I'm fine!'. Up until then I had no self-image at all. Nothing.

Maura, now a teacher herself, has better memories of the convent day school she attended in Dublin in the early 1960s. 'I quite

enjoyed it there. I don't have a horror of it like some girls do. It was a very safe time of my life, very protected. I remember the friendships with the girls – we had great fun, great camaraderie.'
She is, however, critical of the way she was taught:

> We weren't allowed to ask questions about anything. I remember we were doing communism, and we were told about little girls who died with Holy pictures in their hands while the communists beat them to death and burned them and all sorts of things. They were supposed to be martyrs against communism.
>
> I remember in one class being told, 'Right girls, take out your pens and write this down: communism is. . .' I put up my hand and said, 'Why don't you give us the facts and figures and we can decide for ourselves what communism is?' I almost took my life in my hands, I felt, because it wasn't done to ask any questions.

Many women recognise that the problem lay not with individual teachers, whether lay or religious, but with the training they received and the system in which they taught. The education system reflected its religious management not only in its structure but also in its values – the values that dominated the pre-Vatican II Church. Obedience, discipline, humility and chastity were widely accepted as the correct foundation for the education of young people. In addition, nuns who lived in strongly hierarchical orders and who were trained in unquestioning obedience to Church authority inevitably took that experience into the classroom. One former pupil described her impressions of her teachers in these terms:

> The instinct towards style, the enjoyment of food, colour, texture which are a part of every woman's life were curbed under the weight of rules, uniform and regulations. . . Cemented in a basic structure of denial, the nun's capacity to delight in another human being reaching towards pleasure and fulfilment was strained. Within the ethos of obedience the nuns saw development of the child in terms of curbing and pruning.[13]

She added 'trying to undo all that endurance and make way for the growth of love and warmth is a bewildering experience'.
For the girls, the strong religious influence on education meant that schools promoted the Catholic Church's ideal of womanhood.

The highest calling was to be a nun, motherhood was the next best thing and the notion of being an independent working woman was barely entertained.

> *Audrey*: We were supposed to model ourselves on the Blessed Virgin Mary, to have good Christian Catholic values and to be a good wife. I recently picked up an old Victorian book at an auction, and it was about how to prepare a young lady for marriage and all the things she was expected to do. And I didn't see much difference between what it was saying and what we were told in the 1950s in that dreadful convent I was in!

In Audrey's experience as a middle-class girl, the preparation for marriage was moral and intellectual, with very little in the way of practical skills:

> I assumed I would get married shortly after leaving school and that I would marry someone who would keep me in the style that I had been told I would become accustomed to! We had no skills whatever. I didn't even learn domestic subjects because I did music. If you were not going to university – and we didn't see the point – there was no emphasis on a career for a girl at all. So the big thing was to go to the bank and get sent somewhere in the Midlands where you would marry the local solicitor's son or something.

Along with this emphasis on marriage came the reinforcement of the personality characteristics the teachers judged to be suitable for young Catholic women. A former convent pupil describes the ideal held up to her:

> A good girl is tidy. A good girl makes herself pretty. A good girl is polite, docile, demure, submissive, passive, gentle, caring, giving, dependent, chaste. She stays out of trouble. Fighting is for boys, not for girls. Learn these lessons well and you will get a gold star: a boy-friend, a ring, a husband, social approval.[14]

Some of these characteristics are undoubtedly desirable in all adults, but together they create a picture of someone who is immature, emotionally dependent and likely to lack self-assurance.

The job of making girls feel second-class was done very thoroughly, and from such an early age that many girls were not even aware of the process but only wondered, as they grew up, why they did not feel better about themselves.

During the 1960s the education system came under review as more progressive ideas about childhood and schooling began to take root in Ireland, as they did in neighbouring Britain. At the same time, the new emphasis on economic planning meant that politicians began to look at the social and economic effects of the education system and to question its efficiency for an industrialising nation. In 1962 the government set up a Commission to investigate Irish education. The report made depressing reading. It catalogued the poor results of the National schools and showed that large numbers of children were leaving school with no more than a minimal primary education. It also demonstrated a clear association between social class and educational attainment, and showed that the fee structure of secondary schools discriminated against the children from small-farmer and working-class backgrounds.[15]

The Commission's findings spurred on those educationalists who favoured reform, and the following years saw several structural changes to the education system. Free secondary education was introduced in 1967, and new comprehensive schools were built in areas where existing secondary provision was inadequate. As a result the proportion of young people in post-primary education increased rapidly, from one in four 17-year-olds in full-time education in 1964 to one in two in 1979.[16]

The New Curriculum for primary schools, launched in 1971, was a particularly significant development. It introduced the child-centred approach to education, stressing that experience and discovery should be the normal basis of learning. The New Curriculum was a radical departure from traditional methods as it was based on a totally different view of childhood. According to this view children are naturally curious and interested in the world about them. They are capable of self-discipline, and the role of education is to provide them with a secure and stimulating environment in which they can develop at their own pace. It was an approach that owed much to recent developments in child psychology and to the educational theories of Montessori and Froebel, both of whom provided a creative and sympathetic model of child development to replace the Victorian emphasis on discipline and control. The New Curriculum marked a recognition by many teachers and parents that all too often the children's natural gaiety and love of life were lost in long stone corridors and grey uniforms, and their instinctive curiosity defeated by rote learning. When the teacher has all the right answers and the pupil's job is to learn these without asking questions, children have little chance to learn by discovering things for themselves and making up their own minds. It was time for a change.

Although a proportion of teachers were reluctant to relinquish the old methods, the curriculum was introduced into primary schools and much of the traditional harshness and cruelty disappeared. Schools became more colourful, gentler and less austere. To Anne, to whom school was 'fear all the way', the change seems enormous:

My children have no fear of going to school. They may not like it, but the teachers have no fear for them. They are friends with the teachers, they can talk to them. I think the teachers in general have improved an awful lot.

Like many of her contempories, Anne left school at 14. Her children, however, will all go through secondary school and already one has gone on to university.

The clerical grip on education began to loosen a little during the 1970s. While the Church's control over Catholic schools is still very strong, some important changes have been made. The New Curriculum was introduced without any problems with the Hierarchy. From 1973 committees replaced parish priests as managers of National schools, though the priest often stayed on as chairman of the committee. And secondary schools run by religious orders appointed more lay teachers so that by 1979 only one in five secondary teachers was a nun or a brother.[17] Over the same period the gradual secularisation of society was reflected in the attitudes of school pupils, against the efforts of the many religious involved in schools. Research revealed falling numbers of young people at Mass and a sharp decline in school-leavers taking vocations.[18]

A major factor still influencing girls' education is segregated schooling. The proportion of children attending single-sex schools at primary level is still high at 40 per cent.[19] At post-primary level, the segregation between the sexes is even more pronounced. In

1979–80, 63 per cent of girls and 55 per cent of boys were in single-sex institutions.[20] In addition, many mixed schools are not co-educational but co-institutional, providing separate education for boys and girls under the same roof. In spite of the move towards co-education in recent years, the number of young people in genuinely mixed classes is small.

Given traditional attitudes to sexual morality it is no surprise to find a strong tradition of single-sex schools. Schools taught morality by example as well as through religious instruction. Children grew up with the idea that contact between the sexes should be severely limited and that sexual segregation was the norm. Until the 1960s, neither parents nor teachers seriously questioned this approach. The attitude expressed by the Hierarchy in 1910 still held sway: 'Apart altogether from moral considerations, we believe that the mixing of boys and girls in the same school is injurious to the delicacy of feeling, reserve and modesty of demeanour which should characterise young girls'.[21] The bishops' statement also reveals the characteristics they considered appropriate to Catholic girls – characteristics which schools were expected to foster. Even today, the extent of segregated schooling is evidence of its continuing popularity among both parents and teachers. Whether single-sex schools are as popular among the pupils is more doubtful:

Joan: I'd like to be in a co-ed school. I'd like to do some subjects boys do. I'd like to do woodwork.
Josie: If you've never had a brother and you've been to a girls' school all your life you're very, very self-conscious with boys.
Joan: In primary we were in separate schools; the boys were just down the road and if you were seen talking to a boy it was, 'Look at her! She's talking to a boy!' I've never been to a co-ed school, but I've been to Irish college twice and it's brilliant fun mixing with girls and boys. Everyone's more inclined to laugh.
Maeve: People say that in a mixed school people would be distracted because it was mixed, but I tell you people would talk less about boys if it was a mixed school. If a boy over the age of 3 goes past the window everybody's looking at him. They talk about boys *all* the time.
Josie: A boy is someone to be seen with too.
Maeve: So long as you don't have a boy that's got spots or something. As long as you're seen with a fine-looking boy you're all right.

These girls are in no doubt about the disadvantages of being in a girls-only school. Apart from missing out on the companionship of boys, they cannot take certain subjects they would like to, and find it difficult to relate to boys as ordinary human beings. The danger of single-sex schooling is not only that it creates a basic division between the sexes in childhood, but that it also perpetuates the myth that boys and girls should receive a different sort of schooling.

The Employment Equality Agency's report *Schooling and Sex Roles* showed that there are still large differences in the subjects taken by boys and girls in post-primary schools. More boys than girls take mathematics, science and technical subjects and more girls take languages, home economics and other arts subjects. Three factors are at work here: whether or not the school provides a particular subject, how the subjects are timetabled within the school and the choices made by pupils.

The extensive curricular changes at primary level have not, in general, been matched in post-primary schools. There, academic achievement is still the top priority, and the subjects offered for the Intermediate and Leaving Certificates are largely governed by the standards laid down for university entrance and by tradition. Substantial numbers of girls are at schools where certain subjects are simply not available. A majority of girls cannot take physics or technical drawing at Leaving Certificate and a significant minority are excluded from chemistry and higher mathematics.[22] Even where subjects are available in schools, classes may be timetabled on a sex basis. In many mixed schools, for example, girls take home economics while boys take technical subjects. At Leaving-Certificate level, the timetabling of the co-institutional schools prevents over half the girls having option of taking higher mathematics and approximately a quarter from taking chemistry. In the earlier years of post-primary education, 80 per cent of boys and only 20 per cent of girls are obliged to take science.[23]

The researchers of *Schooling and Sex Roles* found some evidence of change in that more girls are taking science than used to be the case and the gap between the sexes has closed slightly in commerce and business subjects. But overall they found a strong bias towards the arts and 'accomplishment' subjects for girls and towards technical and science subjects for boys. The picture is one which would be familiar to researchers in other European countries. As well as showing how strongly schools still adhere to traditional sex-role stereotypes, these differences suggest that the political desire to prepare young people for the world of work and technology has had a far greater influence on boys' education than on girls' education.

This sex bias is not simply a matter of subject provision and allocation but is also reflected in the choices made by individual pupils. For example, of the 20 per cent of girls for whom higher mathematics was an option, only one in four actually took the subject, compared with two out of three offered biology. 'The extent of sex-differentiation is deeply institutionalised in the ideological and cultural presumptions underlying the education system. . . There are generally accepted assumptions as to what is considered to be appropriate to girls and boys on the basis of sex-stereotyped perceptions.'[24]

It is through the hidden curriculum as much as through the subjects on offer that sex stereotypes become institutionalised in schools. The hidden curriculum reflects the attitudes and values of the wider society and affects girls in specific ways. *Schooling and Sex Roles* showed that girls in Ireland, as elsewhere, have poorer self-images and lower expectations of themselves than boys. 75 per cent of boys considered themselves to be 'above average' in class, while girls generally made a much lower assessment of their abilities. Girls also tended to have a more negative attitude towards science and mathematics. This was related to teacher-expectations, as the teachers' attitudes affected the probability of girls choosing certain subjects.[25] In this way, stereotypes repeat themselves as the norms of one generation are transmitted to the next through the teachers' views of what is right and proper for girls and boys.

The Employment Equality Agency was particularly concerned about the influence of sex-stereotypes on the career-choices made by school students. Boys were 50 per cent more likely to aspire to university while four times as many girls as boys aimed for vocational occupations such as teaching and nursing. 'The clear labour-market segregation is almost exactly reproduced in girls' employment expectations.' In practical terms this means that girls enter a much narrower range of jobs than boys. Over half the girls who left school in 1979 found jobs as clerical workers, and a further 21 per cent took service jobs such as hairdressing and shop work.[26] The boys were distributed more evenly over a wider variety of jobs, and had a higher proportion of apprenticeships – 32 per cent, compared with a meagre 6 per cent for girls.[27] The girls' jobs in general bore all the familiar hallmarks of womens' work – limited promotion prospects, poor career development and relatively low adult earnings. The subject choices made by girls, coupled with their underestimation of their abilities, 'gives rise to a very substantial level of under-achievement in terms of girls' potential'.[28]

The implications of this under-achievement are likely to be even more serious in the future as the introduction of microelectronics is causing a rapid reduction in many areas of women's employment, particularly in clerical work. Girls' career aspirations seriously lag behind changes in the employment market. The pattern of girls' subject-choices at school is leaving them at a disadvantage in an increasingly technological job market where traditional 'accomplishments' are of limited value.

The problem carries through to third-level education, where girls are disproportionately concentrated in teacher-training, nursing and secretarial courses. In universities and technical colleges the school pattern is repeated in the large numbers of girls in arts subjects and the biological sciences and a majority of boys in engineering and applied sciences. The only professional degree courses in which women are well-represented are medicine and law. Although college-educated girls are predominantly from middle-class backgrounds and have the advantage of higher education, most are still destined for a relatively predictable and limited set of career opportunities.

Schooling and Sex Roles provides a valuable description of the factors affecting the different patterns of boys' and girls' schooling, but its usefulness is limited by its failure to explore the origins of the hidden curriculum and the reasons for the traditional differences in subjects offered in schools. There is nothing in the report about the ideological importance of the family in Irish society, nor of the role of women as wives and mothers within it. There is no mention of religion, of the effects of religious instruction on the self-images and attitudes of girls, nor of the personality characteristics emphasised in girls' schools. The report calls for important changes such as the elimination of sex-role stereotyping in textbooks and course outlines, in-service training for teachers to promote equality of opportunity, and positive encouragement for girls to take up mathematics and science. But how will such changes come about? Ending sex-stereotyping involves more than in-service courses and

Departmental encouragement (though even these would help); it involves a fundamental shift of attitudes which, in spite of the changes in the 1970s, cuts across widely accepted values about the proper roles of women and men in society.

Schools generally do not lead changes in society but follow them. Schools are conservative institutions, and in many cases do not even reflect attitude changes which have taken place outside the school walls. There is little evidence that schools have adapted to the fact that most girls today will spend a larger proportion of their adult lives in the labour force than at home, or to the difficulties this presents in a period of high unemployment. 'Education for what?' is a question many teachers would like to sit down and discuss, but cannot find the time amidst the rush to cover exam syllabuses and furnish their students with their all-important certificates.

It is also apparent that many schools still adhere to the old-fashioned view of how 'nice young ladies' should behave. They teach a strict moral code in a way that barely acknowledges the debate and upheaval of the 1970s. In a recent case, a woman teacher called Eileen Flynn was dismissed from her post in a convent school because she had a baby by a man to whom she was not married. The principal, a nun, sacked her after she refused to end the relationship. The dismissal caused considerable controversy, and among the comments was one from Father Walsh, Secretary of the Catholic Primary Schools Managers' Association. He stressed 'religion and the ethos in the school is vitally important. One of our prime instruments in implanting religious values in the the children is our Catholic teacher. Religion is a very important part of the school curriculum'.[29] His emphasis on 'implanting religious values' and on teachers as 'instruments' smacks of the authoritarian attitudes of the 1950s, but he was speaking in 1984.

As the discussion of sex education in Chapter 5 showed, there is still a long way to go before many schools take a modern, open look at the moral and personal aspects of the education they offer. Yet because these are precisely the aspects of education which inform the hidden curriculum and therefore the attitudes and expectations of so many girls, it is vital that they are closely examined. The degree of care with which *Schooling and Sex Roles* analysed subject-choice has yet to be applied to the wider influences on girls' education.

At an administrative level it is doubtful whether even the less controversial recommendations of *Schooling and Sex Roles* will be implemented. Educational administration is male-dominated. It is another pyramid to which the usual rule applies – the higher up you look, the fewer women you find. For example, three-quarters of primary-school teachers are women but the majority of school principals are men. Although co-education has been beneficial in many ways, it has not helped women to get top jobs in schools. When schooling is segregated, girls' schools normally have a female principal. In co-educational schools it is rare to find a woman in charge. In 1981 there was only one female principal in over fifty community and comprehensive schools, and less than half a dozen in 250 vocational schools. In the administrative sector there is no female Chief Executive among the thirty-eight Vocational Education Committees in the country. Out of eighty-six primary-school inspectors only six are female, and the only women in the secondary inspectorate are, predictably, in home economics.[30]

As Christina Murphy, education correspondent of the *Irish Times*, comments:

> I think we are in danger of evolving a system which will be administered, managed and run by men for women; a system where the majority of the pupils and teachers will be female – as they are at present – but where the administrators, the inspectors, the school principals will be mainly men; and where the curriculum and the system will be geared to the needs of the male pupils or at least to the needs of the female pupils only as they are perceived by the male decision-makers.[31]

Schools vary enormously in their general approach to teaching, and a comprehensive school with a male principal may provide girls with a much broader, more balanced education than an old-fashioned secondary school. The danger is that steps towards equality in such schools will be confined to the immediately obvious areas of subject availability and timetabling, while the many subtle effects of the hidden curriculum go unnoticed. A male-dominated educational hierarchy is more likely to reinforce sex stereotypes than to challenge them. Such a system is in itself a model of the problem, not of the solution.

8 Working for a Living

It is not easy to write about women and work in the 1980s. The themes of equal pay, equal opportunities and women's rights at work are so well-worn they are almost cliches. Surely we have heard that before? Didn't women get equality years ago? What more do they want? The unfortunate truth is that although women workers did win significant advances in the 1970s, these advances were limited, and are now being undermined by the economic recession of the early 1980s. Women have equality on paper, not in practice.

Women's employment opportunities are clearly related to the economic situation. In a period of economic expansion it is possible for women workers to improve their lot. Male workers are generally less defensive when their jobs are relatively secure and their wages rising, and shortages of labour in certain industries create new job possibilities for women. A low unemployment rate allows a softening of attitudes towards married women working, and as trade-union bargaining-power is increased it can be turned to women's advantage.

All these factors were present to some degree in the 1970s and, combined with the rapid change of attitudes in women themselves, helped to secure anti-discrimination laws and improved working conditions. An attitude shift and an economic shift coincided, and the two together enabled women to achieve useful advances. Trends in the 1980s are different. The attitude shift has continued, in that many women have a greater consciousness of inequality and still have a strong desire for change, but the economic shift has gone into reverse. Women have higher expectations and better educational qualifications and are making more demands on the society

139

around them, yet these demands are increasingly unsatisfied as the recession reduces opportunities and fuels a backlash against the notion of equality.

Fifty years of inequality

From the vantage-point of the late 1970s it was evident that women had come a long way in fifty years, and that the greatest changes had come since 1970. The pattern of women's employment had changed considerably since independence, as had women's attitudes to themselves as workers and trade unionists. In 1926, six out of ten women who were gainfully employed worked in agriculture or in domestic service. Fewer than one in ten worked in industry and only one in twenty was a member of a trade union.[1] These figures are not surprising given the overwhelmingly rural nature of Ireland in the 1920s. The industrial working class was small, and was concentrated in Dublin and a handful of the larger towns. The Dublin area accounted for only 14 per cent of the population of the country.[2] The majority of married women lived and worked with their husbands on farms and did not register in employment statistics. The women who had jobs were predominantly young and single. Many were young women from farms who migrated to the towns in search of work and a better standard of living.

Most women gave up their jobs on marriage, either because it was the social norm to do so, or because of the marriage bars in certain jobs, notably teaching and the Civil Service. Only single women were able to stay in employment for most of their adult lives. Many of these were religious, especially in the female professions of teaching and nursing. But the female workforce also included significant numbers of older women who never married. Migration into the towns by single women in search of work contributed to the population imbalance in which there was an excess of women in urban areas and a corresponding excess of men in the countryside. With little more than one young man to every two young women in the towns, spinsterhood was the inevitable outcome for many. In 1926, for instance, 27 per cent of urban women aged 45–54 were still unmarried, a figure which changed little until the late 1960s.[3]

From the 1930s until 1961, when the population of Ireland hit its

lowest point for a century, the female labour force actually decreased. Domestic service was in decline, and agricultural jobs were disappearing as farming whent through a prolonged period of crisis. There was a slight increase in manufacturing jobs, as the female-dominated industries such as clothing, textiles and footwear managed reasonably well under protectionist government policies. Women in these industries were concentrated in unskilled, repetitive work and earned only 57 per cent of the man's average industrial wage.[4] Even though few married women worked, and women made up only 26 per cent of the total workforce, there were not enough jobs for those who wanted them and many chose to emigrate. Kennedy notes that although women had a very subordinate status in the countryside there was little pressure to keep them there, and girls were at least free as their brothers to emigrate.[5] There were many factors involved in the difficult decision to leave the country – the lack of work and marriage opportunities at home, the better pay and working conditions abroad and the higher status of women in Britain and America.

Bernie, for example, left the west of Ireland in the late 1950s after losing her job there at the age of 18:

> I was a shop assistant. There was no union of course, and we worked from nine till six. I was getting £2.15s a week. I refused to clean the van one day and he said, 'Take your cards'. So I wrote away to England and got a job there. I think practically everyone that I grew up with went to England. It was terrible. They were shipping us out. There wasn't any work here and I hadn't a cat-in-hell's chance of getting another job.
>
> I went to Coventry working in a factory and I was as happy as a lark. I had to work like a slave of course, but the conditions we worked in cannot be compared with here. I was getting £10 a week, which was out of this world, like. I had to pay £2 for my digs and I had the £8 for myself. I enjoyed myself there.

Women in the earlier wave of emigration to the USA had mainly found work in domestic service or in unskilled manual work, whereas the majority of those who went to Britain took clerical, technical and service jobs.

In Ireland, progress towards improving the lot of working women was painfully slow. The unionisation of women increased from the

1930s onwards as women moved out of domestic service into more industrial jobs. The Irish Women Workers' Union took an important lead in organising low-paid and exploited groups such as laundry workers and makers of rosary beads. Other unions, notably the Irish Transport and General Workers' Union, gradually realised the importance of organising women. But there were considerable differences of opinion within the trade-union movement over what constituted rights for women. The need for equal pay for all women was not fully accepted, even among women trade-unionists. There were even debates in the IWWU itself on whether or not married women should be permitted to work.[6]

If one problem for women trade-unionists was a lack of clear objectives, another was the economic situation in the 1940s and 1950s. It was a difficult climate in which to realise advances for women workers. The emergency of the war years was followed by a major economic crisis in which emigration rose to record levels and home industries stagnated. Women were unable to make much headway when there was an acute shortage of jobs for men, and when issues such as equal pay seemed peripheral to the major economic problems of the day. In 1960 the average female wage in transportable goods industries was the same percentage of the male rate as it had been in 1939 – just 53 per cent.[7]

As the economic 'new age' dawned in the 1960s and 1970s, stagnation and crisis gave way at last to change and economic growth. The programmes for economic expansion introduced by the Lemass government in 1958 and 1963 replaced the old protectionist approach with policies designed to attract foreign investment and promote export-oriented private industry. Economically and politically, Ireland was moving into full participation in the European economic system. With the development of these policies came both change and new opportunities for female employment.

The new economic policies emphasised industrialisation through attracting overseas manufacturing companies to Ireland. In its own terms the policy was successful in that by 1977, 25 per cent of the total workforce in manufacturing was in multinational companies which had set up in Ireland between 1952 and 1973 with the assistance of the Industrial Development Authority.[8] Many of the jobs in these electronic, electrical and pharmaceutical companies were for women. Women were attractive as a cheap source of labour, prepared to do the often boring, repetitive semi-skilled and assembly work involved. Although the overall increase in women's industrial jobs between 1961 and 1971 was less than 10 per cent, this figure conceals a considerable redistribution of work away from the old home industries such as footwear and textiles and into the new multinational companies. Women's jobs in metal products, for instance, increased by 83 per cent over this period, and the chemical and plastics industries showed an increase of 45 per cent.[9]

The geography of women's jobs also changed. With the rapid decline of agriculture in many rural areas, the government was under pressure to locate new industry in previously under-developed regions. Areas like Shannon, Galway and North Mayo industrialised rapidly. In the north-west, for example, the new industries provided 60 per cent of the area's manufacturing employment. Dublin and the east coast, which had previously accounted for nearly half the industrial jobs in the country, obtained only 24 per cent of the new jobs.[10] As a result, many of the women taking jobs in factories were from rural areas. They were from families of returned emigrants, or were the daughters (and occasionally wives) of farmers. Some were agricultural workers who had lost their jobs in the accelerated decline of farm work in the 1960s and 1970s.

These women's earnings played an important part in the urbanisation of rural homes. Increased cash incomes enabled many families to build modern bungalows and furnish them with consumer goods. In her study of factory workers in North Mayo, Lorelei Harris describes the importance of the wages to women: 'Money means power: it confers social adulthood and a degree of independence'.[11] The women demonstrate this by spending money on clothes, furnishings and household items. 'Women workers indulge in a flurry of conspicuous consumption, adorning both themselves and their homes from the weekly wage packet. . . In a sense, therefore, material objects have come to stand as the outward symbols of women's social power'.[12]

Although manufacturing employment became the main focus for public attention, the greatest expansion of jobs took place in the service sector. As industrial development gathered speed, the demand for private-sector services such as banking and insurance increased. In addition, sustained economic growth throughout the 1960s and early 1970s enabled the government to expand its expenditure on services such as education, health and social welfare. In all, service jobs showed an average annual increase of 6500, and by 1980 accounted for 49 per cent of all jobs.[13] Again, many of the new jobs were for women, as nurses, teachers, cleaners and clerks.

The distribution of women's occupations in 1979 shows how strongly service jobs had come to dominate the scene. A staggering 28 per cent of all women workers were employed in clerical occupations, followed by 21 per cent in professional and technical jobs (mainly teaching and nursing). Another 15 per cent were in other services. Manufacturing accounted for only 14 per cent of women's occupations, and agricultural work only 6 per cent.[14]

Overall, the number of women at work had risen significantly – by 19 per cent between 1971 and 79 alone.[15] But for the first time in over a century the population of the country had risen too. Many former emigrants returned in the 1970s, and younger men and women who would previously have had little choice but to emigrate now stayed and found work in Ireland. The majority of the women who came into the workforce were single. Overall, Ireland still has a smaller proportion of women in the workforce than most European countries. Although there has been a threefold increase in the proportion of married women at work – from 5.2 per cent in 1961 to 17.4 per cent in 1981 – this is still below the EEC average of 42 per cent.[16] The participation of women in the Republic's labour force drops off rapidly with age as they leave to have their families. In the age group 20–4, two out of three women were out of work in 1979. But for women aged 35 and over, this dropped to one in four, against an EEC average of one in two.[17] In all, 55 per cent of women over the age of 15 are engaged in what the government categorises as 'home duties', and only 28 per cent are out at work, the rest being retired or students.[18]

The industrial developments of the 1960s and 1970s were not the only areas of change for women at work. There was also an important shift in attitudes. Women began to take a more militant stand over their rights at work and to campaign for equal pay and equal opportunities. This upsurge of activity was parallel to that in Britain and many other capitalist countries. Once women started to question their status in society it was inevitable that their conditions as employees should be one of the first areas to receive attention, especially as trade unionism gave women workers a possible means of affecting change. Unions also provided a base from which women could campaign for their rights at a national level. As one woman trade-unionist says: 'It all began to happen with the women's movement here in Ireland about ten years ago. There were women's television programmes and so on and I think women were just beginning to realise that it was us they were talking about. We began to take an interest in ourselves, and one way we could do this was through the union'.

Equal work, equal pay?

Equal pay has long been a contentious issue for women. It is both humiliating and degrading to to be paid less than a man for doing the same work. We may wonder how women in the Civil Service in the 1930s felt when they read the Brennan Commission's justification for paying them a lower rate: 'In those cases in the Civil Service where men and women may be employed indifferently we find special reason for supposing that on the whole when all relevant aspects are taken into account the woman does not give as good a return of work as a man'.[19]

Despite the fact that the first resolution on equal pay was proposed to the Irish Trade Union Congress in 1917, unions made little progress on the issue for almost fifty years. Some women felt strongly about equal pay, but others did not. Given their subordinate role in the workforce, many women were afraid that they would lose their jobs to men once equal pay was established. It was not until the mid-1960s that large numbers of women workers began to adopt a more militant attitude. At the 1964 Trade Union Congress women protested at their exclusion from the minimum-wage increase of the latest wage round, and in 1965 Congress was forced to establish a committee on equal pay. This committee never actually reported, but the issue had been aired and was fast becoming an active campaign. In 1969 several groups of women workers fought for equal pay and for equal increases in the annual wage-round. Some semi-state companies granted equal pay to clerical workers in 1971, and two years later, in the wake of the report of the Commission of the Status of Women, the government agreed to remove the marriage bar from the Civil Service and made a commitment to introduce equal pay.[20]

The Anti-Discrimination (Pay) Act eventually came into force in 1975, in line with EEC requirements. The passing of the Act however, did not guarantee its implementation. A great deal of campaigning, negotiating and strike action was undertaken by many women before their employers conceded equal pay. In 1975, the government itself tried to renege on its commitment to introduce equal pay into the public service, but was forced to back down after a vigorous campaign of opposition. The strength of feeling against the government on this occasion was a timely reminder of how highly many women now valued the concept of equality, and how strongly they were prepared to fight for it.

To Kate and her colleagues working in a large shop, equal pay was a milestone as it was the first time the women had become involved in the union. Management conceded the rises fairly quickly:

There were always two wage structures, the women's and the men's. At that time I was packing orders in despatch alongside this young fella, and he was getting something like £29 more than me, just because he was a lad. When equal pay came in we really went to town on it. We had to investigate all the wage structures and decide who was doing equal work with the fellas. Then the full-time official put in the claim. It was marvellous – my wages went from £26 to £60 in a fortnight.

Employment legislation is never a cure-all, as women workers soon discovered. The law did help to finalise equal-pay agreements for many groups of workers and abolished the practice of separate pay-scales for men and women. But the overall result has been no more than a modest reduction of the wages gap between men and women. In 1970, women's average hourly earnings in manufacturing industry were only 56 per cent of men's. By 1975, they had crept up to 61 per cent. Women's relative position has continued to improve slowly since, to 68 per cent in 1981.[21] The gap in average weekly earnings is even greater because men work longer hours and earn more shift and overtime payments. Women were paid only 59 per cent of the average male weekly wage in 1981.[22]

Why is the wages-gap still so large? There are several reasons. Many employers were notoriously slow in introducing equal pay, and found ways round the law such as altering job descriptions to increase the differences between men's and women's jobs. An equal-pay agreement is a complex matter requiring detailed negotiations by a trade union that is prepared to take the matter seriously. Some women found that although they were supposed to have equal pay they were excluded from certain extra payments or schemes that applied only to the men.

Bernie is a cleaner in a large institution. The male cleaners are all full-time workers on a 40-hour week. They are entitled to increments and are paid an overtime rate for additional hours. The women are called temporary part-time workers. They earn the same hourly rate as the men for a 24-hour week, but are not paid overtime for any extra hours. They are not entitled to increments and they have no unsocial hours payment for starting a 7 in the morning or working on Saturdays. In addition, they are ineligible for the pension scheme.

We are called part-time workers, but I work 39 hours a week. We would like to be on full-time, which would bring us up to the same wage-rate as the men and give us the increments. When the equal pay was discussed the women didn't know anything about increments. It should have been the union man's business to explain that to them, but he didn't. We are the forgotten in every way around here.

Bernie is a 'temporary' worker who has been in the job for eight years. Now she is a shop steward and actively working for a better deal for her women members, who are in an all-too-common situation: they have equal pay on paper but their average weekly earnings are considerably lower than those of their male colleagues.

It has been estimated that even if equal pay was fully implemented women's earnings would rise no higher than 74 per cent of men's.[23] The remaining gap is caused by the different pattern of female employment and the over-proportion of women at the lower end of many salary scales. The real problem for women is not equal pay, but low pay. The majority of women are concentrated in industries and jobs where low pay is the norm. In manufacturing, most of the industries paying high wages to men – industries such as vehicle production, brewing and printing – employ relatively few women. At the other end of the scale, industries such as leather, clothing and food pay the lowest average rates and also have very high proportions of female workers. In 1981, for instance, men in the five highest-paying industries averaged weekly earnings in excess of £164, where women in the five lowest-paying industries averaged under £70 a week.[24] Equal pay legislation is not able to combat these industry-based differences.

Unfortunately, a lack of government statistics makes it difficult to get accurate information on the payment structure in service industries. Figures published by the Department of Public Services in 1983, however, give a revealing picture of the balance between the sexes in the higher grades of one major employer, the Civil Service. At Executive Officer level, women hold their own and comprise 40 per cent of the employees in that grade. Three grades higher, the proportion of women drops to 18 per cent. Only 3 per cent of the next grade are women, only 1 per cent of the grade above that, and in the top grade there are no women at all.[25] The net result is that on average, women in the Civil Service earn considerably less than the men – another earnings gap with which equal-pay legislation could not deal. It is a typical picture, one that could be repeated for education and the health boards, in company management and in most administrative work.

In white-collar and professional jobs where men and women are on the same salary-scale, few women move up the scales as fast as men. The massive drop-out from employment of women over the age of 25, due mostly to child-bearing, coincides with the time when men are beginning to accept promotion and increase their earnings. And for the minority of women who do stay at work, promotion is less frequent. Women tend to stay in lower grades for far longer than men.

Kate: I'd like to see equality in our workplace, not just equal pay. There's an awful lack of promotion for women. For all they are a caring management, you still have the attitude that a man is better than a woman in certain areas. For instance, the hardware section lost its manager recently, and there are four girls who've been there for eight years, and who have done the job when he has been on holiday or whatever, and yet another man was brought in to replace him. He was taken on straight from school, and the women had to show him the ropes! We took it up through the union, and the manager said, 'Oh, it's a traditional male position'.

Equal opportunities

Given the limitations of the equal-pay legislation, the obvious next step was to try and secure equal opportunities for women at work. The Employment Equality Act came into force in 1977 and was designed to prevent discrimination in job recruitment, conditions of work, training and promotion. The Act also set up the Employment Equality Agency to promote equality of opportunity and to review the workings of the law. Once again the legislation proved to be a useful but limited step forward. Equal opportunity is a legal requirement but is sadly lacking in practice.

The Act removed certain blatant forms of discrimination, but it is not easy to legislate away discriminatory attitudes. Stereotyped views of women and sexist attitudes continue happily, untouched by the legislation. Married women are particularly vulnerable to discrimination. Employers, the State and even trade unions have taken the notion of equal opportunities further for single women than for married women.

Maura, a teacher, experienced this problem. She has taught English and French in a comprehensive school for ten years and is a very experienced and respected teacher. Yet she is aware of hostility amongst the male staff towards her as a married woman: 'The headmaster disapproves of us, and the vice-principal goes around saying the women are out more often than the men, and they should be at home looking after their children'. She came across one particular incident which horrified her:

> A diploma student taking a class was having a lot of trouble with my third-form group. The vice-principal went in and I stayed to hear what he was going to say. He said, 'I am a big man with a big voice, and Miss So-and-so is a small woman with a small voice', and he went on about how they should make allowances for women teachers. I was sitting there blushing, getting redder and redder. I felt totally undermined by it. I was raging afterwards, over the fact that he had just fed a prejudice to kids. But there are masses of areas like that.

Although teaching is a profession in which women have been well-established for many years, it is not without its problems. On the one hand, girls' schools enable women to exercise their skills in leadership and administration as well as in teaching. Nuns in charge of large convent schools, for instance, carry a degree of responsibility and authority rarely found elsewhere in women's employment. On the other hand, the ethos of the Catholic school brings contradictions for women, especially if they have children. The morality promoted by the school dictates that women should give priority to their role as mothers, not as teachers. And the stress on the good Catholic teacher in the Catholic school tends to mean that head teachers regard the private lives of women teachers as legitimate areas of concern, as happened in the Eileen Flynn case. The same level of scrutiny does not appear to apply to men.

In industries where management attitudes were favourable, the new emphasis on equal opportunities in the 1970s enabled some women to achieve a great deal. Various bodies ran courses and seminars designed to encourage women to take up management posts and to seek promotion in their organisations. One woman who benefited thereby is Carole, who at the age of 28 holds a senior position in a Dublin-based organisation. She entered an administrative job after taking a post-graduate course in personnel management. In six years she has been promoted twice:

> I'm happy there. I like the responsibility I have. I like the variety, and I meet a lot of people. I expect the position I have now was not all that easy for a woman to get, as the whole organisation is male-dominated really, but I worked hard and they recognised it and I think they treated me as well as anyone else. I'm lucky in that where I am they recognise ability rather than sex.

She is in the first batch of women at executive level, and although she has some ambition to go higher still, she feels the challenge of her present position is quite enough for the moment:

> It is very challenging – sometimes a bit too demanding, too stressful. Some of the responsibilities I have I don't particularly like, such as having to take responsibility for people with the same educational level as my own, the same age as me. I found it very difficult when I got my first promotion because I found an awful lot of resentment against me and I wasn't able to cope with it. I tackle it a lot better now.

She is on target for a high-flying career. But what will happen if she has children?

I very much hope to have children. I would hope to stay at work, but it is very difficult to say at this stage because I see a lot of my friends who were in good professional jobs and who I thought were much more career-oriented than myself who have had children and given up work. My intention would very definitely be to go back to work. I like a challenge, I like meeting people and I think I'd go bananas at home all day.

She may be able to realise her hope if she has just one child, with the help of a sympathetic partner and a good baby-sitter. But if she has two, three, four? This is the crunch for equal opportunities. Motherhood – or active fatherhood – does not mix easily with paid employment. The marriage bar has gone, but most women drop out of the workforce when they have their first baby. As an ITGWU document put it, 'for many women now, the marriage bar has simply been replaced by a "baby bar" which is equally effective and whose removal must be seen as one of the major tasks of the 1980s'.[26]

For years feminists have been saying that women cannot take an equal role in the labour force until men do an equal share of the work at home. But the problem goes deeper still, into the very structure of present employment patterns. Full-time jobs are based on the traditional male pattern of a working life. A man is expected to work a 40 hour week for about forty-eight weeks a year, from the age he leaves school until he retires. This pattern assumes there is a woman in the background to look after his needs – to feed him, wash his clothes, keep house and soothe him after the working day. There is little time left after a full-time job to do all these things *and* have satisfying relationships with children, family and friends *and* to participate in other pursuits (including trade union activities). Rosheen Callender argues this point forcefully in a paper published by the Trade Union Women's Forum: 'It is simply not possible to combine a long and arduous working day with the type of social and human contacts and activities that people *need* throughout their lives'.[27]

In other words, the demanding nature of most full-time jobs actively prevents men from taking an equal share at home even if they want to. As well as making life difficult for women, this diminishes men by cutting them off from their children and from other life-enhancing, satisfying interests.

The model of a 'normal' working-life is a rigid one. It is based on an unchanging routine in which time is chopped up into definite chunks – this many hours at work, that many hours at home. But for women, flexibility is a key requirement. Flexibility to accommodate the changing needs of home and children, flexibility of time within each day and across the years.

Equal opportunities in its truest sense does not mean simply fitting women into the traditions and norms of male work. It means reassessing many aspects of home and working-life to enable both women and men to lead more balanced, fulfilled lives. It is only recently that the debate about equal opportunities in the trade union movement has broadened out from its original concern with removing overt discrimination into a more detailed look at areas such as job-sharing, flexitime, child-care facilities and reduced working-hours. All these are essential areas of concern to women trying to combine employment with home responsibilities.

Because the majority of women have been, and still are, single, trade-union campaigns for equality have tended to emphasise the similarities between women and men, stressing their equal potential and equal ability. They have, in effect, fought for men's wages and conditions for women. While this was appropriate for women who could cope with the demands on time made by traditional full-time work, it did not meet the needs of women who could not conform to this pattern. A woman who has children or who looks after elderly parents will need breaks from work at particular stages of her life and will probably need to work part-time for a number of years. The pattern of her working-life will be very different from the male one, and she is likely to find it very difficult to combine her family responsibilities with a job. This fundamental difference between her situation and that of a man makes the achievement of equal opportunities nigh on impossible.

The 'baby bar'

The first problem for women with children is an acute shortage of part-time work. Only 13 per cent of women in the Republic work part-time – a very low figure compared with Britain and Northern Ireland, where part-time work accounts for 40 per cent of all women's jobs.[28] Many of these jobs are in the public sector, in the school meals service and hospitals, in nurseries and old people's homes. There is also a strong tradition of part-time work in some manufacturing industries in both Britain and Northern Ireland. In the Republic, where the health and social services are less well-developed and where the manufacturing base is smaller, there are fewer jobs of either kind.

Irish trade unions have been reluctant to promote part-time work. Trade-unionists have pointed to the fact that such work is often poorly paid and exploitative, with less job security and fewer promotion prospects than full-time jobs. Only recently, with the recognition that many women will continue to seek part-time work regardless, has the emphasis in some unions shifted towards accepting the need to extend the benefits of trade-union organisation and protection to part-timers. Padragín Ní Murchu explains this change of thinking:

> Traditionally, the trade-union view of part-timers, both at official and shop-floor level, has been to see it as a fringe activity unconnected with real workers' issues or rights . . . This attitude is now being reassessed, for many reasons. One reason is the growth of this phenomenon and the approaches from these workers for trade union protection. Secondly, there is a growing realisation that part-time work is here to stay. . . The trade-union movement must recruit and negotiate on behalf of part-time workers in general.[29]

A related problem is that the ideology of the family is in opposition to the notion of married women working outside the home. A mother who decides to get a job may face considerable hostility from friends and relatives who believe that children need their mothers at home, and that she should put their needs above her own. She may also encounter opposition and discouragement from potential employers and other workers who believe that married women have less right to work than men and single women.

Married women are convenient scapegoats at a time of economic recession. 'One family, one job', thundered a politician in 1983, and of course he meant that women should give up their jobs. In the traditional view of motherhood, women are not individuals with a right to a job, but are seen in relation to their families. If they are single, they can be accepted on equivalent terms to a man. If they are married, they are expected to subsume their own interests to those of their families. Men have no such difficulty. They are readily accepted as individuals who can and should work, regardless of their marital status. Indeed a man who for some reason chooses not to have a job is commonly regarded as either deviant or lazy.

In spite of the increase in the numbers of married women in the labour force, their small overall total has meant that they are still vulnerable to this prejudice. Married women have little trade-union power and politicians are not, in general, ready to spring to their defence. As a result, the movement towards equal opportunities has gone much further for single women, and has left married women lagging behind.

The 1970s challenge to sterotyped male and female roles, however, did result in some steps forward for women with children. In 1981, the Maternity Protection of Employees Act brought women the legal right to fourteen weeks maternity leave and the right to return to the same job after having a child. The length of the statutory leave is minimal compared with other countries. In Northern Ireland and Britain women can take twenty-six weeks after the birth. In Sweden, a country noted for its progressive legislation on women's rights, mothers or fathers can take six months leave, and can work a six-hour day until the child is eight, or take full leave until the baby is eighteen months old.[30] But the Irish legislation did, for the first time, force employers to accommodate a specific aspect of women's lives as mothers.

Maternity leave is significantly different to equality legislation. Instead of assuming that women are equal to men, it recognises that women have special needs. In this sense, maternity leave is an important step towards challenging the norm of the male working lifetime. It is not surprising that many employers have complained about implementing the legislation. They say that it disrupts their manpower [sic] planning, and that it is awkward to keep a job open only to find that the woman does not come back. Such complaints reveal the inflexibility of working arrangements in industry. Few employers are willing to make concessions to parents' needs. The legislation did not, for instance, include any provision for paternity leave, and as yet few negotiated agreements include it.

It is true that only a minority of women go back to work after the birth of a child. For that minority the maternity legislation, and negotiated maternity agreements, are vital. Some other mothers make a clear choice to stay at home with the baby and have no intention of returning to work for some years. But for a large number of women between these two extremes the present situation is unsatisfactory. Maternity leave is too short, or they cannot find suitable child-care facilities to enable them to return to work. Out of the fourteen weeks statutory leave, ten are normally taken after the birth. Yet how many women are physically and emotionally able to cope with their job again just ten weeks after having a baby? And if the mother goes back to work, who will look after the child? The ICTU considers that 'the provision of community child-care facilities [is] an essential prerequisite to enable women to exercise their right to work and to achieve equal opportunities'.[31] Few such facilities exist. With only around eighty subsidised day-care nurseries in the State, most of which cater for disadvantaged children, most parents must rely on private nurseries or child-minders.[32] Some are lucky and find a satisfactory minder, but with no proper registration of facilities and no State subsidies it is matter of luck – and of considerable expense.

According to one estimate, between 10 000 and 16 000 women with children aged up to 3 years old would work if they could find suitable child-care facilities.[33] Many of these would probably prefer part-time work if they could find it.

More married women *are* now working – three times as many as in the early 1960s. Today, the normal pattern is for women to stay at work after marriage, at least until the birth of their first child. In addition, more women are seeking to return to work after having children. Smaller, planned families enable many women to make a definite decision not to have any more children and to go back to work; a choice few of their mothers would have been able to make.

Re-entering the workforce as a mature woman is not easy. The years at home take their toll on women's self-confidence and their belief in themselves as capable, skilled, responsible employees. The isolation of mothers and children in a separate world, cut off from the 'real' world of work and politics and men makes many woman feel apprehensive about making the transition back into working life. A woman who has seen herself solely as a housewife and mother often undervalues her skills and internalises the idea that she has less right to work than a younger woman.

Norma: I haven't worked since I was five months pregnant. I would like to go back to work when my son is settled in school, but I wouldn't have the confidence at the moment to go back. I've been too long away. I mean my typing has gone down to nothing. I'm sure a lot of employers are not that keen to take a woman with children.

AnCO, the Republic's industrial training authority, runs courses for women who want to return to work. The programme started in the 1970s, at a time when some attention was being given to women's special training needs and finance was available from the EEC. The courses assist the transition back into employment, and help women to regain their sense of identity as independent people who can make decisions about their own lives.

Siobhan: The course was the best thing that ever happened. It gave me a different outlook completely towards the future. The longer you are at home, the more confidence you lose. I think the course brought that back and it is a thing I will never lose again. *Anne*: Oh it was marvellous, that course. It was just us – no husbands, no children. It was just our own lives. It has helped me an awful lot. I think I am more outgoing, and I have asserted myself more than I did before.

The popularity of such courses is another indication of the large number of married women who have a strong interest in returning to employment. It the economic situation was more favourable, the rise in the proportion of married women in employment would undoubtedly continue at a more rapid rate, thereby closing another gap between Ireland and other European countries.

Part of the union

For women workers, as for men, union membership is the means by which they can organise together to protect themselves and negotiate with employers. Non-unionised groups of women, notably part-timers and those in small workplaces like shops and restaurants, are vulnerable to the employer's whims and tend to earn poorer wages. But in addition to this basic role of unions, the trade-union movement as a whole has an important function for women. The larger unions and the ICTU have a voice in national political, economic and legislative affairs. As such, they are an important vehicle for campaigns for women's rights. Over the past twenty years, women who have been both union activists and committed to the women's movement have worked hard to get their unions to take up women's issues. The ICTU, for instance, made a substantial submission to the Commission on the Status of Women which outlined priorities for women workers and acknowledged the need for internal change in unions to increase women's representation. In 1976, the ICTU adopted the Working Women's Charter, which contained thirteen principles of equality.[34] Significantly, the Charter included provision for nurseries and family-planning services as well as demands for equality in employment. It committed Congress, on paper at least, to campaign for women's rights on a very wide basis. The larger individual unions have played a similar role, contributing to campaigns for equality through policy-making submissions to government bodies and negotiations with employers.

Women did not win this support without a struggle. Changing attitudes and policies is a slow business. Trade-union men are little different from men in society at large in their distrust of equality for women. 'It is important to recognise', admitted the ICTU in 1978, 'that many long-standing notions and prejudices towards women workers persist even among trade union members.'[35]

One significant development helped the women's cause – their numerical increase as trade-union members. Without women the trade-union movement would not have increased its strength in recent years. With the industrial growth of the 1960s and 1970s, the number of union members in the Republic increased rapidly, Most of these new members werre in white-collar and public-sector unions, and the majority of them were women. Women now make up one third of the membership of general unions and half the membership of white-collar unions. Only in craft and certain other unions are women still a small minority. Overall, out of more than 250 000 women employees, about 158 400, or 63 per cent, are trade union members. [36]

Yet a glance at the proportions of men and women at higher levels in unions shows that women are seriously underrepresented in all decision-making roles. An ITGWU survey of its own branches in 1979 showed that women formed about 30 per cent of the members, but only 19 per cent of the union's shop stewards, 15 per cent of branch committee-members, and 13 per cent of branch trustees. [37] In addition, only one woman sits on the union executive of fifteen. [38] The pattern is a familiar one, common to most unions. Trade unions are strongly hierarchical organisations with well-established procedures for selecting and appointing delegates and representatives at different levels. Few women rise through the hierarchies to influential policy-making posts. Even fewer women become full-time officials serving the membership and negotiating on their behalf. In 1980, there were only thirteen women full-timers in the Republic, four of whom worked for the IWWU (which has since been amalgamated with the Federated Workers Union of Ireland). [39]

Women workers have a double struggle for equality – with their employers and within their unions. An ITGWU pamphlet states the problem:

It is recognised that particular difficulties stand in the way of full and equal participation in union affairs by its women members. Some of these difficulties are practical; some psychological. The latter stem largely from the former: many women regard unions generally as male preserves – and, as we have seen, virtually all key positions in Irish unions *are* held by men. [40]

Some unions, especially those with a majority of women members, have made significant progress towards increasing women's involvement, largely as a result of grass-roots pressure and consistent effort by women activists. Kate, for instance, is a shop representative and chairperson of the local branch of the Irish Distributive and Administrative Trade Union, and has worked hard to get more women involved:

I think equal pay brought the women out. Before that, it never occurred to us that we could get together and better our conditions. We went out and we fought for equal pay and we decided, well, we've done that and we're not going to sit back and let them walk all over us again. Also education has helped – the union has done a great deal of education in the last ten years. I encourage the women, I talk to them, I arrange meetings, and as chairperson I took it on myself to attend the quarterly meetings in each store, so I got known. They identify more with me as a woman – before that it was always men.

Four years ago we had one woman on the National Executive, and we now have six out of twelve, which is great. We had no women full-time officials, and now we have three. The attitude at the top has changed completely. They've seen that women have got something to offer, and they encourage them to participate.

In other workplaces, particularly where women are in a minority, it is still common for women to view unions as a 'man's world'. Talking to factory workers in North Mayo, Lorelei Harris found that 'most women see trade unions as something completely outside their world; as a bureaucratic hierarchy that sometimes fixes things and most of the time does not'.[41] The women workers defined themselves in opposition to both management and male workers. It is easy to see how this situation can arise when, as is so often the case, women and men do different jobs. They therefore have different priorities and concerns, a gender division which is easily exacerbated when women become aware of a lack of union attention to their needs.

Bernie: The men will bond themselves together, but the women won't. They are afraid they are going to lose their jobs, whereas a man isn't afraid. For some reason a man is more aware of that feeling of togetherness and security from a union, but we women are not. My members don't realise that we have the union with us. They feel as if they are on their own. They don't think of the union as 'us'. It is them and us.

To Bernie, brought up in a strong labour family and an active trade unionist herself, her members' lack of interest is frustrating. 'I find it very difficult to get through to them what they are fighting for. They tend to fight for little things, but they are not talking about the pension scheme and things like that.'

It is easy to blame women for their lack of interest, but Bernie is well aware of some of the difficulties both she and her members face. 'I don't think women should put down the way they are. They are ignored generally, and inside the union they are [ignored] to an awful extent.' On one occasion, when the women were trying to change their hours of work, the branch secretary told them they were lucky to have a job and they would have to go where they were put. As Bernie comments, 'he would never say that to men', and his attitude was hardly likely to increase the women's confidence in the union.

Bernie has had a struggle to establish herself in the local union structure:

> They tend to take you here with a grain of salt: 'Ah sure, she's only a woman, she's rambling on again, we won't listen'. But I really assert myself on the branch committee. If I have anything to say I don't care how ludicrous it might sound, I still say it. And they have taken to listening to me now.

For a long time she was not invited to attend shop-stewards' meetings in the workplace, because she was a part-time worker. And after many years of activity in the union, it was only at the latest annual conference that she learned of the existence of the union's womens advisory committee. No one had told her about it. 'I would like to see women treated with the same sort of respect as the men in the union. That the women would not be afraid to stand up and say, "Look, we are not going to tolerate this any more".' She would like to see more women at a national level. 'There is one woman on the executive, that's all. I'd like to see that changed. I think women are quite capable of saying what they have got to say.'

There are other practical problems preventing women becoming active in their unions. Attendance at evening meetings, weekend conferences and residential courses entails complicated arrangements for women with children, and adds an extra stress to the already-difficult situation of trying to combine a job with a family. For full-time officials, the hours spent away from home are often impossibly long. In the words of one woman official: 'The demands of a trade-union official's job are such that it makes it extremely difficult for anyone, male or female, to lead a normal social or family life. This is something that the unions will have to address themselves to'. But she added that 'the unions are way ahead of Irish society in general, in the way they treat women'.[42]

Increasingly, unions are accepting that well-intentioned statements are not enough to secure equality for women, but that positive action is required. Positive action means special provision for women to overcome the barriers to their full involvement in union affairs. Measures range from womens committees and training courses for women shop-stewards, to crèche facilities at conferences and reserved seats on union executives. The aim is to tackle the psychological and the practical problems together. By getting more women into union posts, and giving priority to women's issues, it becomes easier for women members to see the union as relevant to them, as an organisation with which they can identify.

In the early 1980s, women are continuing to make progress towards better representation in union matters. More unions, and the ICTU, are taking up positive action. As more women become involved, they can set up structures to facilitate other women. It remains to be seen whether this impetus can be maintained in the face of falling union memberships and growing unemployment.

Into the 1980s

Can women in the 1980s continue to make progress towards equality in employment? The slow-down in the economy affects women in specific ways. Because of their secondary position in the labour force, women generally feel the squeeze more than men. When redundancies occur, temporary and part-time workers, who are mainly women, are often the first to go. The old argument that married women should go back home rears its ugly head again, and women are supposed to feel guilty for having a job. As competition for jobs increases, it is easier for employers to choose a man and less easy for a woman to prove discrimination in the selection process. A great deal of trade union energy goes into fighting redundancies and trying to maintain real wages, and union leaders have little time for equality issues. As unions lose bargaining power in a recession, it becomes harder for woman to improve their pay in relation to that of men.

All these factors have been in operation in the early 1980s, and have made it increasingly difficult for women workers to take further steps towards equality. In some cases, it has been a major effort just to hang on to the gains of the 1970s. Job security has become the top priority in many industries, often putting equality issues into the background. The disadvantages of relying on foreign companies to provide manufacturing jobs have become apparent as unions have found themselves powerless to defend their members against decisions made outside Ireland. The closure of a manufacturing plant in an area can instantly burst the bubble of prosperity generated in the 1970s. An example of this is the closure of Travenol Laboratories in Castlebar, Co. Mayo in 1985. Travenol is an American company, and became the only large employer in the town when it opened, supported by IDA grants, in the early 1970s. Three quarters of the 700 staff were women, many of them married. The closure announcement shocked the town, and the chances of the workers finding alternative employment in Co. Mayo is minimal. 'It is the end of my working-life,' said one woman, only in her twenties. 'It's going to be very hard for the young single girls but for a married woman like me another job is simply impossible.'[43] Women who gained from the new industrial jobs of the past twenty years are now bearing the brunt of the effects of closures. In addition, women have been severely affected by two other aspects of the current economic situation – the introduction of new technology and cutbacks in public expenditure.

The high concentration of women in a narrow range of jobs leaves them particularly vulnerable to technological change. Over a quarter of all women workers are in clerical jobs, yet there is no possibility of the present level of office work being maintained. One word processor can replace up to five typists; the computerisation of an organisation's administrative system drastically reduces the requirement for typists, clerks and other white-collar staff. Unlike the situation in manufacturing, where the capital investment per new job is very high, office jobs, until now, have been cheap to create. Wages were the main cost, and little machinery was required. Now, the tendency is for management to invest in computerised office systems, and to reduce their staff accordingly. This process is at work in banks and insurance companies, in manufacturing and in the public services. The majority of the workers affected are women.

Many factory jobs too are threatened by microtechnology. A great deal of the work women do in industry is of a repetitive, semi-skilled nature– work such as assembling parts, packing and bottling. These jobs are often the first to be automated. Companies introduce new machines that will perform the given task day in, day out, and without the need for holidays or demands for wage rises.

Professional jobs are not so easy to computerise, but instead face a serious threat from public spending cuts. Teachers, nurses, physiotherapists and social workers all find it increasingly difficult to get jobs. Government cuts have forced schools, health boards and voluntary organisations to freeze vacancies and reduce their spending on staffing. These cuts have a double effect on women. They reduce the number of jobs available and they also increase the load on women as carers in the home. Every lost bed in a geriatric ward is another elderly person to care for at home; every reduction in facilities for mentally-handicapped children means more work for their mothers. As long as women retain the major share of the responsibility for the young, the sick and the elderly, the effect of cuts in public spending will fall disproportionately on them.

As a result of these trends, unemployment among women is increasing more rapidly than among men. Between 1979 and 1982, the number of women registered as unemployed increased by 44 per cent, compared with a 38 per cent increase for men. Official statistics show that fewer women than men are unemployed, but the true number of unemployed women is undoubtedly much larger. Many women are not registered as unemployed because in the eyes of the State they are men's dependents and are not eligible for unemployment benefit. In particular, the figures do not include the many thousands of married women who would return to work if they could find a job, but who remain invisible as long as they are not working.

The outlook for women in employment is not encouraging. At a time when the female workforce is increasing, job opportunities are decreasing. It is likely that unemployment will continue to rise. There is little evidence that girls' education is changing fast enough to prepare young women for modern working life, or to equip at least some of them with the technical and scientific training required to take advantage of jobs in the new technologies. There is a danger of women being left behind in an increasingly technical job market.

Girls are leaving school with a stronger sense of themselves as individuals and with higher expectations. At the other end of the age-scale, more and more married women are looking to rejoin the workforce as soon as their families are settled in school. The aspirations of both groups are being increasingly frustrated by growing unemployment and a troubled economic situation.

9 Finding a Voice: Women in the Church

'People ask me how I can be a feminist and a Roman Catholic. While I recognise it would appear to be a contradiction, it is not a contradiction for me.' Sr Maria has been a nun for twenty-five years and is in no doubt about where she stands:

> I see myself as a woman of the twentieth century, also as a woman who happens to be a Christian. I like to think I am in tune with life around me. As sisters I think we have a great desire to be accepted as women who are struggling to find our own identity within the Church, just as other women are struggling to find their own identity in society. The Church is certainly one of the last bastions of sexism in the world, but things are beginning to happen that are good.

Sr Maria is one of a small but growing number of Christian feminists who, as nuns or as lay women, are committed to a vision of Christianity as a force for justice and against oppression, including the oppression of women. In Ireland, where the women's movement has clashed with the Catholic Church over so many issues – contraception, divorce and family law, to name but a few – it would be tempting to conclude that all feminists are anti-Church. This is not the case. Although the number of women who are both Catholics and feminists is small compared with the USA and Britain, they reflect an important trend. The traditional institutions of the Catholic Church are not only under attack from without, but also from within. Whereas challenges to Church teachings from politicians and campaigning groups are usually made in public and are well reported by the media, much of the internal dissent is less visible. An increasing part of this dissent is coming from women; women who see the contradictions between the Church's view of them and their own attitudes, ambitions and beliefs. They reflect another aspect of the changing position of women in Irish society, and their influence must be included in any assessment of the role of the Catholic Church today.

Feminism has become a lively movement within the Christian churches internationally since the mid-1960s. In the Anglican community women have sustained a vigorous campaign for the right to be ordained, and many churches now have women ministers and deaconesses. In 1984, the General Synod of the Church of Ireland approved the ordination of women as deacons, though women are still debarred from the full ministry of the Church.[1] In the Roman Catholic Church, women have concentrated less on the issue of ordination and more on a broadly-based challenge to the whole masculine orientation of the Church's organisation and teachings. The worldwide upheaval in the Catholic Church following the Second Vatican Council, which called for change and renewal in all parts of the Church, provided the climate in which many women began to question their role within it. The past twenty years have seen particularly dramatic changes for nuns, as the various orders have pulled themselves slowly and painfully out of the nineteenth-century into the twentieth, changing their dress, their rules and their ministries. Most important, nuns have begun to reclaim their full identity as women.

This period coincided with the rise of the women's movement. As more and more women began to define themselves as feminists, the Christians among them inevitably looked at the treatment of women within their Churches. Many left as a result, finding organised religion irrelevant to their needs or feeling that its sexist structures and teachings were insuperable barriers to their continued adherence to the faith. But those women who felt that the basic Christian message remained important in their lives stayed within the Church, determined to change attitudes to women from within.

A few men within the Catholic Church have realised the importance of finding ways of increasing women's involvement in all aspects of the faith. In the early 1970s Dr Donal Flanagan described the problem inherent in the Church's attitudes to women.

'The Church today is still trapped in the Christian women stereotypes she has created. She is not really involved in the struggle for the liberation of women from a man-created, man-controlled, man-centred world system.' As a result, he noted that 'the big ideas about women which will shape her future and the future of man are not originating in Christian circles'.[2] Nine years later, Paul Hynes commented on the continuing lack of interest in women's issues in the Irish Church: 'Over the years I have both heard and read [of] women discussing their role in society and in the Church, but on no occasion have I felt that there is any serious study of the question here'.[3] Meanwhile, a working party on the role of women in the Church had been set up by the National Conference of Priests in Ireland. The report, published in 1982, stressed the urgent need for the Church to re-examine its attitudes to women, and sounded a note of warning: 'By its failure to listen to, dialogue with and reflect on the articulated experience of women the Church is cutting itself off from one of the most vital and radical sources of authentic human development in our time'.[4]

The men behind these statements are, however, the exceptions, and the Irish Catholic Church in general exhibits a complacent attitude to the issue of women's involvement. Even those who promote liberation theology and who are critical of the Church's stand on justice have been slow to include women in their understanding of oppression. In a recent book called *Is Irish Catholicism Dying?*, for instance, the author puts forward a vision of a church committed to confronting inequality and supporting the poor and oppressed, and yet makes no reference to the particular problems faced by women.[5]

Part of this complacency may be due to the fact that surveys of religious behaviour consistently show that women are more religious than men. Women are more regular Mass-goers, and participate more frequently in most religious practices, particularly devotional activities.[6] Yet at a time of rapid decline in religious beliefs in Ireland, and an equally rapid change in women's attitudes, the Church ignores women at its peril. Catholic women are rapidly finding their voices, and many of them are expressing anger and frustration at the way they have been treated.

Christian feminism is now well established in the USA and in some European countries. At its heart is a rejection of the dualistic thinking that underlies much of the Christian tradition, and which was used by the early Fathers of the Church to justify women's inferior status. In their writings the male–female distinction was added to the body–mind dualism to produce an association between the spirit and the male, and between women and the body. Men must strive to be like God, to achieve purity of spirit by controlling the desires of the body. In despising the feminine and sexual sides of themselves men learn to despise women. Sexual woman is the daughter of Eve, the cause of man's fall, the temptress and seducer who will prevent him reaching the state of grace. '*You* are the Devil's gateway', Tertullian told women, '*You* destroyed so easily God's image man.'[7] The implication is clear. Men are made in the image of God; women are not. Worse still, women are to be feared as the path to the devil, to mortality and corruptibility. As symbols of sexuality and maternity, women represent the evil forces of nature which threaten men in their flight away from the body and towards the spirit. Only by casting off these roles and subjugating herself to men can woman hope to achieve salvation, for woman is 'defective and misbegotten' according to Thomas Aquinas.[8] She must strive to be like man, as man must strive to be like God.

Echoes of this fear and loathing of women can still be found in modern stereotypes of sexual woman and in the traditional repression of sexuality in Ireland. They undoubtedly account also for the psychological aversion to the idea of women becoming priests which underlies much theological argument on the subject. Also, as the American theologian Sr Ann Carr points out, the ancient dualism between body and spirit has its modern counterpart in the characteristics attributed to men and women in society. 'Sexual stereotypes in which women are classified as passive, irrational, less organised, incapable of intellectual work or leadership, are often rooted in religious views that are difficult to dislodge.'[9]

Challenging the structures

A starting-point for many women seeking to promote equality within Catholicism is to challenge the hierarchical, male-dominated nature of the Church's structures. The exclusion of women from the priesthood is a fundamental source of inequality. Women are not only thereby prevented from taking on the key role of parish priest, but are barred from the Hierarchy and from most of the major decision-making bodies of the Church. Involvement as laity is the only possibility for women who are not nuns, and the level of lay participation in the Irish Church is generally low. Very few women sit on the various Commissions set up by the Hierarchy to advise on certain areas. Only two members of the eighteen-strong Commission on Justice and Peace are women, and the much larger Commission on Pastoral Matters and Liturgy is composed entirely of men.[10]

It can be difficult for Christian feminists to reconcile their faith with the position of women in Catholicism. Angela, for instance, is active in the women's movement and returned to the Catholic faith a few years ago after a ten-year break:

> I get very angry just thinking about how our power has been suppressed and taken away, at the way that within the Church the role of women has been so restricted and made so passive. I think of the very narrow and rigid way in which we were brought up in the Church in my time. The one role-model was Mary who was so impossibly virtuous and good you couldn't possibly aspire to be like her. She was presented as always very quiet and passive, yet when you explore the Mary of the Gospels you get quite a different picture from this stereotype we were brought up in.
>
> I cannot understand how women can stay in the Church and remain uncritical of it. It involves so much of a denial of yourself to give that much respect to male figures the whole time.

Sr Teresa also considers herself to be a feminist. At the age of 58, she is actively concerned with women's issues:

> I feel great affinity for non-Church young women, because I believe I understand deeply why they are leaving the Church, and I feel they are ridden with guilt and it is not their fault at all. They are leaving because of the tiers, the hierarchical model on which the Church operates in Ireland, and the whole patriarchal system. They can't express their voice, nor can they be treated as equals. They are not going to be insulted.

How then does she sustain her own involvement?

I think it calls for somebody within the Church to locate what is happening, and to change the Church. The others need breathing-space out of it to develop as full persons. I can name what is happening because I have a commitment, and I refuse to allow other models of Church to name themselves as the only reality.

Margaret is an example of a young woman who is hovering on the edge of the Church. She feels strongly that she is a Christian, as she sees in Christ a role-model of someone who was deeply human and aware of oppression. Her struggle is with the langauge and liturgy of the Catholic Church:

It is not something I can relate to. I keep going to Mass and wanting it to be better, then I get there and it hits me – that it is a man up there, and all the altar boys are male, and the prayers have all been made up by men. I'm a working-class woman as well, and that's another thing about the prayers. They are mostly made up by academics. It makes me angry, and I think 'What is the point of coming here and getting angry?' I think the Church and liturgy aren't relating to people any more.

The question of language is a serious one. The consistent use of the terms 'brothers', 'men' and 'he' in hymns, prayers and scripture have a definite effect on women by reinforcing feelings of exclusion and inferiority. As female theologians have pointed out,[11] the language reflects the awareness of its authors, and a complete absence of female terms and imagery reveals a fundamental flaw in the Church's attitude to half its congregation.

Within the structures, the priesthood comes in for particularly strong criticism from feminists, as it does from supporters of other liberation theologies. A feature of post-famine Catholicism in Ireland has been an emphasis on a well-disciplined clergy, somewhat distanced from the people by their authority and their control of all Church-based organisations. Peadar Kirby describes the Irish clergy as resembling 'an efficient and well-marshalled civil service administering and defending a powerful institution'.[12] While the authority of the parish priest has declined in recent years, the clergy in general, and the bishops in particular, retain a very strong hold on the life of the Church. The Catholic Church is not a democracy. It is, as a Vatican document declares, 'a society different from other societies, original in her nature and in her structures'.[13] Decisions in the form of declarations and teachings tend to flow from the top downwards rather than from the grass-roots upwards. With a low level of lay involvement in the Church, there is little to offset the power of the clergy. It is difficult for Catholics who seek changes to make any impact on the existing structures unless they have the support of the Hierarchy. This is especially true in Ireland where the Church is so well established and where faith traditionally meant an unquestioning obedience to the authority of the parish priest.

Add to this the difficulty women experience in getting their voices heard by an all-male body and one can appreciate the problems faced by feminist Christians. It is an unusual priest indeed who, like Paul Hynes, recognises that if the Church is to take women seriously, then priests themselves must be prepared to change:

> We need an openness to discovering just how much we ourselves have been conditioned psychologically, sociologically, economically, by our family upbringing, by our experience of life, by our religious formation, and by the attitudes of the society in which we live. Our attitude to women has been shaped in all these ways so that if we are to face the question of women in the Church we have to allow ourselves to be prised apart painfully, our prejudices exposed and slowly removed.[14]

Not surprisingly, there is some ambivalence among women on the question of their right to be admitted to the priesthood. It is not that women think they are unsuitable for the ministry, but rather that they would not like to see women take on the role of the priest as it is at present construed.

> *Margaret*: I think the priesthood the way it is at the moment is wrong. The fact that they are a cut above everyone, and that they go from school into the seminary and straight out into a parish. It is not the way Jesus meant it to be. Maybe it would be a start for women to get in there, maybe things might start to change slowly. There's that point of view and there's the other – not to go in at all and to start something different. I don't know.

Angela is particularly critical of priests' isolation from women:

I think even a lot of progressive Church groups are not that open to women's experience and I think the fact that we have a celibate clergy has a lot to do with it. It is only when men begin to see what women's experience is like, from being in relationships with women who are struggling for their own identity, that they become aware of the oppression of women.

I would like to see women becoming priests, and I would like to see the priesthood change so that there wasn't such a difference between the laity and the priesthood.

There was a period after Vatican II when women thought there might be some possibility of a move towards accepting them as priests. Their optimism was quashed by the Vatican's Declaration of 1976 on women and the priesthood, which stated firmly that women could not be, and never should be, priests. The Declaration recalled the maleness of Christ and the Apostles, from which the tradition of male priests derives, and refuted arguments for a change. It placed great emphasis on the need for priests to resemble Christ. 'There would not be this "natural resemblance" which must exist between Christ and his minister if the role of Christ were not taken by a man: in such a case it would be difficult to see in the minister the image of Christ. For Christ himself was and remains a man.'[15] As critics have since pointed out, the Vatican did not see any difficulty in a lack of resemblance caused by priests of a different colour, race or size than Jesus – only sex. Sr Maria is one of many women who were disappointed and angered by the Declaration:

In the Vatican Council document of 1965 they tell us that men and women are created equally in the image and likeness of God, and then the same Church structure said that we were *not* created in the image and likeness of God because we didn't bear a physical resemblance to Jesus. That's where the official Church is to me totally inconsistent and wrong, because it is stressing the maleness of Christ rather than his humanness. It is his humanness that needs to be celebrated. I think women should be admitted to the full ministry of the Church.

Sr Teresa shares the view that the role of the priest must change as one part of an overall restructuring:

People are dehumanised in the present model. They are not allowed to grow, and I don't think that is Christian. I'd like the Church to be participatory, much like the New Testament. With leadership, but a leadership in which members genuinely share responsibility and decision-making.

Often people who are working with the poor, the marginalised, who have been broken open in compassion to people in pain, are open to this other model of Church where each person is respected and where the poor can speak for themselves. They are committed to facilitating situations where people can reclaim their own voice. So there is an affinity between the justice movement and the women's movement – they are just operating in different milieux.

As Christian women began to articulate their feelings about their religious beliefs they formed groups similar to those in the secular women's movement. In the USA and in Britain networks, support groups, conferences, newsletters and study groups have grown up within the Christian women's community. In Ireland, such developments are in their infancy. Among women religious in Dublin there is a strong 'Sisters for Justice' group, many members of which are committed to struggling against the oppression of women. In 1983 a group of women religious and lay women set up a Christian women's network, an ecumenical support group for women who wanted to share and develop their spirituality. 'Our identity as women and as Christians is more fundamental than just being members of a particular Church.' Angela is a lay member and finds the network very supportive:

It's a sense of togetherness. When you are on your own you feel very isolated, and being with a group gives you the strength to keep going and put forward your point of view, realising that you are not just some crank but that there are good reasons for thinking the way you do. Since studying feminist theology I have a feeling of continuity, that what we are doing now was done way back in the early days of the Church when you had women ministers. It is very exciting and a little bit scary. I often think we would have been burned for heresy if we had lived in the Middle Ages!

Sr Teresa: I feel that women need to reclaim power over their own lives. If I share something with a group – I think this is the value of women coming together to share their experiences – then I am confirmed and strengthened. Whereas before someone could undermine my self-confidence by saying 'That is not what St Thomas said' or 'That is not what the Church said through the centuries', and I would say, 'Oh, is that so', and I would lose my experience.

Providing an environment in which women can validate their spiritual experience is an important function of groups like the Christian women's network. In such groups, women are open to exploring different views of God, working from the assumption that there is no one correct concept of either God or Christ and that each woman has her own truth. For many women the tradition of referring to God as 'He' is a stumbling-block. Related images of God as all-powerful, angry, judgemental and authoritarian also carry strong masculine connotations. Feminist theologians have pointed out that 'Mother' is not unknown as a title for God. It was used by Julian of Norwich, a woman mystic, and St Teresa of Avila among others. Julian of Norwich also referred to Jesus as both mother and father, 'for like a mother he nurtures us with his own body'.[16] Bringing out these alternative images is part of asserting the feminine in the Churches, finding in both God and Christ tradition- ally 'female' virtues such as caring, loving and peacefulness. As one theologian put it, 'we rather stress the God who turns to us as a partner in love who is gentle, vulnerable and near.'[17]

The changing life of nuns

Christian feminism is not confined to lay women. Many nuns are aware of the issues and are working to promote women's participa- tion within the Church. As a group, nuns have undergone a profound transformation from their pre-Vatican II life-style to their present role.

Throughout the nineteenth and early twentieth centuries the number of nuns in Ireland increased. The peak occurred in 1967, when there were approximately 19 000 Irish nuns.[18] A small proportion of these lived wholly contemplative lives, but the vast majority were in apostolic orders. Founded by women who wanted to find ways of assisting the poor at a time when the State provided few services, the apostolic orders ran schools and hospitals, orphanages and mother-and-baby homes. Irish nuns also joined many emigrant communities in the USA, Canada and Australia and provided a focus for the continuation of the Catholic faith in these countries.

The popularity of vocations as a way of life for Irish women was influenced by several factors. For middle-class girls whose parents could afford to send them to the convent with a dowry, becoming a nun was the main pathway to a professional job. The convent sponsored their training as nurses or teachers and their careers were in no danger of being disrupted by marriage. In addition, the celibate life-style was accorded a high status in a society where sexuality was strongly repressed. Nuns were pure and chaste, they were women in the image of Mary whereas ordinary women were cast as daughters of Eve. The other form of celibacy practised by women – the enforced celibacy of the unmarried – was not so highly regarded. Single women had a low status in society, especially in the rural areas. As Sr Maria describes it, 'the old hierarchical order of the Church was bishops, priests, religious, married people and then single people, and God help you if you were single as you had missed the boat altogether'. The life of a nun offered definite advantages over that of the spinster. Convents, however, tended to reflect the class structure of society. Middle-class girls became 'choir' nuns and might undertake a professional training, whereas girls from poorer backgrounds who had no dowry became 'lay' nuns and played a servicing role within the convent.

The celibate religious life was not without its problems for nuns. The pre-Vatican II understanding of celibacy as an asexual existence was very limiting. As the saying went, there were three sexes – men, women, and nuns. This attitude had two detrimental effects on women. It robbed nuns of part of their womanhood and set them apart from other women, who often found it hard to see nuns as thinking, feeling people like themselves. Also, the more the Church applauded celibacy the more it devalued sexuality and thus reinforced the fear and distrust of non-celibate women.

The harsh interpretation of celibacy was just one aspect of the highly restricted life-style in convents prior to the Second Vatican Council. In spite of the fact that a large proportion of nuns were professional women, some of whom had highly responsible posts, convent life was subject to strict controls. The Canon Law of 1917 laid down rules for the manner of prayer and the general conduct of nuns. A new stress on obedience and rigid hierarchies within convents laid the pattern for the next fifty years. Inside the convent the Mother Superior was the authority figure to whom the nuns must offer obedience. But even she had little power outside the convent, enmeshed as she was within the disciplined hierarchy of priests and bishops.

The life of individual nuns was closely regimented. Friendships were discouraged. Uniformity was the norm, and the expression of individuality through dress, opinions or actions was frowned upon. Sr Maria remembers that 'we taught in school and at four o'clock we locked the door and didn't go out on the streets. We had to get special permission from the bishop if we wanted to go anywhere. It was that structured'.

The 1917 Canons also imposed restrictions on the apostolic work of nuns. Many orders had already drifted away from the often radical ministries of their foundresses into a more Victorian model of charitable institutions in which conformity flourished. 'Up until Vatican II we were brought up in a whole theology of charity. You were charitable to people. You didn't confront them, you didn't argue, you weren't assertive. Obedience and docility were the values within the pre-Vatican Church – the whole thing the women's movement is against' (Sr Teresa). The training of novices was designed to instil these values. In Sr Kathleen's words: 'We came into the novitiate fairly balanced young girls and we were put back into childishness'. Now, she regrets the waste of those years, though at the time she accepted everything as part of what it meant to be a sister:

I had come through the Catholic school system, which was all 'Shut up, don't ask questions'. It was rather like sex – there were things you didn't talk about. That was the way it was, you accepted it. I remember my sister saying, 'Kathleen, why do you have to wear all that old black stuff?' and I said, 'That's the way it is'. No matter what you felt inside, you just pushed it down.

When I think of it now! For three years we were not even allowed to read a newspaper or a novel, and I had loved reading. We were kept on a diet of saints' lives and things on prayer.

Nothing that in any way would make us think. You never asked questions about your faith – it was seen as a great weakness.

In 1965, the Second Vatican Council published its document on the religious orders, *Perfactae Caritatis*. The document suspended the canonical restrictions on religious life and initiated the process of renewal. Each order was to examine its organisation and ministry and was given the freedom to experiment with new ways of living and new areas of work. The stage was set for change, and it was not before time. The number of new vocations each year had begun to fall, and the medieval habit was the outward sign of a life-style that seemed more anachronistic with each passing year. As Sara Maitland points out in *Map of a New Country*, nuns were also affected by two social developments in the 1960s – the introduction of new educational theories and the popularisation of psychoanalysis.[19] Nuns who were schoolteachers were having to adapt to child-centred methods of education. These replaced the old idea of strict discipline with open learning in a secure, stimulating environment. The contrast between these new methods and the nuns' own training was all too obvious. Perhaps the theories could apply to adults too? In addition, popular psychology drew attention to the damage inflicted by sexual repression. Suddenly the whole area of sexuality seemed problematic. Perhaps the vow of chastity was not so straightforward after all? Perhaps the suppression of individuality was not the best foundation for adult religious life?

Nuns began to ask these questions and embark on the difficult process of renewal and change just as the women's movement was developing. As women came together to question and probe, to get angry and demand changes, so nuns inevitably began to look at their position in what is arguably the most male-dominated institution of all. The women's movement also took the argument about sexuality a step further. Feminists maintained that every woman had a choice over how she expressed her sexuality. Celibacy could be a valid option, but only in the context of a sexuality that was acknowledged and understood. The women's movement also encouraged women to stop apologising for themselves, to accept their femaleness and be proud of it. These ideas were not confined to secular women's groups. They were also articulated by women religious, particularly in the USA.

As renewal got under way, it became common practice for nuns to take some time off from their ministries to return to college. Some chose to update their theology, others studied psychology or carried out research. Sr Maria took such an opportunity while teaching abroad and was greatly changed by the experience:

> In the two years of renewal I had to confront my life as a whole. I had to look at who I really was, without any support or props. I had to take a whole second look at the question of my religious life. I came out the other side with a whole new sense of life, and I appropriated to myself a vision of women in the Church. There was no question of wanting to leave religious life. I was set on fire with wanting to stay with it, seeing that the struggle I had was the struggle of every human being around me.
>
> I also discovered the whole meaning of friendship with women in my personal life, which prior to that was non-existent really. Probably my greatest supports now are women.

Sr Maria has seen an enormous change from the time of her novitiate in the 1950s when everything was done according to tradition and rules governed all aspects of life. Now the emphasis is on the personal development of each individual sister, and everyone is expected to be responsible for her own actions.

The change has not been easy. Prior to Vatican II nuns were, as Sr Teresa says, 'reflecting a hierarchical culture and, as we know now, a patriarchal culture, which is even worse. And we imbibed that and believed that, and we are still trying to work ourselves out of it.' Are they succeeding? 'It is a long hard struggle, but my God it is worth it – for self-discovery and self-direction, for personal freedom and the ability to stand up for what you believe in. The whole thing about the truth making you free.'

Sr Teresa had the good fortune to be studying theology in a college abroad when the ferment over Vatican II was at its height in the late 1960s:

> It was a brilliant time to be studying. It completely revolutionised me. It turned me around the opposite way in my whole approach to religious life. I really discovered what it is to be human. I discovered relationships, authentic relationships. It was a mind-

blowing, no, a heart-blowing experience. It was a marvellously freeing and growing thing.

As one of the first women in her group to undertake study of this kind, she had a difficult time when she returned to the convent full of new experiences and ideas. Over the years, as renewal gathered mementum, it became easier. Although it is still hard for the elderly sisters to accept some of the changes, there is a general acceptance within her convent of the new ways in religious life. 'We share responsibility for where we are going. There is give and take, there is mutual support, there is friendship and solidarity. Nobody directs me independently of discussion with me, and ultimately, when the chips are down and there is a conflict, I make my own decisions.'

It is widely accepted that the pace of renewal among religious in Ireland has been slower than in many countries. Two traditional features of Irish Catholicism – anti-intellectualism and deference to clerical authority – prevented the whole-hearted embrace of the challenge of change. In the USA and Canada, where renewal made deep and rapid changes, many nuns have become visible and outspoken as feminists, political activists, writers and peace workers. In contrast to this, Dr Donal Flanagan described nuns in Ireland in 1972 as a 'remarkably silent body'. He went on to say that he would be hard put to find any instance where a female religious superior had expressed any dissatisfaction with the male-dominated ecclesiastical system.[20]

Irish nuns have been catching up since. In 1983 an article in the *Religious Life Review* by a woman superior contained some strong criticisms of the way in which the Irish bishops treat women religious, an event which would have been unthinkable only a decade earlier. One of the author's criticisms was that when women religious meet bishops, they often feel they are received in a 'totally patronising, condescending manner'. She felt that the Church often misunderstands what nuns are doing, and that the traditional theological training of bishops and priests does not equip them to understand women's struggle for equality. 'It is a sorry fact that clergy and laity look with mistrust and scepticism upon women religious as they begin to move into roles and opportunities that until recently have been reserved for ordained men.'[21]

These comments reflect a source of tension between nuns and the clergy. As renewal gathered momentum in Ireland, the process of change was taken much further by nuns than by any other section of the Church – a pattern common to many countries. And once nuns began to shake off their subordinate status in the Church's structures and laws, their many talents and skills found space in which to develop more fully. Nuns are a highly-educated group of women. Over half of those entering religious life in 1978 had honours Leaving Certificates or better, and over a quarter had a university degree.[22] Many nuns undertake professional training or postgraduate research. Others return to college for years of further study or to refresh their skills. As a result, nuns sometimes find themselves more up-to-date in theology than their local priest, and more highly qualified than him as well. Far fewer priests have taken study-years of renewal. In addition, their position in parishes is more isolated than the collective life of nuns, giving them less opportunity to maintain a continuous dialogue with colleagues on aspects of renewal.

Some priests are well aware of this problem. In 1981 the National Conference of Priests in Ireland reported that many priests did not have the vision of the Church central to Vatican II. They did not encourage involvement of the laity, they lacked team work in ministry and they showed a complacent acceptance of the status quo.[23] Prior to the Second Vatican Council, priests in Ireland were generally held in high esteem. They were prestigious figures in local parishes commanding considerable authority. In comparison, nuns seemed old-fashioned and out-of-touch with everyday life. Now the tables are turning. The social changes of the past two decades have undermined the status of the parish priest, and his role is being criticised by liberation theologians among others. Nuns, however, have changed out of all recognition and are to be found alongside radical priests at the forefront of new movements.

Recent photographs in the *Irish Times* have shown nuns in a number of modern roles. One showed a sister being arrested while defending itinerant families against eviction, another was of a group of nuns marching against US foreign policy. A third showed a nun triumphant after completing the Dublin marathon. Their appearance on the front page shows that nuns acting in non-traditional ways are still unusual enough to be newsworthy. No doubt the sight of a nun in running shorts caused a few raised eyebrows. But the pictures revealed something of the changing image of nuns in the 1980s, as women who are not afraid to be identified with political campaigns or to participate with lay people in everyday events.

It would be a mistake to over-emphasise the progressive character of modern Irish nuns. Some individuals and orders are still very traditional. Many convent schools and institutions still operate repressive hierarchies and strongly reinforce traditional Catholic morality. But the effect of renewal has been to break the old patterns of conformity and lessen the suppression of individuality, so that within any group of nuns one can now expect to find a wide range of opinions on religious and political matters, and even individual styles of dress.

Renewal has by no means solved all the problems faced by female religious orders. Ireland shares with many other countries the phenomenon of declining numbers of vocations. By the late 1970s new vocations to convents made up less than half the annual decline in numbers due to departures and deaths. If this trend continues the number of sisters will be reduced by a third by the end of the century. In Ireland, where adherence to traditional Catholic practices is still widespread, the decline in vocations has not been as dramatic as it has elsewhere. In the USA, for instance, the total number of nuns fell by 28 per cent between 1966 and 1975, compared with only 9 per cent in Ireland. With fewer young women joining the religious life the average age of nuns is increasing. By 1975, 54 per cent of Irish nuns were over the age of 50.[24]

It is still a matter of argument whether the decline in vocations was accelerated by the questioning and restructuring caused by renewal, or whether it would have been even worse without it. It is apparent, however, that by the 1960s the way of life for women religious was being challenged, both by nuns themselves and by lay people. Sweeping changes would have been on the agenda whatever the result of the Second Vatican Council. As Sr Joan Chittister, an American nun writes: 'We do not have a vocations crisis. We have a crisis of significance and spirituality'.[25]

Part of this crisis is the difficulty of maintaining religious life as a valid option in societies which are rapidly losing their traditional religious aspect. In Ireland the decline in the regular observance of religious practices and in interest in religious life is particularly pronounced among young people. A survey published in 1969 found that 80 per cent of secondary-school leavers had considered religious life.[26] By 1974, according to a follow-up survey, this had dropped to 46 per cent.[27] Modern comforts discourage people from making sacrifices, said the youngsters, and the decision to join is too final. The authors of the report also noted that the majority of vocations come from children of middle-class families. Yet by the early 1970s the Irish middle classes had wholeheartedly embraced the new materialism, which undermined traditional religious beliefs. Other surveys have confirmed that the practice of religion tends to be strongest amongst those from rural and lower middle-class backgrounds and weakest among better-educated urban people, especially those from white-collar and professional families.[28]

Religious orders also have to face the problems presented by the properties and ministries they have inherited from the past. It is difficult to build a supportive community of women in an austere Victorian mansion. It is hard for nuns to develop and finance new ministries when their orders are saddled with the job of maintaining and staffing large institutions such as girls' schools and nineteenth-century hospitals. Spritual development and organisational change are by no means the only facets of renewal – decisions about practical things like money and resources are also centrally involved.

Sr Kathleen is a member of a teaching order and worked in schools until two years ago, when she became a parish sister – an example of a new, somewhat experimental ministry. She has an open brief to develop her work as she chooses, and lives in the parish in an ordinary house with three other sisters who teach in the local secondary school. Much of her time is spent visiting people, talking and counselling and simply being with them. She also works with groups of parents at the school and is involved in a religious education programme for adults. People are gradually getting used to her, and to her modern dress and ways:

> People will say, 'Isn't it lovely that you can dress in a denim skirt', or 'Isn't it lovely that you don't have to wear a veil'. I was speaking to one woman at a parish meeting, and she said 'I feel much better standing here talking to you when there isn't the barrier of the habit between us'. It is changing with younger people. With older people it's still 'Why aren't you dressed like a nun? I'd like us to be seen as women, not as freaks. I'd like to be seen as someone people in the parish can come to.

Sr Kathleen is very keen on the development of new ministries. But new developments raise new problems. Her order is limited by the problem of financial support for non-salaried posts, by the fact that they continue to run several schools in the town and by the needs of the many elderly nuns in the community:

> We have lost the radicalism in religious life. We were meant to be some kind of prophetic voice in the Church, and I think we've lost it. I'd love us to regain it. OK, we've come a step from the institutional convents and all of that but I still think it's not enough, and I don't know how to go the rest of the way. There are four of us in this town outside teaching, and a few others who feel the same as us about the prophetic voice, and there is always the tension there – should we go off and try something, or would that be deserting the others? Where is the happy medium? There are the physical needs of the old nuns, who are afraid they will be left, and who feel insecure. Several more retire each year, and there are very few younger than 35 or so.
>
> In the schools we are in the rat-race with exams and competitions. We've also got into the middle-class thing. We all have televisions. We watch *Dallas* and *Dynasty*. You might say that's all right, but what do we stand for then? Who are we? What are we doing? I feel personally more committed now than when I became a religious. I really believe in it for myself personally, and I believe in the whole ideal of it. But I am struggling with it, because our whole purpose of being here was to move out into new ways. Religious life was meant to be radical, and it often isn't.

The questions voiced by Sr Kathleen are shared by many other nuns who are exploring and redefining the nature of religious life. The process of renewal is far from over. Nuns have come a long way from their isolated, separate existence towards integration into ordinary life and a greater sense of themselves as women. As new life-styles and ministries continue to develop in the 1980s, the questioning and searching for the meaning and purpose of religious life for women continues too.

As this happens, the problems of being women within the patriarchal structures of the Church are becoming clearer. Some nuns and lay-women are leaving the Church because they feel the difficulties are too great and their religion can no longer offer them what they want. Others are committed to trying to change the

Church from within. Internationally, feminist theology is gaining ground but, with liberation theology, is being condemned by conservatives within the Church. In Ireland, the debate about women's position in the Church is gathering momentum. In areas over which women exert some control, such as the structure within convents, changes and developments will undoubtedly continue. In other aspects of Church life where women have little power and are excluded from the decision-making it is difficult to realise any real change. The Church is, however, under pressure from falling vocations, decreasing congregations and persistent challenges to its authority. Women's voices are adding to the movement for change, and it remains to be seen to what extent the Hierarchy will respond to this pressure or try to quell it, thereby further polarising the situation.

As yet, the growth of Christian feminism has had little impact on the Church's teaching on matters of morality, the family and women's rights. The links between Christian feminists and the rest of the women's movement are tenuous, and women within the Church would not necessarily support campaigns on issues which other feminists see as fundamental to women's liberation. Sr Maria, for instance, thinks that 'the Church is basically right on its teaching on contraception', though she agrees with the principle of individual choice. Similar divergences of opinion undoubtedly exist on issues such as divorce, abortion and sexual choice. Women inside and outside the Church have made progress in recent years towards recognising their common identity as women, but there is still a long way to go before Christian and non-Christian feminists feel that their interests are similar and that they can work together to achieve common goals.

10   Towards Equality: Progress and Problems

The past twenty-five years have been a period of rapid change for women in Ireland. As Irish society has industrialised and urbanised, and as traditional values and ways have been challenged and questioned, every aspect of women's lives has been subject to scrutiny and change. Previous chapters have outlined the main developments. We have seen how women's roles in the countryside were transformed by the decline in farming as a way of life and its replacement by an urban-based culture. As housing improved and living standards rose, the worst aspects of poverty were alleviated but an increase in material possessions meant more housework for women at home. The farmer's wife became a housewife, and women's lives in the countryside became more like those in the towns. Another effect of the economic changes in rural areas was the replacement of arranged marriages with modern marriage, based on a love-relationship. Also, family size began to fall, so that the average number of years women spent as full-time mothers decreased steadily. One result of this, coupled with the growth of new industries, was that the number of married women going out to work tripled between the early 1960s and 1980. Women no longer had to leave their jobs on marriage, and the advent of maternity leave made it possible for some women to combine a job with motherhood, though there were still many problems about doing this, especially while the children were small.

The era of economic change heralded by the *First Programme for Economic Expansion* in 1958 brought with it a period of rapid social change. Traditional Catholic morality, which had been closely associated with an emerging Irish identity in the post-independence period, came under attack as the isolationist stance of the Republic was replaced by more outward-looking politics based on membership of the EEC. The education system also came under review, with pressure to reform the curriculum to meet the needs of an industrialising nation, though the hold of the Catholic Church over schools did not substantially alter. The Church itself, however, was not immune from change as the ferment generated by the Second Vatican Council began to be felt in Ireland, having an especially profound effect on the lives of nuns.

In parallel with these developments, 1970–9 was a decade of debate and controversy about women and women's role in society. As the decade began, the first women's groups met in Dublin and the Government set up a Commission to investigate the status of women. National newspapers introduced women's pages, and programmes about women's issues began to appear on radio and television. As arguments about marriage, motherhood and women's rights were brought out into the open, women became more aware of their oppression, and of the roles of both Church and State in controlling their lives. This increased awareness in turn fuelled the desire for change felt by many women, particularly younger women in urban areas. As the decade progressed women organised campaigns on a number of issues, from equal pay and family law to contraception and welfare rights. Many of the major social controversies of the 1970s centred on issues of particular relevance to women. The ideas of women's liberation were highly controversial because they were fundamentally opposed to the ideology of the family that was enshrined both in the teaching of the Catholic Church and the Constitution of the Republic.

In the mid-1980s, it is pertinent to ask what women have achieved over the past two decades. Do women now have a measure of equality they did not have before? To what extent have sexist structures and institutions been eliminated? Have attitudes towards women really changed? What remains to be achieved, and how likely is further progressive change in the next few years?

These questions are not easy to answer as it is not possible to draw up a simple balance-sheet of gains and losses for women. Over the past two decades, women have pursued different aims at different times. In the 1970s, a great deal of activity was directed towards achieving specific goals such as equal pay and contraceptive rights. The notion of equality was widely discussed, and the term was often used to mean simply equality of opportunity, that is that women should have the same rights as men in areas such as employment, education and public life. Many of the recommendations of the Commision for the Status of Women were based on this relatively narrow understanding of equality. The Commission's task was to pin-point the steps necessary 'to ensure the participation of women on equal terms and conditions with men in the political, social, cultural and economic life of the country'.[1] This was to be achieved through removing discrimination against women, particularly in areas such as employment legislation and social welfare which were under the control of government departments. The Commission emphasised equality in employment, and the majority of the Committee given the task of implementing the recommendations were nominated by the Irish Congress of Trade Unions and the Federated Union of Employers.

Other issues were related to equality in employment, as without certain back-up facilities, women could not realise equal opportunities. Without the means to control their fertility, for example, many working women would not be in a position to take up promotion or retain their jobs after marriage. Similarly, the absence of maternity rights discriminated against mothers at work. The connections between the issues were clear, and it was no accident that demands for maternity leave and the legalisation of contraception appeared alongside demands for equality in employment in the Working Women's Charter, as adopted by the Irish Congress of Trade Unions in 1976.

There is no doubt that in the 1970s women took some useful steps towards equality of opportunity. The equal pay and employment equality legislation facilitated some change; campaigns and educational programmes helped some women to rise up the hierarchies of company management and trade unions. The marriage bar was removed, and the government made a number of changes to the social welfare code and family law. By 1978, the Women's Representative Committee reported that thirty-seven of the original forty-nine recommendations of the Commission for the Status of Women had been partially or wholly implemented.[2]

There were, however, several significant areas in which the notion of equality of opportunity made little progress. The anti-discrimination legislation in Ireland applied only to employment. The fact that important areas such as education and the provision of

State services were not included meant that a great deal of discrimination could continue unchallenged by the law. Another major area untouched by the reforms was the Catholic Church, which still does not recognise women's right to equality within its structures.

In addition, many of the reforms that did take place have had only a limited impact on the overall position of women in society. Although the equal pay legislation removed separate pay scales for men and women, the wages gap between the sexes remains large. In a wide range of organisations, from trade unions and health boards to political parties and the Civil Service, a few more women may now be found in the middle levels but the proportion of women at the top is still very small. Power and authority remain firmly in male hands. In other spheres, such as in craft apprenticeships and technical training, the removal of overt discrimination has done little to aid women's entry into traditionally male areas. Women have equal opportunities in theory but not in practice.

It became apparent in the 1970s that the notion of women being able to achieve equality simply through the ending of discrimination was over-simplistic, and failed to recognise the many complex ways in which women were oppressed. Equality, as many feminists pointed out, is not a simple matter of women having the same education, the same wages or the same career patterns as men. This view of equality sets up men's lives as the ideal to which women should aspire. Many women do not want to live 'male' lives. They are critical of aspects of the accepted male role such as the pressure to engage in full-time work, the distance between many men and their children, and the emphasis on rational thought and achievement at the expense of emotional development. A deeper understanding of equality is based not on copying male norms but on ending the oppression of women; that is, on a situation in which every woman can develop freely and confidently and make genuine choices about her life *as a woman*.

True equality is reflected both internally in the individual and externally in society. Internally, it means a woman having a positive image of herself as a female person, and seeing her abilities and skills clearly. It means feeling that she is of equal worth to other human beings and that she is in charge of her own life. Externally, equality requires a society in which women are taught and encouraged to see themselves as valuable and worthwhile people, and where the social and political structures reflect a recognition of, and constructive use of, women's talents and potential.

A problem of powerlessness

By these criteria, it is apparent that Irish society is still fundamentally unequal. There are several aspects to this inequality which are still problematic for women in the 1980s. The first is the patriarchal nature of most organisations. Bodies such as political parties, the Churches, businesses, government departments and trade unions wield considerable economic and political power. All of these are hierarchical structures with power concentrated at the top. The exclusion of women from the higher levels of the structures renders women essentially powerless over decisions that crucially affect their lives. This applies in many fields: legislative change, employment planning, wage bargaining, medical ethics, the content of education and religious practices. In each case, women are significantly affected by decisions over which they have little or no influence. This powerlessness is a form of structural inequality which affects all women, and which the reforms of the 1970s did little to alter. Equality of opportunity can achieve little for women here, as it simply means incorporating a proportion of women into an existing patriarchal structure. The presence of women does not guarantee any real change in the power structure or in the kind of decisions made. Generally speaking, women who work in large, hierarchical organisations are expected to conform to existing male ways; the structures do not change to accommodate women's particular needs. For example, many employers were reluctant to introduce even the minimal rights to maternity leave required by law, and few will consider the introduction of job-sharing or workplace créches which would make it easier to combine motherhood with a job. As a result, women with children are in the 'all or nothing' situation of which Margaret complained in Chapter 3. Because her employer does not accommodate her dual role as a mother and a worker she must either give up her job and become a full-time mother or she must make child-care arrangements to enable her to conform to the 'normal' male pattern of full-time work. Another example comes from the Catholic Church. Many women are critical of their exclusion from the priesthood, but would not want to become priests themselves until the present rather authoritarian role of the priest has changed. Once again, women do not want an equality that simply offers them a place in an existing structure, but seek changes in the structure itself in order to make it reflect women's particular needs and concerns.

The balance of power between women and men will not be redressed without fundamental change in organisations themselves and the ways in which they operate. The problem is clear, but the solution difficult, because it is hard to achieve the structural change that is necessary for genuine equality between the sexes. Hierarchies tend to be fixed, bureaucratic and slow to adapt. Because power lies with the few at the top it is hard for those lower down to make their voices heard. Such structures are maintained by competitiveness and the use of authority. As a result, any attempt to make a hierarchy more responsive, or to replace it with a more co-operative system, is likely to be perceived as threatening by those holding power within it. This is particularly true where the position of individuals within an organisation is based on status rather than merit, as Joseph Lee shrewdly point out:

The view that women suffer disproportionately from lack of opportunity makes little impact on those whose pockets are lined with rewards of inheritance, seniority, contacts, influence and luck. The less a culture emphasises merit, the more resistant to equality are the males likely to be . . . if only because the supremacy of the dominant males does not depend on superior merit. They are therefore likely to feel vulnerable to what they perceive as a threat posed not so much by women, as by ability in women.[3]

Men in powerful positions are also likely to feel threatened by the fact that when women organise, they tend to do so differently. The women's movement, for instance, is not a fixed organisation but a loose network of groups. Women's groups are rarely structured hierarchically; there are few official leaders and no one with a position which gives her authority over other women. The emphasis is on collective responsibility and decision-making by consensus, with a recognition that every woman's opinion is equally valid. The contrast with most male-dominated organisations is sharp, and indicates the depth to which inequality is embedded in society. Not only are women excluded from existing hierarchical structures, but these structures operate in ways with which many women are not happy.

The family once again

The ideology of the family fructions to support male-dominated hierarchies, and is another source of continuing oppression for women. Although the idea that a woman's main role in life is to be a dedicated wife and mother was strongly challenged in the 1970s, it still has a profound influence in many areas of Irish society. The Churches and the major political parties still adhere to the philosophy that the family is the key unit for a stable society, 'the family' in this case being narrowly defined as two parents and their children within a stable marriage. In their most recent publication, *Love is for Life*, the Irish Bishops quote a Vatican document on this issue: 'According to the plan of God, marriage is the foundation of the wider community of the family, since the very institution of marriage and conjugal love are ordained to the procreation and education of children, in whom they find their crowning'.[4] In the 1980s, the application of this philosophy to social policy still results in discrimination against those who do not fit into the narrow definition of the family. This can be seen, for instance, in the social and economic problems experienced by single parents and in the political difficulties associated with attempts to introduce divorce legislation.

This notion of the family defines a particularly restricted role for married women. This is reflected in the fact that single women have achieved a greater degree of equality of opportunity than married women. Single women have a double advantage. They are generally more free to work full-time and to follow an uninterrupted career, and they are exempt from the home-based roles of wife-and-mother, expected of married women. It is perhaps the treatment of married women, particularly mothers, which best indicates the limits to equality of the sexes. It is here that structural inequalities come home to roost in the expectation that mothers will always subsume their interests to those of their husbands and children, and in the idea that once married, a woman and a man should adopt fundamentally different roles. For the woman, this all-too-often means forfeiting her rights to financial independence and to a job, and losing the freedom to make decisions about her own body.

Today, fewer married women subscribe to a narrow home-based view of their role, or are only prepared to accept it for a few years while their children are small. Also, fewer people live in traditional family units. More unmarried mothers are keeping their children and choosing to live as single parents and the number of separated people is increasing. More couples now live together without getting married. Yet several events of the early 1980s, such as the sacking of the teacher, Eileen Flynn, and the degree of opposition to the liberalisation of the contraception law, show that the traditional Catholic view of marriage still has a great deal of power.

The ideology of the family exerts a strong influence in the area of sexuality. If, as the Church maintains, the procreation of children within marriage is the only moral form of sexual intercourse, then it follows that other forms of sexual expression such as homosexual love and sex between unmarried people will be condemned as immoral and wrong. To maintain the family, sex outside marriage must be repressed as it threatens the exclusiveness of the marriage bond. One reason for the Church's opposition to contraception is that it may facilitate non-marital sex. According to '*Love is for Life*', 'the truth is that, the more contraceptives there are, and the more they are made available to young people, the more sexual indulgence there will be, and the more will irresponsible attitudes towards sex be encouraged'.[5] The Bishops' use of the words 'indulgence' and 'irresponsible' shows that they are still strongly opposed to the feminist view that each woman should be able to choose whether or not to have children, and be free to decide how she wants to express her sexuality. In order for women to be able to exert this choice, sex and procreation must be separated, and women must have access to contraception if they want to use it.

Although as was pointed out above, one argument for contraception was it was a necessary back-up right for equality of opportunity, at a deeper level the campaign for contraception has always been about self-determination for women. As Ann Connolly stated when she was working for the Well Woman Centre in Dublin:

I believe it is very important for women to have this control over their fertility. They must also be free to choose pregnancy; there are two sides to the same coin. Without this ability to have absolute control over their fertility women will not be in a position to exploit other gains that they have achieved to date. Until women are no longer forced into having children they do not want to have, they will never reach true and meaningful equality.[6]

In other words, real equality cannot be achieved until women have the means to self-determination, and fertility control is an essential part of this process. This is a challenge to traditional Catholic teaching. The Irish bishops wrote 'what we have in modern society is not a new morality of sex but rather a radical rejection of the morality of the entire Christian tradition'.[7] While they were not referring specifically to the women's movement in this statement, there is some truth in their assertion. Feminists have criticised the Christian tradition for its treatment of women, and for the way it has reinforced certain aspects of sexual oppression through perpetuating a particular notion of the family and through its teaching on sexuality.

Irish society remains deeply divided on questions of morality. This was starkly revealed during the abortion amendment debate, and can be seen in present-day arguments about divorce, sterilisation and access to contraception. Traditional Catholic morality undoubtedly lost some of its political power during the 1970s; the abortion amendment and subsequent developments can be seen partly as attempts by the moral right to regain this power. At the time that family planning was legalised in 1979, the Bishops accepted that while the Church would continue to make pastoral judgements about the morality of proposed legislation, politicians had the right to make up their own minds on the issues. In other words, they tacitly accepted a degree of separation of Church and State. During the debate on the amendment to the family-planning legislation in 1985, however, certain Bishops appeared to go back on this understanding by arguing that Catholic politicians should legislate according to Catholic morality. This development, together with Pope John Paul II's backing for a traditional approach to morality and the family, means that further liberalisation of the law, particularly on divorce, cannot be taken for granted.

Women together

Despite the problems of structural inequalities and oppressive ideologies there has been a considerable growth of women's organisations and groups over the last few years. The women's movement in Ireland, as in Britain and elsewhere, has grown to encompass a widening spectrum of activity. In addition to campaigning groups on various issues there are now women's writing groups, feminist publishers, self-help therapy groups, women's sports groups, lesbian information services, rape crisis centres, Christian women's networks, women for disarmament, women's arts groups, and many others. There is no doubt that these groups are an important source of strength for many women. Their value lies not only in what they do – offering a service for rape victims or putting on women's art exhibitions, for example – but also in the opportunity they provide for women to develop their own ways of organising. Women-only groups are an alternative environment in which women can explore ideas and support each other away from the constraints imposed by patriarchal structures.

Awareness of and interest in women's issues is not confined to those who define themselves as feminists. Controversial items are regularly aired in the radio magazine programme 'Women Today' and in 'The Women's Programme' on television, both of which command large audiences. Newspapers give extended coverage to debates about morality and women's rights, and to stories such as the death of Ann Lovett and the sacking of Eileen Flynn. There has also proved to be a healthy market for books by and for Irish women, and two new feminist publishing houses have recently set up business in Dublin. Attitudes among women continue to change more rapidly than the structures in society. As quotations in previous chapters have shown, many women are aware of big differences between themselves, their mothers and their daughters. Women today are generally better educated and more articulate, and want to make choices about how they live their lives rather than conform to a particular role. Surveys consistently show that younger people are less religious than their parents. As a result, young women tend to be critical of many of the religious-based standards and values that their mothers took for granted.

As half the population of the Republic is under the age of 25, the attitudes and activities of young people will play a major part in shaping further changes in women's position in Irish society. It cannot be assumed, however, that progressive change will continue steadily. The economic recession of the early 1980s has led to something of a backlash against equality, especially in employment. Employers were more prepared to consider women favourably and employ married women when their industries were expanding. Now, as many industries are contracting and the government is enforcing public spending cuts, many women feel at a disadvantage when competing with men for jobs, especially if they are married. A traditional view of women's role within the family is used by both employers and politicians to give priority to men rather than married women.

The political power built up by women during the 1970s through various campaigning organisations and in the trade-union movement has been weakened by the economic climate. Arguments for facilities such as nurseries and family-planning clinics are frequently opposed on cost grounds, and women at work have less bargaining power when their jobs are at risk. In addition, the power of male-dominated structures continues to provide a barrier to the achievement of full equality. Both Church and State uphold the family as the basis of society, and as each new issue to do with sexuality or marriage arises the same arguments about the family and morality are aired by those opposed to change. Underlying each debate are the more fundamental issues of the power of the Catholic Church and the question of whether or not the Republic is a pluralist State allowing for freedom of belief and action – issues that are still unresolved and which continue to have a profound influence on the position of women in Irish society.

Appendix: A Social Profile of the Interviewees

All interviewees were brought up in the Roman Catholic faith unless otherwise stated.

Molly is 87, a widow, and lives in a town in the west. The eldest of fourteen children, she was brought up in Co. Galway where her father was a gardener on a large estate. She married and had ten children of her own, several of whom live abroad.

Alice is in her seventies, and lives with her husband on a small farm in Co. Clare. Their marriage was arranged. They have no children. Her parents owned a similar small farm a few miles away.

Brid is 58, and lives in Dublin where she is a social worker with a voluntary organisation. Her father was a businessman, and the family was well-off until her father lost most of his money when she was a girl. She is single, and has worked all her adult life.

Sr Teresa is 58, and entered a convent in her early twenties. She returned to Ireland three years ago after spending many years teaching in a Third World country. She now lives in Dublin where she is involved in a variety of projects. She was brought up in Dublin, where her father was a member of the Garda Síochána (the police force).

Audrey is 48. She was brought up in a country area in the west where her father managed a small factory. As a young woman she worked abroad as a secretary until returning to Dublin, where she married. Her husband is a professional man, and she has worked for periods throughout her married life. They have two school-age children.

Sr Kathleen is 46, and entered a convent soon after leaving school. She is a graduate and taught for many years in a convent school in the countryside. She is now a parish sister working in an urban housing estate. Her family owned a small farm.

Bernie is 45, and comes from a working-class family in the west, where her father was a docker. She worked in England for many years, and returned to Ireland after separating from her husband. She has four children and works as a cleaner.

Siobhan is 44 and lives with her husband on their medium-sized farm in Co. Galway. She has three teenage children. Her own parents owned a small farm, and she was one of 11 children.

195

Sr Maria is 43, and has been a nun for twenty-five years. She taught abroad for many years and returned to Ireland four years ago. She now teaches in a girls' secondary school run by her Order. She was brought up in the west of Ireland, where her father was a member of the Garda Síochána.

Ann is 41, married with seven children. She left school at the age of 13 and did various jobs until getting married. Her husband has a white-collar job in a town in Co. Mayo, where they live. Her father ran a small shop and her mother took in sewing.

Elizabeth is 41, and lives in a town in Co. Limerick. She was brought up in the countryside nearby. Her father was a soldier. After getting married she lived in the USA for some years before divorcing her husband and moving back to Ireland. She has three children, one of whom still lives with her. She has worked in offices throughout her adult life and currently works as a bookkeeper.

Tricia is 35. She grew up in a middle-class Catholic family in England and came to live in Ireland when she was 22. She is a single parent with two young children and lives near a town in the west where she works in adult education.

Angela is 34. A single parent, she lives with her son and her mother in Dublin. She is a graduate and until recently worked as a teacher in a secondary school.

Clare is 32, and was brought up in Dublin. Her father was a professional engineer and her mother was a graduate, though she never had a job. Clare trained as a nurse in England, and now works in Dublin. She is separated from her husband and has one child.

Kate is 31, and comes from a working-class family in a western town. When her father died she had to leave school at the age of 12 and work in a local shop. She has done similar work ever since. She is single and lives with her mother.

Maura is 30, and teaches in a Dublin comprehensive school. Her father was a clerical worker in Dublin, and her mother came from a small farm in the countryside. She is married to another teacher and they have one child. At the time of interview she was pregnant.

Mary is 29, and was brought up in a town in the west. Her father was a clerical worker. She is single, and works as a secretary/administrator in a local office.

Tracy is 29, married with two young children. She lives in Dublin where she went to university and trained as a music teacher. She teaches the piano part-time.

Carole is 28, and has a senior administrative post in a Dublin-based organisation. She has a degree and a post-graduate qualification in personnel management. She comes from Co. Kildare, where her father owned a shop.

Carmel is 27, unmarried, and lives with her son in Co. Mayo. She was brought up in a farming and shop-owning family in Connemara. She left school with her Leaving Certificate and had a variety of jobs before having her son. She is not working, and lives on the Unmarried Mother's Allowance.

Margaret is 27, and comes from a working-class Dublin family. She is married with one child, and lives an a Dublin suburb. She recently returned to college as a mature student and took a degree.

Síle is 26, a single parent who lives with her son in a small flat. She comes from a farming family in the west and is the eldest of seven children. She left school after taking Leaving Certificate. She is not working, and lives on the Unmarried Mother's Allowance.

Norma is 25, and separated from her husband. She has one child, whom she looks after at home. Her family moved to England when she was young, and returned to Dublin when she was a teenager. Her father keeps a shop. Before her marriage she was a typist.

Susan is 21, single and unemployed. She was brought up in a working-class Dublin family and left home as a teenager. She has lived in hostels and flats since, and has served a prison sentence.

Maeve is 14, and in her second year at a convent secondary school in the west. She spent much of her childhood in London, until her family moved back to Ireland a few years ago. She is the eldest of seven children.

Josie is 14 and in the same class as Maeve. She comes from a professional, Protestant family which moved from England to Ireland ten years ago.

Joan is 14 and in the same secondary school. She lives with her parents and one brother in a village a few miles from town.

Notes and References

1. Introduction: women and the family

1. Basil Chubb, *The Government and Politics of Ireland*, 2nd edn (London and New York: Longman, 1982) p.v.
2. June Levine, *Sisters* (Dublin: Ward River Press, 1982) p. 265.
3. Women's Representative Committee, *Second Progress Report of the Implementation of the Recommendations in the Report of the Commission on the Status of Women* (Dublin: Stationery Office, 1978) p. 1.
4. M. MacCurtain, 'Women, the Vote and Revolution', in M. MacCurtain and D. Ó. Corráin (eds) *Women in Irish Society* (Dublin: Arlen House, 1978) p. 53.
5. Central Statistics Office, *Census of Population of Ireland*, 1926.
6. Terence Brown, *Ireland: A Social and Cultural History* (Glasgow: Fontana Paperbacks, 1981) p. 26.
7. *Bunreacht na hÉireann (Constitution of Ireland)*, (Dublin: Stationery Office, 1980) p. 136.
8. J. H. Whyte, *Church and State in Modern Ireland 1923–1979*, 2nd edn (Dublin: Gill & Macmillan, 1980) p. 172.
9. Ibid, p. 103.
10. *Bunreacht na hÉireann*, pp. 136–8. ——
11. J. H. Whyte, *Church and State*, p. 27.
12. Ibid, p. 50.
13. Margaret Ward, *Unmanageable Revolutionaries*, (Dingle: Brandon Books, 1983) pp. 238–43.
14. *Irish Times*, 11 September 1979.
15. D. B. Rottman and P. J. O'Connell, 'The Changing Social Structure', in F. Litton (ed.) *Unequal Achievement* (Dublin: Institute of Public Administration, 1982) pp. 70–2.
16. C. Murphy, 'The New Feminism', *Irish Times*, 9 January 1978.
17. J. H. Whyte, *Church and State*, pp. 399–400.
18. B. M. E. McMahon, 'The Law Relating to Contraception in Ireland',

in D. M. Clarke (ed.) *Morality and the Law* (Dublin and Cork: Mercier Press, 1982) ch. 2, p. 22.

19. J. H. Whyte, *Church and State*, p. 405.
20. Peadar Kirby, *Is Irish Catholicism Dying?* (Dublin and Cork: Mercier Press, 1984) p. 35.
21. D. M. Clarke, 'Moral Disagreement', in D. M. Clarke (ed.) *Morality and the Law*, ch. 1, p. 11.
22. J. H. Whyte, *Church and State*, p. 382.
23. P. Kirby, *Is Irish Catholicism Dying?*, p. 37.
24. *Irish Times*, 21 March 1984.
25. Ibid.
26. P. Kirby, *Is Irish Catholicism Dying?*, p. 35.
27. Ibid, p. 36.
28. *The Pope in Ireland. Addresses and Homilies.* (Dublin: Veritas Publications, 1979) p. 79.
29. *Irish Times*, 13 February 1985.
30. *Irish Times*, 18 February 1985.
31. *Irish Times*, 8 February 1985.
32. *Irish Times*, 14 December 1984.
33. Inside Tribune, *Sunday Tribune*, 25 September 1983.

2. Maidens and myths: women in rural life

1. *Irish Press*, 18 March 1943.
2. Central Statistics Office, *Census of Population of Ireland 1926*.
3. Central Statistics Office, *Census of Population of Ireland 1946*.
4. Conrad Arensberg and S. T. Kimball, *Family and Community in Ireland*, 2nd edn (Cambridge, Massachusetts: Harvard University Press, 1968).
5. P. Gibbon, 'Arensberg and Kimball Revisited', *Economy and Society*, vol. 2, no. 4, November 1973, pp. 479–98.
6. Robert E. Kennedy, *The Irish: Emigration, Marriage and Fertility*, (Berkeley, Los Angeles and London: University of California Press, 1973) p. 212.
7. F. S. L. Lyons, *Ireland Since the Famine* (London: Fontana, 1973). First published by Weidenfield & Nicholson, 1971.
8. D. Fitzpatrick, 'Irish Farming Families before the First World War', *Comparative Studies in Society and History*, vol. 25, no. 2, April 1983, pp. 339–74.
9. J. J. Lee, 'Women and the Church since the Famine', in M. MacCurtain and D. Ó Corráin (eds) *Women in Irish Society*, p. 37.
10. R. E. Kennedy, *The Irish: Emigration, Marriage and Fertility*.
11. Conrad Arensberg, *The Irish Countryman*, (New York: American Museum Science Books, 1968) p. 62. First published by Macmillan, 1937.
12. Walter Macken, *The Bogman*, (London: Pan Books, 1972) pp. 92–7.

13. Máirtín Ó. Cadhain, 'The Hare-Lip', in Máirtín Ó Cadhain, *The Road to Brightcity* (Dublin: Poolbeg Press, 1981) p. 88.
14. Ibid, p. 87.
15. Ibid, p. 91.
16. C. Arensberg and S. T. Kimball, *Family and Community*, p. 131.
17. Hugh Brody, *Inishkillane*, (London: Jill Norman & Hobhouse, 1979) p. 112. First published by Allen Lane, 1973.
18. C. Arensberg, *The Irish Countryman*, pp. 55–8.
19. C. Arensberg and S. T. Kimball, *Family and Community*, p. 48.
20. R. E. Kennedy, *The Irish: Emigration, Marriage and Fertility*, p. 141.
21. Ibid, p. 144.
22. H. Brody, *Inishkillane* p. 88.
23. R. E. Kennedy, *The Irish: Emigration, Marriage and Fertility*. p. 145.
24. Frank O'Connor, 'The Impossible Marriage', in Frank O'Connor, *A Life of Your Own*, (London: Pan Books, 1972) p. 15. First published by Macmillan, 1969.
25. Ibid, p. 10.
26. Patrick Kavanagh, 'The Great Hunger', in Patrick Kavanagh, *Collected Poems*, (London: Martin Brian & O'Keefe, 1972) p. 36.
27. Ibid, p. 35.
28. R. E. Kennedy, *The Irish: Emigration, Marriage and Fertility*, p. 69.
29. Ibid, p. 73.
30. T. Brown, *Ireland: A Social and Cultural History*, p. 20.
31. R. E. Kennedy, *The Irish: Emigration, Marriage and Fertility*, p. 77.
32. Ibid, p. 73.
33. Liam O'Flaherty, 'Going into Exile', in *Liam O'Flaherty's Short Stories: Volume 1* (London: New English Library, 1981) p. 100. First published by Jonathan Cape, 1937.
34. Ibid, p. 101.
35. H. Brody, *Inishkillane*, p. 10.
36. *Irish Times*, 8 April 1983.
37. M. Ó. Cadhain, *The Road to Brightcity*, p. 65.
38. Ibid, p. 68.
39. Robin Flower, *The Western Island* (Oxford: Oxford University Press, 1978) p. 59. First published by Oxford University Press, 1944.
40. Liam O'Flaherty, 'Spring Sowing', in *Liam O'Flaherty's Short Stories: Volume 1*, pp. 11–12.
41. D. Hannon, 'Kinship, Neighbourhood and Social Change in Irish Rural Communities', *Economic and Social Review*, vol. 3, no. 2, January 1972, 163–88.
42. Central Statistics Office, *Census of Population of Ireland 1956*.
43. D. B. Rottman and P. J. O'Connell, 'The Changing Social Structure', p. 78.
44. *Commission on Emigration and other Population Problems 1948–1954*, (Dublin: Stationery Office) p. 135.
45. Ibid, p. 136.
46. D. Hannon, 'Kinship, Neighbourhood and Social Change', p. 179.

3. Of housewives, mothers and Mary

1. D. F. Hannon and L. A. Katsiaouni, 'Traditional Families? From Culturally Prescribed to Negotiated Roles in Farm Families', *Economic and Social Research Institute*, paper no. 87, 1977.
2. Ibid, p. 188.
3. Ibid, p. 26.
4. Alexander J. Humphries, *New Dubliners – Urbanisation and the Irish Family* (London: Routledge & Kegan Paul, 1966).
5. Ibid, p. 237.
6. Ann Oakley, *Housewife* (Harmondsworth: Penguin Books, 1976) p. 6. First published by Allen Lane, 1974.
7. A. J. Humphries, *New Dubliners*, p. 237.
8. Jean Tansey, *Women in Ireland. A Compilation of Relevant Data* (Dublin: The Council for the Status of Women, 1984) p. 190.
9. *The Pope in Ireland*, pp. 80–1
10. Simone de Beauvoir, *The Second Sex* (Harmondsworth: Penguin Books, 1974) p. 203. First published 1949.
11. Marina Warner, *Alone of All her Sex – The Myth and Cult of the Virgin Mary* (London: Weidenfield & Nicholson, 1976) p. 191.
12. J. Tansey, *Women in Ireland*, Table 3.3, p. 80.
13. Ibid, Table 1.7, p. 13.
14. Derived from John Blackwell, 'Digest of Statistics on Women in the Labour Force and Related Subjects', first draft.
15. Michael Tynan, *Catechism for Catholics* (Dublin: Four Courts Press, 1983) p. 57.
16. B. M. Walsh, 'Ireland's Demographic Transformation 1958–70', *Economic and Social Review*, vol. 3, no. 2 (January 1972) pp. 251–75.
17. *Irish Times*, 29 February 1984.
18. *Sunday Tribune*, 12 February 1984.
19. Irish Bishops' Pastoral Letter, *Human Life is Sacred*, 1975.
20. Andrew Rynne and Liam Lacey, *A Survey of 249 Irish Women Interviewed while Pregnant and out of Wedlock between September 1982 and July 1983*, Table 20. Paper obtained from Dr A. Rynne, Clane, Co. Kildare. Results summarised in *Irish Times*, 29 February 1984.
21. Pauline Jackson, *The Deadly Solution to an Irish Problem – Backstreet Abortion* (Dublin: Women's Right to Choose Campaign, 1983) p. 2.
22. Cherish, *Singled Out – Single Mothers in Ireland* (Dublin: Women's Community Press, 1983) p. 10.
23. Ibid, p. 47.
24. A. Rynne and L. Lacey, *A Survey*, Tables 9 and 13.

4. Marriage: a new partnership?

1. Nancy Sheper-Hughes, *Saints, Scholars and Schizophrenics*, (London, Berkeley and Los Angeles: University of California Press, 1982) pp. 114–15.

202   *Notes and References*

2. Central Statistics Office, *Report on Vital Statistics 1975* (Dublin: Stationery Office, 1979) p. ix.
3. T. Baggot, 'Relationship Rather than Contract', in AIM Group for Family Law Reform, *Modern Marriage – A Fresh Approach*, (Dublin: 1983) p. 10.
4. Liam O'Flaherty, 'Going into Exile', in *Liam O'Flaherty's Short Stories* p. 100.
5. Ibid, p. 105.
6. Irish Bishops' Pastoral Letter, *Human Life is Sacred*, p. 50.
7. Marina Warner, *Alone of All Her Sex*, p. 77.
8. W. B. Yeats, *Selected Poetry* (London: Macmillan, 1970) p. 161.
9. James Joyce, *A Portrait of the Artist as a Young Man.* (St Albans: Granada Publishing, 1977) p. 91. First published 1916.
10. Ibid, p. 97.
11. Patrick Pearse, 'The Mother', in B. Kennelly (ed.) *The Penguin Book of Irish Verse*, 2nd edn (Harmondsworth: Penguin, 1981) p. 296.
12. June Levine, *Sisters*, p. 156.
13. Ibid, p. 157.
14. Irish Bishops' Pastoral Letter, *Human Life is Sacred*, p. 48.
15. Ibid, p. 24.
16. Sacred Congregation for Catholic Education, *Educational Guidance in Human Love*, (London: Catholic Truth Society, 1983) p. 4.
17. Sacred Congregation for the Doctrine of the Faith, *Declaration on the Question of the Admission of Women to the Ministerial Priesthood* (Vatican City: Vatican Polyglot Press, 1976) p. 14.
18. Irish Bishops' Pastoral Letter, *Love is for life* (Dublin: Veritas Publications, 1985) p. 16.
19. Irish Bishops' Pastoral Letter, *Human Life is Sacred*, p. 49.
20. Ibid, pp. 49–50.
21. The Rape Crisis Centre in Dublin is campaigning for the law to be amended to recognise rape within marriage.
22. *Bunreacht Na hÉireann*, Article 41.3.2.
23. Nuala Fennell, Deirdre McDevitt and Bernadette Quinn, *Can You Stay Married?* (Dublin: Kincora Press, 1980) p. 13.
24. John O'Connor (ed.) *Social Reform of Marriage in Ireland* (Divorce Action Group, 1983) p. 1.
25. N. Fennell, D. McDevitt and B. Quinn, *Can You Stay Married?* p. 28.
26. William Duncan, *The Case for Divorce in the Irish Republic*, revised edn (Dublin: Irish Council for Civil Liberties, 1982) p. 12.
27. Ibid, p. 15.
28. *Irish Times*, 12 February 1985.
29. M. Tynan, *Catechism* p. 57.
30. Ibid, p. 57.
31. *Irish Times*, 10 February 1984.
32. John A. Murphy, 'The Church, Morality and the Law', in D. M. Clarke (ed) *Morality and the Law*, p. 112.
33. W. Duncan, *The Case for Divorce*, p. 52.
34. Ibid, p. 17.

5.   Sexuality I: a matter of choice

1. Leaflet distributed by Women's Right to Choose Campaign at the Irish Women's Conference, Dublin 1984.
2. Sacred Congregation for Catholic Education, *Educational Guidance in Human Love*, p. 4
3. Women's right to Choose Campaign leaflet.
4. Sacred Congregation for Catholic Education, *Educational Guidance*, p. 1.
5. *Irish Times*, 13 September 1983.
6. A. Rynne and L. Lacey, *A Survey*, p. 5.
7. Sacred Congregation for Catholic Education, *Educational Guidance*, p. 30.
8. Ibid, p. 31.
9. Ibid, p. 32.
10. Irish Bishops' Pastoral Letter, *Human Life is Sacred*, p. 43.
11. Sacred Congregation for Catholic Education, *Educational Guidance*, p. 4.
12. Ibid, p. 7.
13. M. Warner, *Alone of All Her Sex*, p. 71.
14. Sacred Congregation for Catholic Education, *Educational Guidance*, p. 32.
15. Irish Bishops' Pastoral Letter, *Love is for Life*, p. 37.
16. Sacred Congregation for Catholic Education, *Educational Guidance*, p. 8.
17. *Irish Times*, 30 August 1984.

6.   Sexuality: contraception and abortion

1. *Irish Times*, 27 March 1984.
2. *Irish Times*, 21 February 1978.
3. J. H. Whyte, *Church and State*, p. 407.
4. Ibid, p. 413.
5. Ibid, p. 413.
6. *Irish Times*, 8 February 1985.
7. A. Rynne and L. Lacey, *A Survey*, Table 27.
8. Ibid, Tables 26 and 29.
9. Irish Bishops' Pastoral Letter, *Human Life is Sacred*, p. 59.
10. Irish Bishops' Pastoral Letter, *Love is for Life*, p. 31.
11. Irish Bishops' Pastoral Letter, *Human Life is Sacred*, p. 56.
12. J. H. Whyte, *Church and State*, p. 400.
13. Irish Women's Right to Choose Group, *Abortion – A Choice for Irish Women*, 2nd edn, 1981, p. 1.
14. Ibid, p. 1.
15. *The Pope in Ireland*, pp. 77–8.
16. Ibid, p. 80.
17. *Magill*, September 1983, p. 11.
18. *Irish Times*, 23 August 1983.

19. *In Dublin*, 25 August 1983.
20. *Irish Times*, 5 September 1983.
21. *Irish Times*, 4 February 1983.
22. Open Door Counselling, *First Client Profile Report*, July–September, 1983.
23. Ibid, p. 32.
24. *Irish Times*, 24 August 1984.

7. **Girls in school**

1. Employment Equality Agency, *Schooling and Sex Roles – Agency Comment, Recommendations and Summary Findings of Report*, 1983.
2. Primary School Curriculum, *Teacher's Handbook*, Part 1 (Dublin: Stationery Office, 1971) p. 14.
3. *Irish Times*, 26 October 1983.
4. J. J. Lee, 'Women and the Church Since the Famine', in M. MacCurtain and D. Ó. Corráin (eds) *Women in Irish Society*, p. 41.
5. J. H. Whyte, *Church and State*, p. 20.
6. Council for Education Report, *The Curriculum of the Secondary School* (Dublin: Stationery Office, 1969) p. 80.
7. Ibid, p. 80.
8. Ibid, p. 88.
9. T. Brown, *Ireland: A Social and Cultural History*, p. 249.
10. Council for Education Report, *Curriculum of the Secondary School*, p. 92.
11. Ibid, p. 182.
12. Ibid, p. 192.
13. *WICCA*, no. 4 (no date) p. 5.
14. *WICCA*, no. 11. (no date) p. 4.
15. *Investment in Education* (Dublin: Stationery Office, 1966).
16. D. B. Rottman and P. J. O'Connell, 'The Changing Social Structure', p. 73.
17. C. Murphy, 'Education – A Review of the Decade', *Irish Times*, 28 December 1979, p. xiii.
18. See, for example, T. Inglis, 'How Religious are Irish University Students?, *Doctrine and Life*, vol. 30, no. 7, 1978, pp. 404–32.
19. *Irish Times*, 16 February 1984.
20. Employment Equality Agency, *Schooling and Sex Roles*, p. 28.
21. D. H. Akenson, *A Mirror to Kathleen's Face – Education in Independent Ireland 1922–1968* (Montreal and London: McGill–Queen's University Press, 1975) p. 137.
22. Employment Equality Agency, *Schooling and Sex Roles*, p. 32.
23. Ibid, p. 31.
24. Ibid, p. 34.
25. Ibid, p. 35.
26. Ibid, p. 35–6.
27. Ibid, p. 17.

28. Ibid, p. 37.
29. *Irish Times*, 9 February 1984.
30. C. Murphy, 'Women and Education', in *Women's Political Association Magazine*, no. 18, p. 7.
31. Ibid, p. 7.

8. Working for a living

1. Irish Congress of Trade Unions, *Trade Union Information*, September 1968, p. 3.
2. R. E. Kennedy, *The Irish: Emigration, Marriage and Fertility*, p. 214, Appendix Table 3.
3. Ibid, p. 169, Table 57.
4. Irish Congress of Trade Unions, *Trade Union Information*, no. 72, 1956.
5. R. E. Kennedy, *The Irish: Emigration, Marriage and Fertility*, p. 84.
6. M. E. Daly, 'Women, Work and Trade Unionism', in M. MacCurtain and D. Ó. Corráin (eds) p. 77.
7. Irish Congress of Trade Unions, *Trade Union Information*, November 1970.
8. J. Blackwell, 'Government, Economy and Society', in F. Litton (ed.) *Unequal Achievement: The Irish Experience 1957–1982*, p. 56.
9. J. Blackwell, *Digest of Statistics*, Table 4.3B.
10. A. Wickham, 'Women, Industrial Transition and Training Policy in the Republic of Ireland', in M. Kelly, L. O'Dowd and J. Wickham (eds) *Power, Conflict and Inequality* (Dublin: Turoe Press, 1982) p. 151.
11. L. Harris, 'Industrialisation, Women and Working Class Politics in the West of Ireland', *Capital and Class*, no. 19, Spring 1983, p. 113.
12. Ibid, p. 112.
13. J. Blackwell, 'Government, Economy and Society', p. 47.
14. Derived from Table 4.4A in J. Blackwell, *Digest of Statistics*.
15. Ibid, p. 3.2.
16. J. Tansey, *Women in Ireland*, Table 3.3 p. 80.
17. J. Blackwell, *Digest of Statistics*, Table 3.11.
18. Ibid, Table 3.2.
19. *Commission of Inquiry into the Civil Service 1932–5*, vol. 1 (Dublin: Stationery Office).
20. *Report of the Commission on the Status of Women* (Dublin: Stationery Office, 1972), Recommendation no. 1.
21. J. Blackwell, *Digest of Statistics*, Table 6.3.
22. Ibid, Table 6.2.
23. Irish Transport and General Workers Union, *Equality for Women*, April 1980, p. 17.
24. J. Blackwell, *Digest of Statistics*, Table 6.2.
25. J. Tansey, *Women in Ireland*, Table 3.11, p. 99.
26. Irish Transport and General Workers Union, *Equality for Women*, p. 22.

27. Rosheen Callender, 'Time versus Money and the Need for the Reorganisation of Work', in Trade Union Women's Forum, *Topical Issues for Women at Work*, February 1983, p. 30.
28. J. Blackwell, *Digest of Statistics*, Table 3.5.
29. Padraigín Ní Mhurchu, 'A Trade Union Approach to Part-time Workers', in Trade Union Women's Forum, *Topical Issues*, pp. 8–10.
30. Trade Union Congress, *Working Women* (London: Trade Union Congress, 1983) p. 19.
31. Irish Congress of Trade Unions, *Submission to the Government Working Party on Child-care for Working Parents*, p. 5.
32. Ibid, p. 3.
33. Ibid, p. 5.
34. Irish Transport and General Workers Union, *Equality for Women*, p. 57.
35. Irish Congress of Trade Unions, *Equality for Women Workers, 1978*, p. 3.
36. Irish Transport and General Workers Union, *Equality for Women*, p. 42.
37. Ibid, p. 45.
38. J. Tansey, *Women in Ireland*, Table 3.18, p. 115.
39. Irish Transport and General Workers Union, *Equality for Women*, p. 43.
40. Ibid, p. 47.
41. L. Harris, p. 109.
42. Interview with Padraigín Ní Mhurchu, *Irish Times*, 21 March 1984.
43. *Irish Times*, 11 January 1985.
44. J. Blackwell, *Digest of Statistics*, Table 5.1.

9. Finding a voice: women in the Church

1. *Irish Times*, 23 May 1984.
2. D. Flanagan, 'Nuns – The Silent Majority', *Ireland Today*, November 1972, quoted in M. MacCurtain, 'Women – Irish Style', *Doctrine and Life*, vol. 24, no. 4, April 74, p. 194.
3. P. Hynes, 'Women in the Church', *Doctrine and Life*, vol. 31 no. 8, 1981, p. 521.
4. National Conference of Priests in Ireland, 'The Role of Women in the Church', *Religious Life Review*, vol. 21 no. 99, November/December 1982, p. 336.
5. Peadar Kirby, *Is Irish Catholicism Dying?* (Dublin and Cork: Mercier Press, 1984).
6. See, for example, T. Inglis, 'How Religious are Irish University Students?, and M. Nic Ghiolla Phádraig, 'Roman Catholics in England, Wales and Ireland: Surveys Compared', *Doctrine & Life*, vol. 31. no. 10, pp. 612–21.
7. Rosemary Radford Ruether, *Sexism and God-Talk: Towards a Feminist Theology* (London: SCM Press, 1983) p. 167.

8. A. Carr, 'Coming of Age in Christianity: Women and the Churches', *The Furrow*, vol. 34, no. 6, June 1983, p. 348.
9. Ibid, p. 356.
10. National Conference of Priests in Ireland, *The Role of Women in the Church*, p. 336.
11. See for example A. Carr, p. 354 and R. R. Ruether, *Sexism and God-Talk*, pp. 47–68.
12. P. Kirby, *Is Irish Catholicism Dying?* p. 61.
13. Sacred Congregation for the Doctrine of the Faith, *Declaration on Admission of Women to Priesthood*, p. 16.
14. P. Hynes, *Women in the Church*, p. 523.
15. Sacred Congregation for the Doctrine of the Faith, *Declaration on Admission of Women to Priesthood*, p. 13.
16. R. R. Reuther, *Sexism and God-Talk*, p. 128.
17. C. Halkes, 'Feminist Theology: An Interim Assessment', in V. Elizonda and H. Greinacher (eds) *Concilium: Women in a Men's Church* (Edinburgh: T. & T. Clerk, 1980) p. 115.
18. T. Inglis, 'Decline in Numbers of Priests and Religious in Ireland', *Doctrine and Life*, vol. 29, no. 2, February 1979, pp. 79–98.
19. Sara Maitland, *A Map of the New Country: Women and Christianity* (London: Routledge & Kegan Paul, 1983) pp. 61–3.
20. D. Flanagan, quoted in M. MacCurtain, 'Women – Irish Style', pp. 193–4.
21. K. Macdonald, 'Women Religious and Bishops – Some Experiences', *Religious Life Review*, vol. 22 no. 100, January/February 1983, pp. 15–23.
22. T. Inglis. 'Decline in the Number of Priests and Religious in Ireland', p. 82.
23. P. Kirby, *Is Irish Catholicism Dying?*, p. 32.
24. T. Inglis, 'Decline in the Number of Priests and Religious in Ireland', p. 82.
25. Joan Chittister, *Women, Ministry and the Church* (New York and Ramsey: Paulist Press, 1983) p. 35.
26. J. Newman, D. Ward and L. Ryan, 'Vocations Survey 1971', Research and Development Commission (Dublin, 1971), unpublished. Quoted in T. Inglis, 'Decline in Number of Priests and Religious in Ireland', p. 94.
27. Rita Heeran, 'Attitudes of School Leavers to Missionary Religious Vocation', Irish Missionary Union (Dublin 1976). Quoted in T. Inglis, 'Decline in Numbers of Priests and Religious in Ireland', p. 95.
28. See T. Inglis, 'How Religious are Irish University Students?' and P. Kirby, *Is Irish Catholicism Dying?*, pp. 35–7.

10. Towards equality: progress and problems

1. Women's Representative Committee, *Second Progress Report*, p. 1.
2. Ibid, pp. 4–39.

3. J. Lee, 'Society and Culture' in F. Litton, p. 10.
4. Irish Bishops' Pastoral Letter, *Love is for Life*, p. 26.
5. Ibid, p. 30.
6. A. Rynne, *Abortion: the Irish Question*, (Dublin: Ward River Press, 1982) p. 150.
7. Irish Bishops' Pastoral Letter, *Love is for life*, pp. 30–1.

Bibliography

AIM Group for Family Law Reform, *Education is Everybody's Business*, Seminar Report, 1979.

AIM Group for Family Law Reform, *Modern Marriage: A Fresh Approach*, Seminar Report, 1983.

Akenson, D. H. (1975) *A Mirror to Kathleen's Face: Education in Independent Ireland 1922–1968* (Montreal and London: McGill–Queen's University Press).

Arensberg, Conrad, (1968) *The Irish Countryman* (New York: American Museum Science Books). First published by Macmillan, 1937.

Arensberg, Conrad and Kimball, S. T. (1968) *Family and Community in Ireland* 2nd edn (Cambridge, Massachusetts: Harvard University Press).

Blackwell, J. (1982) *Digest of Statistics on Women in the Labour Force and Related Subjects*, first draft.

Brody, Hugh, (1973) *Inishkillane: Change and Decline in the West of Ireland* (London: Jill Norman & Hobhouse). First published by Allen Lane, 1973.

Brown, Terence, (1981) *Ireland: A Social and Cultural History 1922–79* (Fontana Paperbacks).

Carr, A. (1983) 'Coming of Age in Christianity: Women and the Churches', *The Furrow*, vol. 34, no. 6, June, pp. 345–58.

Cherish, *Singled Out* (1983) (Dublin: Women's Community Press).

Chubb, Basil, (1982) *The Government and Politics of Ireland*, 2nd edn (London and New York: Longman).

Clark, Clara, (1982) *Coping Alone* (Dublin: Arlen House).

Clarke, Desmond M. (1982) *Morality and the Law* (Cork and Dublin: Mercier Press).

Curtain, Chris, Kelly, Mary and O'Dowd, Liam (eds) (1984) *Culture and Ideology in Ireland* (Galway: University Press).

Council for Social Welfare, Dublin (1974) *A Statement on Family Law Reform*.

Council for Education Report (1969) *The Curriculum of the Secondary School* (Dublin: Stationery Office).

Council for the Status of Women (1981) *Irish Women Speak Out: A Plan of Action from the National Women's Forum* (Dublin: Co-op Books).

Council for the Status of Women, *Women at Home: A Report on Nationwide Get-Togethers of Women* (booklet, no date).

Council for the Status of Women, *Women in Rural Ireland: A Report of Get-Togethers held in 1982.*

Duncan, William, (1982) *The Case for Divorce in the Irish Republic*, revised edn (Dublin: Irish Council for Civil Liberties).

Employment Equality Agency (1983) *Schooling and Sex Roles: Agency Comment, Recommendations and Summary Findings of Report* (Dublin: Employment Equality Agency).

Fennell, Nuala, McDevitt, Deirdre and Quinn, Bernadette (1980) *Can You Stay Married?* (Dublin: Kincora Press).

Fine-Davis, Margaret, (1983) *Women and Work in Ireland: A Social Psychological Perspective* (Dublin: Council for the Status of Women).

Gallagher, M. (1974) 'Atheism Irish Style' *The Furrow*, vol. 25, no. 4, April, pp. 183–92.

Gannon, Ita and Jack, (1980) *Prostitution: The Oldest Male Crime?* (pamphlet).

Hannon, D. F. (1970) *Rural Exodus: A Study of the Forces Influencing the Large-Scale Migration of Irish Rural Youth* (London: Geoffrey Chapman).

Hannon, D. F. (1972) 'Kinship, Neighbourhood and Social Change in Irish rural Communities', *Economic and Social Review*, vol. 3, no. 2, January, pp. 163–88.

Hannon, D. F. and Katsiaouni, L. A. (1977) 'Traditional Families? From Culturally Prescribed to Negotiated Roles in Farm Families', Economic and Social Research Institute paper no. 87.

Harris, L. (1983) 'Industrialisation, Women and Working Class Politics in the West of Ireland', *Capital and Class*, no. 19, Spring 1983, pp. 100–17.

Humphries, Alexander, J. (1966) *New Dubliners: Urbanisation and the Irish Family* (London: Routledge & Kegan Paul).

Hynes, P. (1981) 'Women in the Church', *Doctrine and Life*, vol. 31, no. 8, pp. 521–4.

Inglis, T. (1979) 'Decline in Numbers of Priests and Religious in Ireland', *Doctrine and Life*, vol. 30, no. 2, February, pp. 79–98.

Inglis, T. (1978) 'How Religious are Irish University Students?' *Doctrine and Life*, vol. 29, no. 7, pp. 404–32.

Investment in Education, report of the survey team appointed by the Minister of Education in 1962 (Dublin: Stationery Office).

Irish Bishops' Pastoral Letter, (1975) *Human Life is Sacred*.

Irish Bishops' Pastoral ·Letter, (1985) *Love is for Life* (Dublin: Veritas Publications).

Irish Council for Civil Liberties, (1983) *Women's Rights in Ireland* (Dublin: Ward River Press).

Irish Feminist Review 1984, (Dublin: Women's Community Press).

Irish Transport and General Workers Union, (1980) *Equality for Women*, April.

Irish Women's Right to Choose Group, (1981) *Abortion – A Choice for Irish Women*, 2nd edn (Women's Right to Choose Group).

Jackson, Pauline, (1983) *The Deadly Solution to an Irish Problem – Backstreet Abortion* (Dublin: Women's Right to Choose Campaign pamphlet).

Kelly, M., O'Dowd, L. and Wickham, J. (eds) (1982) *Power, Conflict and Inequality* (Dublin: Turoe Press).

Kennedy, R. E. (1973) *The Irish: Emigration, Marriage and Fertility* (Berkeley/Los Angeles/London: University of California Press).

Kirby, Peadar, (1984) *Is Irish Catholicism Dying?* (Dublin and Cork: Mercier Press).

Levine, J. (1982) *Sisters* (Dublin: Ward River Press).

Litton, F. (1982) *Unequal Achievement, The Irish Experience 1957–1982* (Dublin: Institute of Public Administration).

Lyons, F. S. L. (1982) *Ireland Since the Famine* (London: Fontana). First published by Weidenfeld & Nicholson, 1971.

MacCurtain, M. (1974) 'Women – Irish Style', *Doctrine and Life*, vol. 24, no. 4, April, pp. 182–97.

MacCurtain, Margaret and Ó Corráin, Donncha. (1978) *Women in Irish Society: The Historical Dimension* (Dublin: Arlen House).

Missing Pieces: Women in Irish History (1983) (Dublin: Irish Feminist Information Publications with Women's Community Press).

Murphy, John A. (1975) *Ireland in the Twentieth Century* (Dublin: Gill & Macmillan).

National Conference of Priests in Ireland (1982) 'The Role of Women in the Church', *Religious Life Review*, vol. 21, no. 99, November/December, pp. 335–40.

Nevin, Donal, (1980) *Trade Unions and Change in Irish Society* (Dublin and Cork: Mercier Press).

Newman, Josephine, (1984) 'The Women's Movement in the Church and in the World', *Doctrine and Life*, vol. 34, no. 3, pp. 108–18.

Nulty, Christine, ed. (1980) *Images of Irish Women, The Crane Bag*, vol. 4, no. 1.

O'Connor, John, (ed.) (1983) *Social Reform of Marriage in Ireland* (Divorce Action Group pamphlet).
Open Door Counselling (1983) *First Client Profile Report*, July–September.

The Pope in Ireland: Addresses and Homilies (1979) (Dublin: Veritas Publications).
Rape Crisis Centre, Dublin, First Report 1979 and Second Report 1981.
Rose, Catherine, (1975) *The Female Experience: the Story of the Women's Movement in Ireland* (Dublin: Arlen House).
Rynne, Andrew, (1984) *Abortion: The Irish Question* (Dublin: Ward River Press).
Rynne, A. and Lacey, L. (n.d.) 'A Survey of 249 Irish Women Interviewed while Pregnant and out of Wedlock between September 1982 and July 1983'. Paper obtained from Dr A. Rynne, Clane, Co. Kildare.

Sacred Congregation for Catholic Education (1983) *Educational Guidance in Human Love: Outlines for Sex Education* (London: Catholic Truth Society).
Sacred Congregation for the Doctrine of the Faith (1976) *Declaration on the Question of the Admission of Women to the Ministerial Priesthood* (London: Catholic Truth Society).
Scheper-Hughes, Nancy, (1982) *Saints, Scholars and Schizophrenics* (Berkeley, Los Angeles and London: University of California Press).
Steinet-Scott, Liz, (1985) *Personally Speaking: Women's Thoughts on Women's Issues* (Dublin: Attic Press).
Sweetman, Rosita, (1979) *On Our Backs: Sexual Attitudes in a Changing Ireland* (London: Pan Books).

Tansey, Jean, (1984) *Women in Ireland: A Compilation of Relevant Data* (Dublin: Council for the Status of Women).
Trade Union Women's Forum (1983) *Topical Issues for Women at Work*, February.
Tynan, Michael, (1983) *Catechism for Catholics* (Co. Dublin: Four Courts Press).

Ward, Margaret, (1983) *Unmanageable Revolutionaries* (Dingle: Brandon Books).
Walsh, B. M. (1972) 'Ireland's Demographic Transformation 1958–70', *Economic and Social Review*, vol. 3, no. 2, January, pp. 251–75.
Whyte, J. H. (1980) *Church and State in Modern Ireland 1923–1979* 2nd edn (Dublin: Gill & Macmillan).
Women's Representative Committee (1978) *Second Progress Report on the Recommendations in the Report of the Commission on the Status of Women* (Dublin: Stationery Office).

Index